John Franklin Genung

Handbook of Rhetorical Analysis

Studies in Style and Invention

John Franklin Genung

Handbook of Rhetorical Analysis
Studies in Style and Invention

ISBN/EAN: 9783337139049

Printed in Europe, USA, Canada, Australia, Japan

Cover: Foto ©Thomas Meinert / pixelio.de

More available books at **www.hansebooks.com**

HANDBOOK

OF

RHETORICAL ANALYSIS.

STUDIES IN STYLE AND INVENTION,

*DESIGNED TO ACCOMPANY THE AUTHOR'S PRACTICAL
ELEMENTS OF RHETORIC.*

BY

JOHN F. GENUNG,

Ph.D. of the University of Leipsic; Professor of Rhetoric
in Amherst College.

BOSTON, U.S.A.:
GINN & COMPANY, PUBLISHERS.
1889.

CONTENTS.

PART I.—STUDIES IN STYLE.

		PAGE
I.	JOHN BUNYAN. Christian's Fight with Apollyon	1
II.	THOMAS DE QUINCEY. On the Knocking at the Gate in Macbeth	8
	Study Introductory to Following Selections	17
III.	EDMUND BURKE. The Age of Chivalry is gone!	18
IV.	WILLIAM MAKEPEACE THACKERAY. On Letts's Diary	24
V.	JOHN RUSKIN. Description of St. Mark's, Venice	36
VI.	JAMES RUSSELL LOWELL. **The Poetry of St.** Peter's, Rome	48
VII.	THOMAS CARLYLE. **Coleridge** as a Talker	56
	Study of Figures in Previous Selections	64
VIII.	THOMAS HENRY HUXLEY. **A Liberal Education**	67
IX.	JOHN HENRY, CARDINAL NEWMAN. I. Accuracy of Mind.	
	II. **Ideal** Authorship described	80
	Study of **Fundamental Processes in Previous Selections**	86
X.	NATHANIEL HAWTHORNE. **The** Custom-House Inspector	89
XI.	MATTHEW ARNOLD. The Literary **Spirit of the English** and of the French compared	97
	Study of Sentences in Previous Selections	110
XII.	THOMAS BABINGTON, LORD MACAULAY. **The Work of the** Imagination in writing History	114
	Study of Paragraphs in Previous Selections	128

PART II.—STUDIES IN INVENTION.

XIII.	JOHN MORLEY. Progressive Tendencies **of the Age of Burke**	133
XIV.	JOSEPH ADDISON. Lucidus Ordo	141
XV.	SIR ARTHUR HELPS. On the Art of Living with Others	147

CONTENTS.

		PAGE
XVI.	RICHARD DODDRIDGE BLACKMORE. Description of Glen Doone	156
XVII.	ARTHUR PENRHYN STANLEY. Triumphal Entry of Christ to Jerusalem	161
XVIII.	JOHN RICHARD GREEN. The Character of Queen Elizabeth	169
	Notes on Description in Previous Selections	185
XIX.	THOMAS HUGHES. St. Ambrose Crew win their First Race	187
XX.	JOSEPH HENRY SHORTHOUSE. A Mysterious Incident	198
XXI.	SIR WALTER SCOTT. An Historical Incident Retold	206
XXII.	JOHN STUART MILL. The Meaning of the Term Nature	225
XXIII.	JOHN RUSKIN. Of the Pathetic Fallacy	233
	Notes on Exposition in Previous Selections	253
XXIV.	JOHN TYNDALL. The Meteoric Theory of the Sun's Heat	255
XXV.	THOMAS BABINGTON, LORD MACAULAY. Queen Elizabeth a Persecutor	266
XXVI.	GEORGE WILLIAM CURTIS. The Public Duty of Educated Men	275
Directory of Selections		305

PREFACE.

THE selections that make up this Handbook, while fairly representative, so far as they go, of the authors from whose works they are taken, are not to be regarded as introductions to the authors as such, still less as studies in the history and development of English prose literature. They are simply, as the title indicates, extracts to be analyzed, in style and structure, for the purpose of forming, from actual examples, some intelligent conception of what the making of good literature **involves**: taken from the best writers, because it is safer to study models of excellence than examples of error; taken from several writers, because it is not wise to make an exclusive model of any one author's work, however excellent; and taken for the most part from recent writers, not because these are better than writers of earlier time, but because they are more likely to illustrate the usages practically needed in this century.

"I think, as far as my observation has gone," says Mr. John Morley, "that men will do better for reaching precision by studying carefully and with an open mind **and a vigilant eye the** great models of writing, than by excessive practice of writing on their own account." In a general way such testimony as this to **the** value of the study of literary models is universal. Biographies **of** authors are full of it; reports, gleaned from every available source, of " books **which have** influenced me," and accounts of the great literary works which have been at eminent writers' elbows, constant companions and inspirers, are eagerly read and treasured for their helpfulness to workers who aspire to like eminence. But while the question of the what is so copiously answered, the question of the how remains for the most part unapproached. Its answer has hardly got farther than the general **idea that all one has to do is to** choose, with proper respect for one's tastes and aptitudes, some great masterpiece or some great author's works, and then read, read, read, until the general indefinite influence of **the style** has soaked into and thoroughly saturated **the** reader's **mind.** To this, as one way of study, no objection is here offered, provided the works be wisely, and perhaps it ought **to be** said variously, chosen. For one kind of discipline it undoubtedly has its value. Such reading as this may, however, be so pursued as to be anything but "studying carefully and with an open mind and a vigilant eye," and so it may miss its vaunted value; indeed, it begins to benefit the student only when he begins to interpret the vague impressions that he has received, by referring them to definite principles, only when there begins to be evolved in his mind some scientific explanation, however crude, of the literary phenomena he has observed. This is the main secret of the benefit derived from literary study by those great authors who write with Virgil and Milton and Burke at their elbows. Their own constant efforts in the same kind of work have sharpened their vision to recognize in their favorite models concrete solutions of their daily literary problems. Thus they have come to answer, each for himself, the question how to study models; and in each case the answer means that the student has evolved from his research some kind of a *science of rhetoric*, — one-sided, it may be, and inadequate, but still such a science as he can utilize in his own work. Valuable indeed such a result **is,** and it is interesting to all readers to know what great masterpiece of literature infused its influence into each eminent author's style. **Unfortunately, however,** such result answers the question of the how for only one person; it does not contribute to progress all along the line. Each new student must begin as helplessly and as much at sea **as** if nothing of the kind had ever been done; he has to make the way he finds. **And the reason** why so many students who enter hopefully on a course of study of this kind find it a delusion and a disappointment — for such is the fact — is, that they have not pursued it intelligently enough **or sys-**

tematically enough to have reached definite practical deductions for their own guidance in matters literary.

Nor is the problem fully solved by making the deductions and presenting them, in scientific form and order, to the student. The study of the text-book of rhetoric is indeed, like the study of literary models, one important element in the circuit of rhetorical training; nor should either element be thrown away for the sake of the other. "This ought ye to have done, and not to leave the other undone." But to complete the circuit, connection must be made. It is not because theory is bad, but because theory alone, without its application in practice or in the concrete, is inadequate, that the text-book is so often found a failure. One cannot become a writer, it is justly urged, by learning rules and conning ready-made philosophizings on style and invention. It is not so often urged, because the thing has not so often been tried, but it is equally true, that one cannot become a writer by studying models of writing, without evolving therefrom the very rules and philosophizings that in their abstracted form people are so ready to reject. Becoming a writer, that is, actual practice in subduing the detailed requisites of expression until they become pliant and ready servants of the writer's will, occupies a position distinct from either of these, being the third element in the rhetorical circuit. Theory, example, practice, — these are the three.

The present Handbook is an attempt to supply the second of these, in a series of selections from the best prose writers; and so to connect these with the theory, as found in the text-book, that the student may be enabled to make, or to discover, his own rhetoric. Thus the book aims to supply, in some degree and from the constructive point of view, what has hitherto seemed most lacking, namely, a practical answer to the question how to study literary models. How far the attempt has succeeded, can be ascertained, of course, only by the test of actual study, being an attempt hitherto for the most part untried. What lies on the surface, as the most obvious feature of the book, is the ordered and progressive character of the selections and of the annotations thereto, which begin with the simpler investigations and go on, step by step, to what is more comprehensive and complex. It may be noted further that each succeeding study investigates not only the distinctive principles for which it is introduced, but whatever have been noted in selections preceding; while also frequent return is made to the re-examination of earlier selections, whenever the student has advanced far enough in the rhetoric to have new principles to apply. And what needs especially to be observed, as a preventive of mistake, is, that he who takes up these studies with the idea of finding in the notes a body of information about the text will be disappointed: the notes are intended rather to elicit and direct study, and from beginning to end (to use the phrase so often employed in the book) "pre-suppose a knowledge of the rhetoric." They are just what they purport to be, studies; and study is the only way to master them.

This kind of annotation has been deliberately adopted, in spite of some real disadvantages that inhere in it. It would have been much easier to trace out in detail the various felicities of expression than to bring them out **by** means of questions; it is often hard so to shape a question as not to suggest the answer in the very attempt to secure the study necessary thereto; nor can the student be trusted to find out so much for himself as could easily have been found out for him and presented ready-made. But would the other way, after all, have been so useful? This book is frankly committed to the conviction that it is much better to discover a thing than to be told it, even though one does not discover so much. And it aims so to promote the attitude of research and study that when the student has found what these notes guide him to, he may have the impulse and the ability to go on and discover more. To this end — to rouse thought and set it growing, if this may be — the form of annotation by question and reference is chosen. It is worth while to compel attention to the details of expression, if for no other object than to secure the time spent in study. Many things can be worked out by the student himself if he will only stop long enough;

nay, if he will tarry a little and go to work rightly, he may make his study of English as valuable a mental discipline as the study of Latin and Greek, — hard as this is to realize in the absence of grammar and lexicon work, and in the universal breakneck pace of reading that now obtains. A corresponding expenditure of time, and a corresponding minuteness of attention, wisely directed, would, I am sure, place English fully side by side, as a disciplinary study, with the classic languages. But the first requisite is to call in the student's thought from the vague excursions that the easy mother-tongue leaves it so free to make, and give it something to do, something toward which the very time spent is time gained. What Wordsworth found in the contemplation of nature is equally needed, in these hurrying days, in the study of literature, — " the harvest of a *quiet* eye."

Accordingly, the student of this book may sometimes be asked questions whose answers are so obvious as to seem hardly worth the delay; but some time he will find, I am confident, that the very attention necessary to consider them has in some degree increased his insight and sharpened his literary sense. Besides, no one can tell what questions here so easily resolved may not, on occasions of his own future work, be perplexing problems, requiring for their solution all the keenness he can command.

Some of the questions herein asked may be too hard for the student, in his present stage, to answer; some indeed, appealing perhaps to individual taste, may not be susceptible of an indubitable decision, one way or the other; but the mere exercise of thought thereon has its value, greater than we are apt to realize. One large element in the study of literature is the development of what may be called *tact:* the student comes to *feel* the rightness, or the strength, or the felicity of an expression, and thus to justify it. Such feeling often lies too deep to find a reason in words, and yet it has all the certitude of a demonstration. It is of great importance that this tact, this feeling, be well grounded; not resting on whim, nor on merely individual standards, but on deep and universal principle. This is one of the objects to which this book aspires to contribute; its desire being, not to finish off the student in rhetoric, but to open the gate and set him on the way to those delights of literary study which are to be had in "privateness and retiring."

With the same object in view the book may sometimes direct the student to subtle points of criticism not treated of in the rhetoric. These may be caviare to the general, and yet be adapted to find and bring out the elect. In all study of literature the best and finest discoveries are only for those who have ears to hear; may it not be worth while to make occasional appeal to such?

Yet with whatever is here attempted, it is not for a moment claimed that this rhetorical analysis lays bare, or adequately interprets, the secret life of literature. "There is something about the best rhetoric which baffles the analysis of the critic, as life evades the scalpel of the anatomist." Let this be confessed at the outset. To many, perhaps to the majority, the secret must remain incommunicable; they have no ear for such music. But even these will do better to learn something definite, albeit elementary, about literary laws, than to strain their immature critical powers toward something that must of necessity be to them only vague and luminously cloudy; while the elect few who by an inborn yet educated tact come to feel the throbbing life of literature, will feel it all the more keenly and truly for knowing also the prosaic constructive principles at the foundation, the principles to which it is the lowly aim of this book to guide them.

Acknowledgments are due, and are hereby gratefully made, to Messrs. Houghton, Mifflin & Co., for permission to copy selections from Lowell and Hawthorne; and to Mr. George William Curtis, both for kindly placing at my disposal his oration on "The Public Duty of Educated Men," and for the warm interest he has taken in the general project of the book. Nor should I leave unmentioned Mr. J. S. Cushing, the printer, whose taste speaks for itself, and whose uniform kindness has made the mechanical preparation of this volume a delight.

AMHERST, January 7, 1889.

I.

STUDIES IN STYLE.

HOW THESE STUDIES ARE CONNECTED WITH THE RHETORIC.

ON CHOICE OF WORDS: RHETORIC, TO PAGE 48. — Bunyan, p. 1; De Quincey, p. 8.

ON KINDS OF DICTION: RHETORIC, TO PAGE 84. — Study Introductory to Following Selections, p. 17; Burke, p. 18; Thackeray, p. 24; Ruskin, p. 36.

ON FIGURES OF SPEECH: RHETORIC, TO PAGE 107. — Lowell, p. 48; Carlyle, p. 56; Study of Figures in Previous Selections, p. 64.

ON FUNDAMENTAL PROCESSES: RHETORIC, TO PAGE 171. — Huxley, p. 67; Newman, p. 76; Study of Fundamental Processes in Previous Selections, p. 86.

ON THE SENTENCE: RHETORIC, TO PAGE 192. — Hawthorne, p. 89; Matthew Arnold, p. 97; Study of Sentences in Previous Selections, p. 110.

ON THE PARAGRAPH: RHETORIC, TO PAGE 214. — Macaulay, p. 114; Study of Paragraphs in Previous Selections, p. 128.

I.

JOHN BUNYAN.

CHRISTIAN'S FIGHT WITH APOLLYON.

"The style of Bunyan is delightful to every reader, and invaluable as a study to every person who wishes to obtain a wide command over the English language. The vocabulary is the vocabulary of the common people. There is not an expression, if we except a few technical terms of theology, which would puzzle the rudest peasant. We have observed several pages which do not contain a single word of more than two syllables. Yet no writer has said more exactly what he meant to say. For magnificence, for pathos, for vehement exhortation, for subtle disquisition, for every purpose of the poet, the orator, and the divine, this homely dialect, the dialect of plain working men, was perfectly sufficient. There is no book in our literature on which we would so readily stake the fame of the old unpolluted English language, no book which shows so well how rich that language is in its own proper wealth, and how little it has been improved by all that it has borrowed." — MACAULAY.

BUT now, in this Valley of Humiliation, poor Christian was hard put to it; for he had gone but a little way before

---

This Selection and the one following are studied for the manner in which they illustrate Choice of Words; and presuppose a knowledge of the Rhetoric as far as page 48.

To aid in estimating how the style of this extract accords with its purpose, bear the following facts in mind: 1. It is a simple narrative, written by an unlearned man, for plain, common people. 2. The diction takes its coloring from the book in which Bunyan was most deeply read, the Bible. 3. The Pilgrim's Progress, from which this selection is taken, is an allegory (see Rhetoric, p. 94); from which fact we naturally look to see many words and turns of expression determined or influenced by the double sense that allegory contains.

Line 2. Hard put to it, — an idiom; see Rhet. p. 46, rule 14. Why so called? — **A little way,** — what is the more formal and less

he espied a foul fiend coming over the field to meet him: his name is **Apollyon**. Then did Christian begin to be afraid, **and to cast in** his mind whether to go back **or** to stand his ground. But he considered again that he had no armor for his back, and therefore thought that to turn the back to him might give him the greater advantage with ease to pierce him with his darts. Therefore he resolved to venture and stand his ground; for, thought he, had I no more in mine eye than the saving of my life, 'twould be the best way to stand.

So he went on, and Apollyon met him. Now the monster was hideous to behold: he was clothed with scales like a fish (and they are his pride); **he** had wings like a dragon, feet like a bear, and out of his belly came fire and smoke; and his mouth was as the mouth of a lion. When he was come up to Christian, he beheld him with a disdainful countenance, and thus began to question with him.

Apol. Whence come you? and whither are you bound?

Chr. I am come from the City of Destruction, which is the place of all evil, and am going to the City of Zion.

---

idiomatic expression? Try the effect of rewriting the whole sentence in more learned terms; is the style improved thereby? — **3. Espied**, what equivalent Latin derivative **is more used** now? — **Foul**, — how is the choice of this word probably **influenced by** Mark ix. 25? — **5.** What idiom in this line? How is the **same idea** repeated in the next line? See Rhet. p. 30, rule **2.** — Modernize the idioms in ll. **11, 12.**

17. As. Note how the term of comparison is varied from *like* in previous lines. Which of the two terms is more used with a verb, and which with a noun? — **18. Was come.** Cf. ll. 21, 36. What equivalent form of the verb is more used now? — Find a Latin equivalent for **disdainful.**

20. The dialogue form is very frequent with Bunyan; it is a mark of the vivid imagination which led him to identify himself with the feelings and thoughts of his characters. Note how natural it is for

Apol. By this I perceive thou art one of my subjects; for all that country is mine, and I am the prince and god of it. How is it then that thou hast run away from thy king? Were it not that I hope thou mayest do me more service, I would strike thee now at one blow to the ground.

Chr. I was born indeed in your dominions, but your service was hard, and your wages such as a man could not live on; for the wages of sin is death. Therefore when I was come to years, I did as other considerate persons do, look out, if perhaps I might mend myself.

[In the dialogue that ensues, Apollyon tries by promises and threats to reclaim Christian to his service; but Christian steadily maintains his allegiance to the Prince whom he now follows.]

Apol. Then Apollyon broke out into a grievous rage, saying, I am an enemy to this Prince; I hate his person, his laws, and people; I am come out on purpose to withstand thee.

Chr. Apollyon, beware what you do, for I am in the

---

him to slip into direct discourse in l. 10, and how the vivacity is increased thereby; cf. Rhet. p. 127. In some of his dialogue passages he includes more than the actual words spoken; see ll. 34, 41.

23. Does the omission of the conjunction before thou occasion any disadvantage here? — 24. Why is not god spelled with a capital?

33. **Look out,** — what auxiliary should be **understood with** this, to give the proper construction? — **Mend myself,** — find a more modern expression.

34. **Broke out, grievous,** — substitute Latinized terms for these, and note the loss of energy. — 36. **Withstand,** — derivation, see Skeat, Etymological Dict. *s. v.* What is the equivalent Latin derivative?

38. **Beware** means what here? Is it exactly modern usage?

41-45. What words of Saxon derivation are especially energetic in this paragraph? Try to find more learned terms, and note the difference in effect.

King's highway, the way of holiness; therefore take heed
40 to yourself.

Apol. Then Apollyon straddled quite over the whole breadth of the way, and said, I am void of fear **in** this matter. Prepare thyself to die; for I swear **by my infernal den** that thou shalt go no **further; here** will I **spill** thy soul.
45 And with that he threw a flaming dart at **his** breast; but Christian had a shield in his hand, with which he caught it, and so prevented the danger of that.

Then did Christian draw, for he saw 'twas time to **bestir** him; and Apollyon as fast made at him, throwing
50 darts as thick as hail; by the which, notwithstanding all that Christian could do to avoid it, Apollyon wounded him in his head, his hand, and foot. This made Christian give a little back; Apollyon **therefore** followed his work amain, and Christian again took courage, **and re-**
55 **sisted** as manfully as he could. This sore combat lasted for above half a day, even till Christian was almost quite

---

45. **And with that,**—note that this is the prevailing connective through this more narrative portion; cf. ll. 61, 63, 69, 73. What connectives would **be** more used now?

48-58. Note the vigorous Saxon words in ll. **48, 55, 57,** and see if you can find other words so good.—Put in other terms the idioms in **49, 53, 58,** and **note** the effect.—**48. Draw,**—a technical term— meaning what? Does it transgress Rhet. p. 40, rule 10?—'**Twas,**— **notice** that Bunyan was freer in the use of contractions **than writers** nowadays; see also ll. **11,** 83.—**50. The which,**—see also l. 98. The article is no longer used thus with **the relative,** except perhaps by Carlyle, who **is an** exception to **all rules.**—**54. Amain,**—derivation; see Skeat, *s. v.*—**Resisted,**—compare this word with *withstand,* l. 36, and note the similarity **of** the roots from which they are derived. Synonyms, see Rhet. p. 30, 2. "We oppose by active *force.* We resist **by** inherent *power.* We withstand by inherent *firmness.*"—C. J. SMITH. Can you **trace** anything of this distinction here?—**56. Almost quite,**—is **this** expression redundant? Com-

spent; **for** you must know that Christian, by reason of **his** wounds, must needs grow weaker and weaker.

Then Apollyon, espying his opportunity, began to gather **up** close to Christian, and wrestling with him, gave him a dreadful fall; and with that Christian's sword flew out of his hand. Then **said** Apollyon, I am sure of thee now; and with that he had almost pressed him to death, **so that** Christian **began** to despair **of life.** But as **God** would **have it,** while Apollyon was fetching **of his** last blow, **thereby** to make a full end of this good man, Christian nimbly reached **out** his hand for his sword, **and caught** it, saying, Rejoice not against me, O mine enemy! **when** I fall **I** shall **arise;** and with that gave him **a deadly thrust, which** made him give back, as one that had received his mortal wound. Christian perceiving that, **made at him** again, saying, Nay, in all these things, we are more than conquerors, through him that loved us. And with that Apollyon spread forth his dragon's wings, and sped him away, that Christian for a season saw him no more.

In this combat **no man** can imagine, unless he had seen and heard as I did, what yelling and hideous roaring Apollyon made all the time of the fight;—he spake like a dragon; and on the other side, what sighs and groans burst **from** Christian's heart. I never saw **him** all the

---

pare ll. **41, 105** for the proper **use of** *quite*. How do we Americans sometimes use the word improperly? — **59. Gather up close,** — what would be the modern equivalent of this idiom? — **65.** Note the idiom in this line. — **Fetching of,** — why is the "of" wrong here and right in **line 11**? — **68.** Quoted from Micah vii. 8. What enemy is meant in the original? — **71.** Note the idiom. — Quotation from Romans viii. 37. — **74. Dragon's wings,** — would we use the possessive in such case now? — **Sped him away,** — find an equivalent expression.

while give so much as one pleasant look, till he perceived he had wounded Apollyon with his two-edged sword; then indeed he did smile and look upward. But 'twas the dreadfullest sight that ever I saw.

85 So when the battle was over, Christian said, **I** will here give thanks to Him that hath delivered me out of the mouth **of** the lion, to Him that did help me against Apollyon. And so he did, saying,

> Great Beelzebub, **the** Captain of this fiend,
> 90 Design'd my **ruin**; therefore to this end
> He sent him harness'd **out**; and he with rage
> That hellish was, did fiercely me engage:
> But blessed Michael helped me, and I
> By dint of sword did quickly **make** him fly.
> 95 Therefore to Him let me give lasting praise,
> **And** thank and bless His holy name always.

Then there came to him a hand with some of the leaves of the Tree of **Life**, the which Christian **took** and applied to the wounds that he had received in the battle, and was 100 healed immediately. He also sat down in that place to eat bread, and to drink of the bottle that **was** given him a little before: so being refreshed, **he** addressed himself to his journey, with his sword drawn **in** his hand; for he said, **I** know not but some other enemy **may** be at hand. But he 105 met with **no** other affront from Apollyon quite through this **valley**.

From PILGRIM'S PROGRESS.

---

83. Compare the sense of this **indeed** with the **one** in l. 29; for which latter see Rhet. p. 138, 38. What two uses of the word thus revealed? — **91. Harness'd**, — an old technical term, for which there is no more occasion. — **94. Dint of**, — analyze the idiom, and find an equivalent.

Of the narrative just studied, Richard Grant White says, "No person who has read 'The Pilgrim's Progress' can have forgotten the fight of Christian with Apollyon, which, for vividness of description and dramatic interest, puts to shame all the combats between knights and giants, and men and dragons, that can be found elsewhere in romance or poetry; but there are probably many who do not remember, and not a few perhaps who, in the very enjoyment of it, did not notice, the clearness, the spirit, the strength, and the simple beauty of the style in which that passage is written." Here are ascribed to the extract all the fundamental qualities of style mentioned in Rhet. pp. 19-25. Let us test some of them.

How does Bunyan show adaptation of style to thought (Rhet. p. 17, 1)? How to the reader (17, 2)? Does the nature of the thought require fine shades of meaning, such as we associate with precision (20)? Test some of the sentences for perspicuity (20); e.g. ll. 13-17; 48-52; 64-71; 76-80; 100-104 (the longest sentences in the extract). Are there any complexities in their structure?

As to choice of words, test the sentences for force (21, 1). Put e.g. ll. 61-78 into other words, choosing Latinized terms for the Saxon where possible, and see if it is as vigorous.

"Simple beauty" (23),—what evidence of that? Are the sentences smooth? Do you *notice* the felicity of the expression,—or indeed think of it as style at all? What does this fact indicate?

II.

THOMAS DE QUINCEY.

ON THE KNOCKING AT THE GATE IN MACBETH.

"Exactness, rather than perspicuity, is his peculiar merit. **On this he openly prides himself.** . . . He certainly had reason to glory. None of our writers in general literature have shown themselves so scrupulously precise. His works are still the crowning delicacy for lovers of formal, punctilious exactness." — W. MINTO.

"Whence is that knocking?
How is't with me, when every **noise** appals me?
What hands are here? ha! they **pluck out** mine eyes.
Will all great Neptune's ocean wash **this** blood
Clean from my hand? No, this my hand will rather
The multitudinous seas incarnadine,
Making the green one red."

MACBETH, *Act II. Scene I.*

FROM my boyish days I had always felt a great perplexity on one point in Macbeth. It was this: the knocking at

---

This selection is studied as illustrating **the Choice of Words**, especially as regards fine and exact usage. **To aid** in the study, bear in mind the following facts: **1.** Published in the London Magazine, **in** October, 1823, this paper was evidently intended for educated readers, and did not need to simplify on their account. **2.** The subject, being expository (see Rhet. p. 383), **requires** accurate, discriminating language; and from Rhet. p. 44, 2 we naturally expect that words of Classical origin will **be freely employed.** The conditions are thus quite different from **those** which governed **the previous** selection.

Line 1. **Boyish,** — why is this word **better than** "boyhood's"? — **I had always felt,** — pluperfect, because the author wishes to place it before the fact mentioned l. 13. — **Perplexity,** — compare with synonyms, *embarrassment, bewilderment, confusion.* Why is *perplexity*

the gate, which **succeeds** to the murder of **Duncan**, produced to my **feelings** an effect for which I never could account. The effect was, that **it** reflected back upon the murder a peculiar awfulness and a depth of solemnity; yet, however obstinately I endeavored with my understanding to comprehend this, for many years I never could see *why* it should produce such an effect. . . .

In fact, my understanding said positively **that it** could **not** produce any effect. But I knew better; **I felt** that it did; and I waited and clung to the problem until further knowledge should enable me to solve it. At length, in 1812, Mr. Williams made his *début* on the stage of Ratcliffe Highway, and executed **those** unparalleled **murders** which have **procured for him such a** brilliant and undying

---

better here? — **3. Succeeds to,** — a more formal word than *follows*. Is it exacter? — **4. For which, etc.,** — cf. *that I never could account for*. Which sounds more colloquial, and which better fitted for such a paper as this? — **6. Peculiar awfulness, etc.** Would *awe* be accurate here? What **is** the good of two nearly synonymous expressions? See Rhet. p. 32. — **7. With my understanding.** This phrase is made prominent by its order (cf. Rhet. p. 181, 4); to what is it antithetic (l. 4)?

9. The periods indicate **that** something is **omitted. It** is a paragraph of digression, beginning, "Here I pause **for** one moment **to** exhort the reader never to pay any attention to his understanding, when it stands in opposition to any other faculty of his mind." The beginning of the next paragraph will indicate how easily it can be left out; cf. Rhet. p. 207, *note*.

10. Positively. This is set over against something negatively expressed **or** implied; find what it is. — **12. Problem.** Compare *question*. **Why is this** better? What verb is used with this (cf. also l. 36), and what would be the fitting verb with *question?* — **14. Début.** Why italicized? Is it admissible under Rhet. rule 11, p. 41? This word, with several words in the twelve lines succeeding, are chosen to accord with the ironical view that De Quincey chooses here to take **of** murder;

reputation. On which murders, by the way, I must observe, that in one respect they have had an ill effect, by making the connoisseur in murder very fastidious in his taste, and dissatisfied by anything that has since been done in that line. All other murders look pale by the deep crimson of his; and, as an amateur once said to me in a querulous tone, "There **has** been absolutely nothing *doing* since his time, or nothing that's worth speaking of." But this is wrong; for it is unreasonable to expect all men to be great artists, and born **with** the genius of Mr. Williams. Now it will be remembered, that in the first of these murders, (that of the Marrs,) the same incident (of a knocking at the door, soon after the work of extermination was complete) did actually occur, which the genius of Shakspeare has invented; and all good judges, **and** the most eminent dilettanti, acknowledged the felicity of Shakspeare's suggestion, as soon as it was actually realized. Here, then, was a fresh proof that I was right in relying on my own feeling, in opposition to my understanding; and I again set myself to study the problem; at length I solved it to my own satisfaction; and my solution is this. Murder, in ordinary cases, where the sympathy **is** wholly directed to

---

see note on this figure, p. 65 below. — **19. Connoisseur,** — derivation and use? — **19. Fastidious in his taste; 22. Amateur; 25. Great artists; 26. Genius,** — **from** what department of thought are these words chosen? How do they change the suggestion of the thought here? — **28. Incident.** Cf. synonyms *event, occurrence,* — why is this better? — **29. Extermination.** — is this merely a synonym for murder, or does it intentionally express more? See De Quincey's Works, Vol. XI. pp. 614–620. — **30. Did actually,** — to what is this in antithesis? — **32.** Derivation of **dilettanti,** — as a foreign word, why not italicized? — **Acknowledged.** — how different from *recognized?* — **Felicity,** — literally what? Why better than *happiness?* — **33. Actually realized,** — to what is this in antithesis? — **38. Sympathy.** Study this

the case of the murdered person, is an incident of coarse
and vulgar horror; and for this reason, that it flings the 40
interest exclusively upon the natural but ignoble instinct
by which we cleave to life; an instinct, which, as being
indispensable to the primal law of self-preservation, is the
same in kind, (though different in degree,) amongst all
living creatures; this instinct, therefore, because it anni- 45
hilates all distinctions, and degrades the greatest of men
to the level of "the poor beetle that we tread on," exhibits
human nature in its most abject and humiliating attitude.
Such an attitude would little suit the purposes of the poet.
What then must he do? He must throw the interest on 50
the murderer. Our sympathy must be with *him;* (of course

---

word in connection with its later use, ll. 51 sq.—**39. Coarse and vulgar,**—try if the sense can be adequately expressed by one of these words alone; cf. Rhet. p. 31.—**41. Exclusively,**—how is this more specific than *wholly?*—**Ignoble,**—what previous adjective softens the use of this?—**42. Cleave to life,**—compare the verb *clung* used with *problem,* l. 12, and note fineness of use.—**43. Primal,**—discriminate between synonyms *primary, primal, primitive.*—**45, 46, 47, Annihilates, degrades, exhibits,**—trace the derivation of each of these words, and show in each case how congruous is the object to the verb. —**48. Abject and humiliating,**—what is the good of using both terms?—**50. Throw,**—compare *flings,* l. 40, and see Rhet. p. 31.— **51. Sympathy,**—what is the derivation, and what in the derivation makes "sympathy *for*" a barbarism (see De Quincey's note below)? On the use of the word sympathy here, De Quincey has the following note: "It seems almost ludicrous to guard and explain my use of a word, in a situation where it would naturally explain itself. But it has become necessary to do so, in consequence of the unscholarlike use of the word sympathy, at present so general, by which, instead of taking it in its proper sense, as the act of reproducing in our minds the feelings of another, whether for hatred, indignation, love, pity, or approbation, it is made a mere synonym of the word *pity;* and hence, instead of saying 'sympathy *with* another,' many writers adopt the monstrous bar-

I mean a sympathy of comprehension, a sympathy by which we enter into his feelings, and are made to understand them, — not a sympathy of pity or approbation). In the murdered person, all strife of thought, all flux and reflux of passion and of purpose, are crushed by one overwhelming panic; the fear of instant death smites him "with its petrific mace." But in the murderer, such a murderer as a poet will condescend to, there must be raging some great storm of passion, — jealousy, ambition, vengeance, hatred, — which will create a hell within him; and into this hell we are to look.

In Macbeth, for the sake of gratifying his own enormous and teeming faculty of creation, Shakspeare has introduced two murderers; and, as usual in his hands, they are remarkably discriminated: but, though in Macbeth the strife of mind is greater than in his wife, the tiger spirit not so awake, and his feelings caught **chiefly** by contagion from her, — yet, as both were finally involved in the guilt of

---

barism of 'sympathy *for* another.'" — **52. Comprehension,** — point out how this word is defined in the repetition that follows. — **55.** What idea is here developed by two nearly synonymous expressions? — **Flux and reflux**; technical terms, — are they too difficult for the class to whom the paper is addressed? — **58. Petrific,** — derive this word, and show its adaptedness to the idea. — **59. Condescend to,** — what more is suggested than if De Quincey had said *describe* or *depict?* Cf. ll. 31, 33. — **60. Storm of passion,** — what makes this term more fitting here than the weaker term "flux and reflux of passion," l. 55, and why is the other more fitting there?

63. **Enormous,**—derivation?—**64.** Define **teeming**, and show how it advances on the idea expressed in *enormous*. — **66. Discriminated,** — compare *distinguished*, and show how the derivation makes this word better here. — **67.** What strong epithet in this line? — **68. Contagion,** — a technical term — from what source? — **69. Involved,** — show how

murder, the murderous mind of necessity is finally to be 70
presumed in both. This was to be expressed; and on its
own account, as well as to make it a more proportionable
antagonist to the unoffending nature of their victim, "the
gracious Duncan," and adequately to expound "the deep
damnation of his taking off," this was to be expressed with 75
peculiar energy. We were to be made to feel that the
human nature, that is, the divine nature of love and mercy,
spread through the hearts of all creatures, and seldom
utterly withdrawn from man,—was gone, vanished, extinct;
and that the fiendish nature had taken its place. And, as 80
this effect is marvellously accomplished in the *dialogues*
and *soliloquies* themselves, so it is finally consummated by
the expedient under consideration; and it is to this that

---

the word, by its derivation, is fitted to the context.— **70. Of necessity,**—why not *necessarily?* Try and see.— **71.** How does **presumed** fit its derivation here? — **Expressed,**—why would not *said* or *told* be fitting here?— **72. A more proportionable antagonist,**—can this be put in simpler terms without circumlocution?— **74.** How does **adequately** fit its derivation here?— **Expound,**—why not *explain* or *interpret?*— **77. Divine,**—what antithetic **word answers** to this below? **79. Gone, vanished, extinct,**—trace degrees of meaning and climax (see Rhet. p. 105). Does the **use of** three words answer to the idea's prominence?— **81, 82. Dialogues and soliloquies,**—what is the difference in these two words? Derive them. — **Accomplished, consummated,**—discriminate degrees of meaning in these two.— **83. Expedient under consideration,**—a repetition of what, and why the variation in repetition?— **84-103.** Read these sentences carefully aloud, **and note how** elaborate is the diction, owing to the presence of elegant words. Try the effect of substituting simpler terms, and see if the passage remains as suggestive. Is there a suspicion of fine writing (Rhet. p. 45, rule 13) in "a vast metropolis" (why not *great city?*), "great national idol" (why not *honored citizen?*), "carried in funeral pomp to his grave" (why not simply *buried?*)? See if the simpler words would adequately portray the scene De Quincey here wishes to

I now solicit the reader's attention. If the reader has ever
85 witnessed a wife, daughter, or sister, in a fainting fit, he
may chance to have observed that the most affecting moment in such a spectacle, is *that* in which a sigh and a
stirring announce the recommencement of suspended life.
Or, if the reader has ever been present in a vast metropo-
90 lis, on the day when some great national idol was carried
in funeral pomp to his grave, and chancing to walk near
the course through which it passed, has felt powerfully, in
the silence and desertion of the streets, and in the stagnation of ordinary business, the deep interest which at that
95 moment was possessing the heart of man, — if all at once
he should hear the death-like stillness broken up by the
sound of wheels rattling away from the scene, **and making
known that** the transitory vision was dissolved, **he** will be
aware that **at** no moment was his sense of **the complete**
100 **suspension** and pause in ordinary human concerns so **full**
and affecting, as at **that** moment when the suspension
ceases, and the goings-on of **human** life are suddenly
resumed. All action in any direction is best expounded,
measured, and made apprehensible, by reaction. **Now**
105 apply this to the case in Macbeth. Here, as **I have said,**

---

impress. — **93. Note the number of words used to portray** the one idea
— silence, desertion, stagnation, **96,** stillness, and **100, suspension,
pause; and** trace the particular aspect **of the scene** with which each
word is used. — **96, 97.** What words in these two lines are picturesque
or descriptive **words** (cf. Rhet. pp. 62, 168)? See if you can discern
the descriptive quality in the sound. — **98. Be aware,** — would it be
accurate to say here, as is often said nowadays, *be conscious?* — **101. Suspension ceases,** — note that one elaborate word naturally consorts
with another, as belonging to the same stratum of diction (see Rhet.
p. 83); thus, *ceases* here is better than *stops*. — **103.** Trace the stages
of the idea presented **by the three verbs. Does the importance of the**

the retiring of the human heart, and the entrance of the
fiendish heart, was to be expressed and made sensible.
Another world has stept in; and the murderers are taken
out of the region of human things, human purposes, human
desires. They are transfigured: Lady Macbeth is "un- 110
sexed"; Macbeth has forgot that he was born of woman;
both are conformed to the image of devils; and the world
of devils is suddenly revealed. But how shall this be
conveyed and made palpable? In order that a new world
may step in, this world must for a time disappear. The 115
murderers, and the murder, must be insulated — cut off by
an immeasurable gulph from the ordinary tide and succession of human affairs — locked up and sequestered in some
deep recess; we must be made sensible that the world of
ordinary life is suddenly arrested — laid asleep — tranced 120
— racked into a dread armistice; time must be annihilated;
relation to things without abolished; and all must pass
self-withdrawn into a deep syncope and suspension of earthly

---

thought **justify so minute expression?** — 107. **Expressed,** — repeated from l. 71, with a word added. What is the use of the words **made sensible?** — **Fiendish is set** over against **human** here; compare what is added to the idea, ll. 76–80. — 110. **Transfigured,** — an unusual use of the word; in what respect? — 114. **Conveyed and made palpable,** — compare these words with the verbs in ll. 103, 104, and trace the difference. — 116. **Insulated,** — note how this technical term is immediately defined for the present purpose in the parenthesis. — 115–124. Note the different ways of saying essentially the same thing, in these lines. — 121. **Armistice,** — derivation? — **Annihilated, abolished,** — discriminate these, and note **their** fitness to their subjects. — 123. **Syncope,** — a technical term; **from** what source? Does the succeeding phrase explain it sufficiently **to** justify it? Note the synonym for this employed in l. 121. (It will be noted, by the way, how the unusual words here, — insulated, sequestered, armistice, syncope — **are all** made intelligible by equivalent expressions in the context.) —

passion. **Hence it is, that** when the deed is done, when
125 the work of darkness is perfect, then the world of darkness
passes away like a pageantry in the clouds; the knocking
at the gate is heard; and it makes known audibly that the
reaction has commenced: the human has made its reflux
upon the fiendish; the pulses of life are beginning to beat
130 again; and the re-establishment of the goings-on of the
world in which we live, first makes us profoundly sensible
of the awful parenthesis that had suspended them.

O, mighty poet! **Thy** works are not as those of other
men, simply and merely great works of art; but are also
135 like the phenomena of nature, like the sun and the sea, the
stars and the flowers,— like frost and **snow,** rain and dew,
hail-storm and thunder, which are to be studied with entire
submission of our own faculties, and in the perfect faith
that in them there can be no too much or too little, nothing
140 useless or inert,— but that, the further we press in our
discoveries, the more we shall see proofs of design and self-
supporting arrangement where the careless eye **had seen**
nothing but accident.

From ESSAYS IN LITERARY CRITICISM, Works Vol. IV.

---

128. Human, fiendish,— the adjectives are used without their substantives; would it be as impressive if any substantive, as in ll. 77, 80, 106, 107, were employed?

134. Simply and merely,— point out the derivation of these words, **whose root-meanings** were identical. What distinction do you notice between **them here?**— **135. Phenomena,**— derive, and note how defined **and** particularized in the succeeding (cf. Rhet. p. 290). — **140. Useless or inert,**— **an** example of **what has** been very prominent throughout, — adjectives in pairs. Is **it obtrusive** enough to be called a mannerism? — **143. Accident,**— **what terms** constitute the antithesis to this?

STUDY INTRODUCTORY TO FOLLOWING SELECTIONS.

The three Selections that follow will be studied in a somewhat broader way, as illustrating some of the characteristics that diction takes, according to the prevailing mood or emotion in which the work is written; and presuppose a knowledge of the Rhetoric as far as page 84.

Before proceeding to these Selections, however, let us see what characteristics of this kind are revealed in the two Selections that have already been given.

Bunyan: pages 1-6. — Bunyan has a simple and intelligible story to tell; as it were, a recital of plain fact. His appeal, therefore, is merely to the intellect; and the diction, in the regularity and restraint of its structure, is of the Intellectual Type; see Rhet. p. 69. Can you discern, in ll. 35-44, any evidences of increased emotion? Note the short, trenchant clauses, all direct assertions, and the strong words and figures; e.g., "I hate his person," etc.; "Prepare thyself to die;" "Here will I spill thy soul." The exclamation in l. 68, also, is natural to the heightened feeling of this part of the story.

De Quincey: pages 8-16. — The selection from De Quincey, being concerned with expounding ideas, is also prevailingly of the Intellectual Type, but in a manner very different from that of Bunyan. You have already observed how exact he is, in the choice of words and in the discrimination of shades in the idea; this is called for largely by the nature of his task. But also, as an individual trait, his diction is very elaborate. We see here illustrated what critics have noted, that "his language naturally and unavoidably shaped itself into stately phrases"; and sometimes we can feel, with the critics, "their occasionally somewhat inappropriate pomp and elegance." Observe if this is in any degree the case in ll. 80-102; 113-132.

The last paragraph shows the effect of emotion, and is distinctly an approach to the Impassioned Type. What is there that indicates a heightened style? Read it aloud, and observe the flow of it, its euphony and rhythm (cf. Rhet. p. 169), the omission of the article in l. 136 (see Rhet. p. 51), the imaginative delight in the impressive phenomena of nature, which gives the passage a poetic touch.

III.

EDMUND BURKE.

THE AGE OF CHIVALRY IS GONE!

"In all its varieties Burke's style is noble, earnest, deep-flowing, because his sentiment was lofty and fervid, and went with sincerity and ardent disciplined travail of judgment. . . . Burke had the style of his subjects, the amplitude, **the weightiness, the** laboriousness, the **sense, the** high flight, the grandeur, proper to a man dealing with imperial themes, the freedom of nations, the justice of rulers, the fortunes of great societies, the sacredness of law." — JOHN MORLEY.

IT is now sixteen or seventeen **years since I** saw the Queen of France, then the Dauphiness, at Versailles; and

---

The "Reflections on the Revolution in France," from which **this** Selection **is** taken, was first published in October, 1790. The mood in which the present passage was written is well indicated in the following passage from a letter of Burke's to Sir P. Francis, under date of Feb. 20, 1790: "I tell you again, that the recollection of the manner in which I saw the Queen of France, in the year 1774, and the contrast between that brilliancy, splendor, and beauty, with the prostrate homage of a nation to her — and the abominable scene of 1789, which I was describing, *did* draw tears from me, and wetted my paper. These tears came again into my eyes, almost as often as I looked at the description; they may again. **You do** not believe this fact, nor that these are my **real** feelings: but that the whole is affected, or, as you express it, downright foppery."

Let us see how such emotion **and such vivid** realization reveal themselves in the diction.

1. **Notes on the prevailing types of the Diction.** — Lines **1-7** are descriptive; point out how they **agree** with the characteristics of descriptive language mentioned Rhet. p. **338**, bottom. — What do you

surely never lighted on this orb, which she hardly seemed
to touch, a more delightful vision. I saw her **just above
the** horizon, decorating and cheering the elevated sphere 5
she just began to move **in**; glittering like the morning
star, full of life, and splendor, and joy. Oh, what **a** revolution! **and what a** heart must I have, to contemplate without

---

discern of poetic structure in l. **3?** — What word from the **poetic vocabulary?** — Explain the figure that lines **1–7** embody; is **it suitable to** ordinary plain prose, such prose, for instance, as Bunyan's? — Do you discern in these lines words chosen in part for their euphony or picturesqueness? — Read the clauses aloud; do you observe a tendency to regularity of rhythm? — Consider how all these things help the imagination to realize the **passage.** It will be observed that, although the **diction is** brilliant and **noble, there are** few if any words that belong exclusively **to** the poetic *vocabulary*; **and** this agrees with what **Hazlitt** says: "It has always appeared to me that the most perfect prose style, the most powerful, the most **dazzling, the most** daring, that which went nearest to the verge of poetry, and yet never fell over, was Burke's."

Lines **7–31** are not so much description as comment; and they are obviously more impassioned than preceding or following. Point out the irregularities of expression due to emotion; see Rhet. p. 71. Notice **first the** exclamatory **sentences;** cf. Rhet. **p.** 97. Try the effect of putting ll. **7–9** in a mere assertion. What repetition makes ll. **24–26** exclamatory (cf. l. **18)?** Notice next **how the repetitions aid** the emphasis; (cf. Rhet. p. 161, 74); see e.g. ll. **9, 13, 14, 15, 20, 26.** Notice finally **how** much is expressed **by** circumlocutions that give **the real significance** of the thought. What circumlocution for "became **queen**" in l. **10?** for "poison" (some say "a dagger") in l. **12?** — For what **is** the bold figure (taken perhaps from Milton, Par. Lost, I. 664) in ll. **16, 17,** a circumlocution? Lines **18–31** are quoted, Rhet. p. 292, as example of amplification by repetition. Point out in these lines the different equivalents for *chivalry.* — From such details as these, we observe **that the impassioned character of the** passage is expressed **mostly** by repetition: first **of the note,** "Little did I dream" (ll. **9–15), then** of the note, "**Never,** never more" (ll. 20–24), finally of the note, "**It is gone**" (ll. 18, 26). Notice how these expressions, or their equivalents, are reiterated as the dominating elements of their sentences, somewhat like **a musical refrain.**

emotion that elevation and that fall! Little did I dream, when she added titles of veneration to those of enthusiastic, distant, respectful love, that she should ever be obliged to carry the sharp antidote against disgrace concealed in that bosom; little did I dream that I should have lived to see such disasters fallen upon her in a nation of gallant men, in a nation of men of honour, and of cavaliers. I thought ten thousand swords must have leaped from their scabbards to avenge even a look that threatened her with insult. But the age of chivalry is gone. That of sophisters, economists, and calculators, has succeeded; and the glory of Europe is extinguished for ever. Never, never

---

Do you find the rest of the Selection so impassioned as what has been examined? Do you note any of the irregular, or abrupt, or poetic expressions due to impassioned style? Let us see why. Do the thoughts with which it deals come so much home to *personal* feelings and concerns, or is it more abstract? Give the main underlying thought of paragraph, ll. 32-51. Of ll. 52-64. Of ll. 65-76. Of ll. 77-99. Are these thoughts, as here treated, well adapted to fervid passion?

2. **Notes on choice of Words.** — In the Selection from Bunyan we have seen words employed for plain and simple information; in the Selection from De Quincey, for exactness and fineness. In this Selection we shall find many of the unusual words employed partly for strength, partly for rhythm.

The strength is due for the most part to the suggestive, thought-producing quality of the expressions chosen. See Rhet. p. 21. II. 1. — 12. The sharp antidote against disgrace, — how much more does this suggest than the word *poison?* — 16. Ten thousand swords, — try some indefinite number, like *multitudes* of swords, and note the change of effect. — 16. Leaped from their scabbards, — how does the word *leaped* aid the vigor of the expression? — 20-23. Point out the epithets that rouse thought by means of paradox or antithesis. — Point out similar ones in l. 53. — What strong Saxon verb in l. 58? — Suggestive epithets in l. 62? — In l. 78? — Note how all is summed up and strengthened (l. 98) by a short, striking sentence.

more, shall we behold that generous loyalty to rank and sex, that proud submission, that dignified obedience, that subordination of the heart, which kept alive, even in servitude itself, the spirit of an exalted freedom. The unbought grace of life, the cheap defence of nations, the nurse of manly sentiment and heroic enterprise, is gone! It is gone, that sensibility of principle, that chastity of honour, which felt a stain like a wound, which inspired courage whilst it mitigated ferocity, which ennobled whatever it touched, and under which vice itself lost half its evil, by losing all its grossness.

This mixed system of opinion and sentiment had its origin in the ancient chivalry; and the principle, though varied in its appearance by the varying state of human affairs, subsisted and influenced through a long succession of generations, even to the time we live in. If it should ever be totally extinguished, the loss I fear will be great. It is this which has given its character to modern Europe. It is this which has distinguished it under all its forms of government, and distinguished it to its advantage, from the states of Asia, and possibly from those states which flourished in the most brilliant periods of the antique world.

Of course the words that promote the rhythm and euphony are also suggestive and exact; they would not be chosen, by so earnest a writer as Burke, for their sound alone. But test some of the lines by reading aloud, or by trying to substitute equivalent words. Note the rhythm of lines 3 and 4. — Of 6 and 7. Substitute a monosyllable for *splendor*, and note the effect. — How would *rise* for *elevation*, in l. 9, affect the sound of it? — Read carefully ll. 20–31, and mark how accented and unaccented syllables follow one another (cf. Rhet. p. 170). How does this regularity of accent correspond with the sentiment of the passage?

The passage ll. 47–64 is quoted, Rhet. p. 187, to illustrate how short sentences may be interspersed with long, to aid in ease of interpretation.

It was this, which, without confounding ranks, had produced a noble equality, and handed **it down through** all the gradations of social life. **It was this** opinion which mitigated kings into companions, and raised private men to **be fellows with** kings. Without force, or opposition, it subdued **the** fierceness of pride and power; it obliged sovereigns **to** submit to the soft collar of social esteem, compelled **stern** authority to submit to elegance, and gave a dominating vanquisher of laws to be subdued by manners.

But now all is to be changed. All the pleasing illusions, which made **power** gentle, **and** obedience liberal, which harmonized the different shades **of** life, and which, by a bland assimilation, incorporated into politics the sentiments which beautify and soften private society, are to be dissolved by this new conquering empire of light and reason. All the decent drapery of life is to be rudely torn off. All the superadded ideas, furnished from the wardrobe **of a moral** imagination, which the heart owns, and the understanding ratifies, as necessary to cover the **defects of our** naked, shivering nature, and to raise it to dignity in **our** own estimation, are to be exploded as **a** ridiculous, absurd, and antiquated fashion.

On this scheme **of** things, a **king is but** a man; a queen is but a woman; a woman is but an animal, and an animal not of the highest order. All homage paid to the sex in

---

50. On this passage Mr. Joseph **Payne** ("Studies in English Prose," p. 325) **has** the following note: "There is probably some misprint here, which must have escaped the author's notice. The phraseology as we find it, is impossible, though **the meaning** is easily seen. It may be thus paraphrased — 'made him, **who had** proudly overthrown all laws, submit in his turn to the dominion of manners.' Perhaps 'gave'— which is the real difficulty — ought to be 'made,' though, in that case, the construction would still be awkward."

general as such, and without distinct views, is to be regarded as romance and folly. **Regicide, and** parricide, and sacrilege, are **but** fictions of superstition, corrupting jurisprudence by destroying its simplicity. The murder of a king, or a queen, or a bishop, or a father, is only common homicide; and if the people are by any chance, or **in any way, gainers** by it, a sort of homicide much the most pardonable, **and** into which we ought not to make too severe a scrutiny.

On the scheme of this barbarous philosophy, which is the offspring of cold hearts and muddy understandings, and which is as void of solid wisdom, as it is destitute of all taste and elegance, laws are to be supported only by their own terrors, and by the concern which each individual may find in them from his own private **speculations, or can spare** to them from his own private interests. **In the** groves **of** *their* academy, at the end of every vista, you see nothing but the gallows. Nothing is left which engages the affections on the part of the commonwealth. On the principles of this **mechanic philosophy,** our institutions can never be embodied, **if I may use the** expression, in persons; so as **to create in us love, veneration, admiration, or** attachment. But that sort of reason which **banishes the affections** is incapable of filling their place. These public affections, combined with manners, are required sometimes **as supplements**, sometimes as correctives, always as aids **to law.** The precept **given** by a wise man, as well as a great critic, for the construction of poems, is equally true as to states: *Non satis est pulchra esse poemata, dulcia sunto.* There ought to be a system of manners in every nation, which a well-formed mind would be disposed to relish. To make us love our country, our country ought to be lovely.

From REFLECTIONS ON THE REVOLUTION IN FRANCE.

IV.

WILLIAM MAKEPEACE THACKERAY.

ON LETTS'S DIARY.

"**The** charm comes from the writer, and his mode of treatment. The wit and the humor, so 'bitter-sweet'; the fine fancy **and** delicate observation; the eye for ludicrous situations; the richness, raciness, and occasional wildness of the comic vein; **the** subtlety **of the** unexpected strokes of pathos; the perfect obedience of **the** style to the mind it expresses; **and** the continual presence of the writer himself, making himself the companion of the reader, — gossiping, hinting, sneering, laughing, crying, as the narrative proceeds, — combine to produce an effect which **nobody, to say** the least, ever found dull. The grace, flexibility, and easy elegance **of the** style are especially notable. It is utterly without pretension, and partakes **of the** absolute sincerity of the writer; it is talk in **print**, seemingly as simple as the most familiar private **chat, and as** delicate **in its** felicities as the most elaborate composition." — E. P. WHIPPLE.

MINE is **one** of your No. 12 diaries, **three shillings cloth boards**; silk limp, gilt edges, three-and-six; **French mo-**

The selection from **Burke, just studied, being largely oratorical** and impassioned, combined, **as** we have seen, some of the abrupt and irregular characteristics of **spoken** discourse, with some of the elegances of **poetry.** **The present** selection, though **also** spoken discourse, is very different **from the style of** Burke; pitched, **as** it were, in a different key. It is what Whipple **calls** Thackeray's style above, " talk in print." We **expect** accordingly to **find** in it the chattiness, the freedom, the raciness, of conversation, both in the words chosen, which **are** free to be colloquial or learned, and in the way they are put together, which may at will be formal or irregular. **See Rhet.** pp. 76-78.

Line 1. One of your, — a colloquial idiom; how would it be expressed in more formal **style?** — **1-3.** In what spirit **is** this memorandum

rocco, tuck ditto, four-and-six. It has two pages, ruled
with faint lines for memoranda, for every week, and a ruled
account at the end, for the twelve months from January to
December, where you may set down your incomings and
your expenses. I hope yours, my respected reader, are
large; that there are many fine round sums of figures on
each side of the page: liberal on the expenditure side,
greater still on the receipt. I hope, sir, you will be "a
better man," as they say, in '62 than in this moribund '61,
whose career of life is just coming to its terminus. A
better man in purse? in body? in soul's health? Amen,
good sir, in all. Who is there so good in mind, body or
estate, but bettering won't still be good for him? O
unknown Fate, presiding over next year, if you will give
me better health, a better appetite, a better digestion, a

---

of prices, like an inventory, dictated? Is it given merely to impart
useful information? — 3. Is the word ditto a strictly literary word, —
would it sound fitting, for example, in such a passage as we have just
studied from Burke? — 6. Incomings, — what is the equivalent of this
in business language? — 7. Yours, my respected reader, — this
strikes the personal, colloquial note which is the tone of the piece, a
mutual intercourse with the reader. In Burke there is the first person,
but no second; in De Quincey there is only a distant relation to his
reader; see, for instance, De Quincey, l. 84. Here the writer and reader
are at close quarters, and the whole style is correspondingly more familiar. — 8. Fine round sums, — how does this expression illustrate
Rhet. p. 34, rule 4, remark? — 11. Moribund, — derivation? —
12. Terminus, — what is the meaning of this Latin word, and how
does it correspond with the root-meaning of career? — for which latter,
see Skeat's Etym. Dict. Does this suggestiveness justify the use of the
unusual word, and remove it from "fine writing"? (Cf. Rhet. p. 45.) —
What characteristics of spoken diction and structure do you discern in
ll. 12–41? (Cf. Rhet. p. 77.) — 13. What is the primary meaning of
amen, and how does it fit this passage? — 15–20. A half whimsical
prayer, differing from a real invocation in not being in the solemn or

better income, a better temper in '62 than you have bestowed in '61, I think your servant will be the better for
20 the changes. For instance, I should be the better for a new coat. This one, I acknowledge, is very old. The family says so. My good friend, who amongst us would not be the better if he would give up some old habits? Yes, yes. You agree with me. You take the allegory?
25 Alas! at our time of life we don't like to give up those old habits, do we? It is ill to change. There is the good old loose, easy, slovenly bedgown, laziness, for example. What man of sense likes to fling it off and put on a tight *guindé* prim dress-coat that pinches him? There is the cozy wrap-
30 rascal, self-indulgence — how easy it is! How warm! How it always seems to fit! You can walk out in it; you can go down to dinner in it. You can say of such what Tully says of his books: *Pernoctat nobiscum, pereginatur, rusticatur.* It is a little slatternly — it is a good deal stained —
35 it isn't becoming — it smells of cigar-smoke; but, *allons donc!* let the world call me idle and sloven. I love my ease better than my neighbor's opinion. I live to please myself; not you, Mr. Dandy, with your supercilious airs. I am a philosopher. Perhaps I live in my tub, and don't

---

thou-style. — 20. **A new coat**, — it becomes evident, in l. 23, why exactly this instance is chosen. — 23. What double meaning in the word **habits**, to suggest the allegory, as it is called in the next line? — 28. *Guindé*, — does this technicalism make the passage obscure, and does it add enough to pay for its use, though not understood? — 29–31. Express this sentence in a more formal style. — Would wrap-rascal be fitting in a severely literary style? See Webster's Dict. — 35. *Allons donc!* — a French idiom or colloquialism, equivalent to *who cares?* or *nonsense!* Throughout his works Thackeray evinces a very intimate knowledge of the French language. — 40. The sentence is broken off abruptly, much in the manner of Charles Lamb. Observe that the very abruptness increases the effect of what is thus broken off.

make any other use of it—. **We won't** pursue further
this unsavory metaphor. . . .

A diary. Dies. Hodie. How queer to read are some of the entries in the journal! Here are the records of dinners eaten, and gone the way of flesh. The lights burn blue somehow, and we sit before the ghosts of victuals. Hark at the dead jokes resurging! Memory greets them **with the** ghost of a smile. Here are the lists **of** the individuals who have dined at your own humble table. The agonies endured before and during those entertainments are renewed, and smart again. What a failure that special grand dinner was! How those dreadful occasional waiters did break the old china! What a dismal hash poor Mary, the cook, made of the French dish which she *would* try **out of** *Francatelli!* How angry Mrs. Pope was at **not** going down to dinner before Mrs. Bishop! How Trimalchio sneered at your absurd attempt to give a feast; and Harpagon cried out at your extravagance and ostentation!

— 41. **What is** there "unsavory" in the metaphor?— Here, for lack of space, a list of bad habits, with comments, all in the same half-whimsical spirit, is omitted.

42. The **Latin words from which the word** diary **is derived,** — how is the significance of the passage increased by the use **of** them? — 43. What right has **journal**, from its derivation, to be used here **as** equivalent for *diary?* — **44. Gone the way of flesh,** — from what universal event is this expression adopted here? — For the significance of **the lights burn blue**, compare Shakespeare, Richard III. Act V. sc. 3. — **46. Resurging,** — Thackeray coins this word, from the suggestion of the Latin word *resurgam, I shall rise again*, used in religious literature of the resurrection from the dead. Does the figure in which he is speaking, together with the freedom of conversational style, justify the coinage? (See **Rhet. p.** 36, 6.) — **47**. What humorous word-play in this line?— What does **individual** primarily signify, and for what **word** is it often incorrectly used? Is the use accurate here? — **54–62.** The

How Lady Almack bullied the other ladies in **the** drawing-room (when **no** gentlemen were **present**) : **never** asked you
60 back to dinner again : left **her card by her** footman : and took not the slightest notice of your wife and daughters at Lady Hustleby's assembly ! On the other hand, how easy, cozy, merry, comfortable, those little dinners were ; got up at one or two days' notice ; when everybody was contented ;
65 the soup as clear as amber : the wine as good as Trimalchio's own ; and the people kept their carriages waiting, and would not go away till midnight !

Along with the catalogue of bygone pleasures, balls, banquets, and the like, which **the pages record,** comes a
70 list of much more important **occurrences, and** remembrances of graver import. On two days of Dives' diary **are** printed notices that " **Dividends are due at the** Bank." **Let us** hope, dear sir, that this announcement considerably interests you ; in which case, probably, you have no need
75 **of** the almanack-maker's printed reminder. **If you look over poor** Jack Reckless's note-book, amongst his memoranda **of** racing odds given and taken, **perhaps you may** read : — " Nabbam's bill, due 29th September, 142 *l.* 15 *s.* 6 *d.*" Let us trust, as the **day has passed, that the little**

---

proper names used **in these lines** are characteristic of Thackeray, who always made even **his most** casual instances concrete by well-chosen names which play a very felicitous part in aiding the suggestiveness of the passage. What suggestiveness is there in " Mrs. Pope " and " Mrs. Bishop " ? **Trimalchio** was a celebrated cook in the reign of Nero ; see Brewer's " Reader's Handbook." Harpagon, a character of Moliere's, the type of utter miserliness ; see *ibid.* Almack's, the former name of Willis's Rooms, King St., London, famous for aristocratic and exclusive balls. The significance of Hustleby, as antithetical to Almack, is obvious. See other well-invented **names,** ll. 71, 76, 78, 100.

70, 71. Important . . . import, — is it felicitous to employ these two similar words so near together ? — 79. **Little transaction,** — what

transaction here noted has been satisfactorily terminated. If you are paterfamilias, and a worthy kind gentleman, no doubt you have marked down on your register, 17th December (say), "Boys come home." Ah, how carefully that blessed day is marked in *their* little calendars! In my time it used to be, Wednesday, 13th November, "5 *weeks from the holidays*"; Wednesday, 20th November, "4 *weeks from the holidays*"; until sluggish time sped on, and we came to WEDNESDAY, 18th DECEMBER. O rapture! Do you remember pea-shooters? I think we only had them on going home for holidays from private schools, — at public schools, men are too dignified. And then came that glorious announcement, Wednesday, 27th, "Papa took us **to** the Pantomime;" **or** if not papa, perhaps you condescended to go to the pit, under charge of the footman.

That was near the end of the year — **and** mamma gave you a new pocket-book, perhaps, with a little coin, God bless her, in the pocket. And that pocket-book was for next year, you know; and, in that pocket-book you had to **write down** that sad day, Wednesday, January 24th, eighteen hundred and never mind what, — when Dr. Birch's young friends were expected to **reassemble.**

---

expression of dunning creditors is here imitated? — **81. Paterfamilias,** — derivation? Is it suited to all kinds of style? — **89. Pea-shooters,** — the use of pea-shooters will be found explained in " School Days at Rugby," Chap. IV.: — "'What do they do with pea-shooters?' inquires **Tom.** 'Do wi' 'em! why, peppers every one's faces as we comes near, 'cept the young gals, and breaks windows wi' them too, some on 'em shoots so hard.'" — Do you find, in the adjectives, ll. **84, 92,** and in the exclamation, l. **88,** an illustration of Rhet. p. 77, 4?

What is there in the paragraph, ll. **95-101,** to indicate that Thackeray entered thoroughly into the feelings of childhood, with regard to school and home life? One leading characteristic of Thackeray was that he was always young in spirit.

Ah me! Every person who turns this page over has his own little diary, in paper or ruled in his memory tablets, and in which are set down the transactions of the now dying year. Boys and men, we have our calendar, mothers and maidens. For example, in your calendar pocket-book, my good Eliza, what a sad, sad day that is — how fondly and bitterly remembered — when your boy went off to his regiment, to India, to danger, to battle perhaps. What a day was that last day at home, when the tall brother sat yet amongst the family, the little ones round about him wondering at saddle-boxes, uniforms, sword-cases, gun-cases, and other wondrous apparatus of war and travel which poured in and filled the hall; the new dressing-case for the beard not yet grown; the great sword-case at which little brother Tom looks so admiringly! **What a dinner** that was, that last dinner, when little and grown children assembled together, and all tried to be cheerful! What a **night** was that last night, when the young ones were at **roost for** the last time together under the same roof, and **the** mother lay alone in her chamber counting the fatal hours as they tolled one after another, amidst her tears, her watching, her fond prayers. What a night that was,

---

102. **Ah me!** — This interjection indicates what change in the mood of the piece? **In what** figurative sense is the word *diary*, or *calendar*, henceforth understood? — 105. **Mothers and maidens,** — why is this a more graceful **expression** than *mothers and daughters* would be? — 113. **Wondrous** apparatus, — this expression indicates that Thackeray is looking through whose eyes? **and** in what mood? — What humorous touches do you discern in this description? — **What touches** of pathos? — 119. **At roost,** — this word adds strangely both to the humor and the pathos of the account. — 121. **The fatal hours,** — what feeling does this well-chosen epithet help us to realize? — 123. Observe how naturally the sadness of the scene makes the passage run into exclamation. So also **131.**

and yet how quickly the melancholy dawn came! Only
too soon the sun rose over the houses. And now in a 125
moment more the city seemed to wake. The house began
to stir. The family gathers together for the last meal.
For the last time in the midst of them the widow kneels
amongst her kneeling children, and falters a prayer in
which she commits her dearest, her eldest born, to the care 130
of the Father of all. O night, what tears you hide — what
prayers you hear! And so the nights pass and the days
succeed, until that one comes when tears and parting shall
be no more.

In your diary, as in mine, there are days marked with 135
sadness, not for this year only, but for all. On a certain
day — and the sun, perhaps, shining ever so brightly — the
house-mother comes down to her family with a sad face,
which scares the children round about in the midst of
their laughter and prattle. They may have forgotten — 140
but she has not — a day which came, twenty years ago it
may be, and which she remembers only too well: the long
night-watch; the dreadful dawning and the rain beating at
the pane; the infant speechless, but moaning in its little
crib, and then the awful calm, the awful smile on the sweet 145
cherub face, when the cries have ceased, and the little suffering breast heaves no more. Then the children, as they see
their mother's face, remember this was the day on which their

---

The paragraph, ll. **135-158 is genuinely and** deeply pathetic, **but
marked** by few peculiarities of expression to bring out the pathos, it
being so deeply ingrained in the thought. Note what there **is** — what
antithesis in l. **137, and 139,** — the common word **scares**, l. **139**, so
much more vivid than *frightens*, — the epithet in **143**, — the repeated
epithet in **145**, — the epithets in **146, 147**. Notice also how frequently
the adjective **little** recurs (ll. **144, 146, 149, 151**), and what vivid reali-
zation of the scene gave rise to its employment in each case. —

little brother died. It was before they were born ; but she
150 remembers it. And as they pray together, it seems almost
as if the spirit of the little lost one was hovering round the
group. So they pass away : friends, kindred, the **dearest-
loved**, grown people, aged, infants. As we go on the
down-hill journey, the mile-stones are grave-stones, and on
155 each more and more names are written ; unless haply you
live beyond man's common age, when friends have dropped
off, and, tottering, and feeble, and unpitied, you reach the
terminus alone.

In this past year's diary **is** there any precious day noted
160 **on which** you have made a new friend? This is a piece of
good fortune bestowed but grudgingly on the old. After
a certain age a new friend is a wonder, like Sarah's child.
Aged persons are seldom capable **of** bearing friendships.
Do you remember how warmly you loved Jack and Tom
165 when you were at school; what a passionate regard **you
had for Ned when** you were at college, and the immense
letters you wrote to each other? How often do you write,
now that postage costs nothing? There is the age of
blossoms and sweet budding green : the age of generous
170 summer ; the autumn when the leaves drop ; and then
winter, shivering **and bare**. Quick, children, and sit at my
feet ; for they are cold, very cold : and it seems as if neither
wine **nor worsted will warm** 'em.

In this past year's diary is there any dismal day noted in

---

155. Haply, — somewhat archaic, but **not** unfitting in this descriptive and somewhat emotional passage.

164–166. How is this passage helped by using particular names of persons? — **166. Immense,** — what makes this a well-chosen word? — **171.** In what assumed character is this sentence spoken? — **173.** Does the alliteration aid the effect **of the** passage? What do you suppose **prompted the** contraction at the end of the sentence?

which you have lost a friend? In mine there is. I do not 175
mean by death. Those who are gone, you have. Those
who departed loving you, love you still; and you love them
always. They are not really gone, those dear hearts and
true; they are only gone into the next room: and you will
presently get up and follow them, and yonder door will 180
close upon *you*, and you will be no more seen. As I am in
this cheerful mood, I will tell you a fine and touching story
of a doctor which I heard lately. About two years since
there was, in **our** or some other city, a famous doctor, into
whose consulting-room crowds came daily, so that they 185
might be healed. Now this doctor had a suspicion that
there was something vitally wrong with himself, and he
went to consult another famous physician at Dublin, or it
may be at Edinburgh. And he of Edinburgh punched his
comrade's sides; **and listened at his** heart and lungs; and 190
felt his pulse, **I suppose**; and looked at his tongue; and

175-181. The idea **of these lines** Thackeray has enlarged upon in
" The Newcomes," Vol. II. Chap. VII. : " If love lives through all life;
and survives through all sorrow; and remains steadfast with us through
all changes; **and in all darkness** of spirit burns brightly; **and,** if we die,
deplores us **for** ever, and loves still equally; and **exists with the very
last** gasp and throb of the faithful bosom — whence it passes **with the
pure** soul, beyond death; surely it shall be immortal! Though we **who**
remain are separated from it, is it not ours in Heaven? If we love still
those we lose, can we altogether lose those we love?" — **182-212.** Much
of the charm of this beautiful story lies in the studied simplicity of its
sentence-structure. Notice that **nearly** every sentence begins with
" and," and that **all consist of simple declarative** propositions, one after
the other; in this **respect** imitating **the simple** narratives of children,
or perhaps the unstudied narrative style of the Bible. It is a good example of an incident **well** told; compare Rhet. p. 358. — **189. Punched
his comrade's sides,** — this detail is given not so much for humor as
in imitation of the unscientific description of a common, unlearned

when he had done, Doctor **London said to** Doctor Edinburgh, **" Doctor, how long have I to live ? "** And Doctor Edinburgh said to Doctor London, " Doctor, you may last
195 a year."

Then Doctor London came home, knowing that **what** Doctor Edinburgh said was true. And he made up his accounts, with man and heaven, I trust. And he visited his patients as usual. And he went about healing, and
200 cheering, and soothing and doctoring; and thousands of sick people were benefited by him. And he said not **a word to** his family at **home;** but lived amongst them cheerful, and tender, and calm, and loving; though he knew the night was at hand when he should see them and work no
205 more.

And it was winter time, and they **came and** told him that some man **at** a distance — **very sick, but very rich — wanted** him ; and, though Doctor London knew that he was him**self at death's door, he went to the sick man;** for he knew
210 the **large fee would be good for his** children **after him.** And **he died; and** his family never knew until he was gone, that he had been long aware of the inevitable doom.

This is a cheerful carol **for** Christmas, is it not ? You see, in regard to these **Roundabout** discourses, I never know
215 whether they **are to be merry or** dismal. My hobby has

---

observer; **though a trace** of humor there is indeed in **it. — 200.** Doc**toring,** — would **the** use of *doctor* as a verb be admissible, for instance, in the previous Selection? What **justifies** it here? See Webster's Dict. *s. v.*

213-231. Observe how, with the transition to the general **chatty** tone of the discourse, the racy, free, conversational style, full **of exclamations and interrogatories,** humorous figures, **anecdotes, and the** like, is resumed. Point out some of the *words* that contain a spirit of humor, and explain how they help the passages where they occur. —

the bit in his mouth; goes his own way; and sometimes trots through a park, and sometimes paces by a cemetery. Two days since came the printer's little emissary, with a note saying, "We are waiting for the Roundabout paper!" A Roundabout paper about what or whom? How stale it [220] has become, that printed jollity about Christmas! Carols, and wassail-bowls, and holly, and mistletoe, and yule logs *de commande* — what heaps of these have we not had for years past! Well, year after year the season comes. Come frost, come thaw, come snow, come rain, year after year [225] my neighbor the parson has to make his sermon. They are getting together the bonbons, iced cakes, Christmas trees at Fortnum and Mason's now. The genii of the theatres are composing the Christmas pantomime, which our young folks will see and note anon in their little [230] diaries. . . .

From ROUNDABOUT PAPERS.

---

218. **Little emissary,**—what is the derivation of this word, and from what part of the vocabulary taken? An example of what has been noticed in the style of Hawthorne, Rhet. p. 46, of humor expressed by using a word somewhat larger than its occasion. — 226. **The parson,** — what word would more naturally be used in **formal style?**

231. The piece is broken off here a little **before the end;** but the present is a hardly less appropriate stopping-place than **the other.** The conversational freedom of the "Roundabout Papers" is as evident in their general structure as in their diction. They are just the opposite of formal, severe composition.

V.

JOHN RUSKIN.

DESCRIPTION OF SAINT MARK'S, VENICE.

"Of Ruskin the writer, aside from the art critic, it is surely superfluous for me to say anything: for mastery of our language, the greater authorities long ago have given him his place; the multitude of petty critics and pinchbeck rhetoricians who pay him the tribute of tawdry imitation is the ever-present testimony to his power and masterhood. Probably no prose writer of this century has had so many choice extracts made from his writings, — passages of gorgeous description, passionate exhortation, pathetic appeal, or apostolic denunciation; and certainly no one has so molded the style of all the writers of a class as he." — W. J. STILLMAN.

AND now I wish that the reader, before I bring him into St. Mark's Place, would imagine himself for a little time in a quiet English cathedral town, and walk with me

---

The selections from Burke and Thackeray, just studied, were adduced as examples, in different kinds, of spoken style. Very different they are in most respects, the one being impassioned, the other colloquial; but they agree in presenting the idea in short, simple, direct utterances, easily apprehensible by a hearer. In this respect the present selection is quite in contrast to them. Its long and involved sentences, with their multitudes of minor clauses and phrases, making wide excursions from the principal subject and predicate, are very little adapted to a hearer; they contemplate only a reader who can linger over their intricate details. See Rhet. p. 80; and test the diction by rewriting the first paragraph, ll. 1-47, in spoken style, shortening the sentences and retaining merely what is striking and effective for oral public discourse.

Note also how different is the task undertaken in this selection from that undertaken in Burke and Thackeray. This is descriptive: it seeks

to the west front of its cathedral. **Let us** go together up
the more retired street, at the end of which we can see
the pinnacles of one of the towers, and then through the
low grey gateway, with its battlemented top and small
latticed window in the centre, into the inner private-looking
road or close, where nothing goes in but the carts of the
tradesmen who supply the bishop and the chapter, and where
there are little shaven grassplots, fenced in by neat rails,
before old-fashioned groups of somewhat diminutive **and**
excessively trim houses, with little oriel and bay windows
jutting out here and there, and deep wooden cornices and
eaves painted cream color and white, and small porches to
their doors in the shape of cockle-shells, or little, crooked,
thick, indescribable wooden gables warped a little on one
side; and so forward till we come to larger houses, also
old-fashioned, but of red brick, and with gardens behind
them, and fruit walls, which show here and there, among
the nectarines, the vestiges of an old cloister arch or shaft,
and looking in front on the cathedral square itself, laid out
in rigid divisions of smooth grass **and** gravel walk, yet not
uncheerful, especially on the sunny side where the canon's
children are walking with their nurserymaids. And **so**,

---

to arouse the reader's imagination so as to make him realize the scene
before him like a picture. We look therefore for the *picturing* power
of word and phrase, for imaginative diction; and are not surprised to
see it **taking on** something of the **richness of** poetry. See **Rhet.**
pp. 73-75.

The most **prominent** feature of Ruskin's **style is his copious use of**
adjectives; note this **in** the first paragraph. In the first two sentences,
ll. **1-24**, are these adjectives picturesque, or merely defining? Note in
the sentence, ll. **25-47, where the adjectives begin to become** more descriptive, to take more the nature of epithet; see Rhet. pp. 56-58. **Do
you** find any epithets that are less suited to prose than to poetry? What

taking care not to tread on the grass, **we** will go along the straight walk to the west front, and there stand for a time, looking up at its deep-pointed **porches and** the dark places between their pillars where there were statues **once,** and
30 where the fragments, here and there, of a stately figure **are** still left, which has in it the likeness of a king, perhaps indeed a king on earth, perhaps a saintly king long ago in heaven; and so higher and higher up to the great mouldering wall of rugged sculpture and confused arcades, shat-
35 tered, and grey, and grisly with heads of dragons **and** mocking fiends, worn by the rain and swirling winds **into** yet unseemlier shape, and colored on their stony scales by the deep russet-orange lichen, **melancholy** gold; and so, higher still, to **the** bleak towers, **so far** above that the eye
40 loses itself among the **bosses of their traceries,** though they are rude and strong, **and only sees like** a drift of eddying black points, **now** closing, **now** scattering, and now settling suddenly into **invisible** places among **the** bosses and flowers, the crowd of restless birds that fill the
45 whole square with that strange clangor of theirs, so **harsh** and yet so soothing, like the cries of birds on a solitary coast between the cliffs and sea.

    Think for a little while of that scene, **and the meaning** of all its **small formalisms,** mixed with **its serene sublimity.**
50 Estimate **its** secluded, continuous, **drowsy felicities, and its evidence of the sense and steady** performance of such kind **of** duties as **can be regulated by the** cathedral clock;

---

picturesque and poetic details in ll. **30–38**? **What curious poetic phrase in l. 38?** What poetic detail in ll. **44–46**? Consider now **why this** particular part should employ such heightened expression.

    Would you call the adjectives in l. **50** defining adjectives or epithets? that is, do they point out some quality essential to the main idea, or

and weigh the influence of those dark towers on all who
have passed through the lonely square at their feet for
centuries, and on all who have seen them rising far away
over the wooded plain, or catching on their square masses
the last rays of the sunset, when the city at their feet was
indicated only by the mist at the bend of the river. And
then let us quickly recollect that we are in Venice, and
land at the extremity of the Calle Lunga San Moisè, which
may be considered as there answering to the secluded street
that led us to our English cathedral gateway.

We find ourselves in a paved alley, some seven feet wide
where it is widest, full of people, and resonant with cries
of itinerant salesmen, — a shriek in their beginning, and
dying away into a kind of brazen ringing, all the worse for
its confinement between the high houses of the passage
along which we have to make our way. Over-head an inextricable confusion of rugged shutters, and iron balconies
and chimney flues pushed out on brackets to save room,
and arched windows with projecting sills of Istrian stone,
and gleams of green leaves here and there where a fig-tree
branch escapes over a lower wall from some inner cortile,
leading the eye up to the narrow stream of blue sky high
over all. On each side, a row of shops, as densely set as
may be, occupying, in fact, intervals between the square
stone shafts, about eight feet high, which carry the first
floors: intervals of which one is narrow and serves as a

---

only something secondary and descriptive? **Distinguish between the ordinary adjectives and epithets that occur in ll. 52-58.**

The paragraph, ll. **63-111**, which describes the approach to St. Mark's, is to be compared with ll. 1-25, which describe the approach to the English cathedral. Both passages are of course preparatory and secondary **to what follows them.** The difference of idiom between

door; the other is, in the more respectable shops, wainscoted to the height of the counter and glazed above, but in those of the poorer tradesmen left open to the ground, and the wares laid on benches and tables in the open air, the light in all cases entering at the front only, and fading away in a few feet from the threshold into a gloom which the eye from without cannot penetrate, but which is generally broken by a ray or two from a feeble lamp at the back of the shop, suspended before a print of the Virgin. The less pious shopkeeper sometimes leaves his lamp unlighted, and is contented with a penny print; the more religious one has his print colored and set in a little shrine with a gilded or figured fringe, with perhaps a faded flower or two on each side, and his lamp burning brilliantly. Here at the fruiterer's, where the dark-green water-melons are heaped upon the counter like cannon balls, the Madonna has a tabernacle of fresh laurel leaves; but the pewterer next door has let his lamp out, and there is nothing to be seen in his shop but the dull gleam of the studded patterns on the copper pans, hanging from his roof in the darkness. Next comes a "Vendita Frittole e Liquori," where the Virgin, enthroned in a very humble manner beside a tallow candle on a back shelf, presides over certain ambrosial morsels of a nature too ambiguous to be defined or enumerated. But a few steps farther on, at the regular wine-shop of the calle, where we are offered "Vino Nostrani a Soldi 28.32," the Madonna is in great glory, en-

---

ll. 1–25 and ll. 25–47 has already been noted as due to the difference in the character of the adjectives and to the decidedly more poetic expression, every way, of the latter passage. Note now carefully the adjectives in this paragraph, and see if there are any that are not essentially defining and prosaic.

throned above ten or a dozen large red casks of three-year-old vintage, and flanked by goodly ranks of bottles of Maraschino, and two crimson lamps; and for the evening, when the gondoliers will come to drink out, under her auspices, the money they **have** gained during the day, she will have a whole chandelier.

A yard or two farther, we pass the hostelry of the Black Eagle, and, glancing as we pass through the square door of marble, deeply moulded, in the outer wall, we **see** the shadows of its pergola of vines resting on **an ancient** well, **with** a pointed shield carved on its side; and **so** presently emerge on the bridge and Campo San Moisè, whence to the entrance into St. Mark's Place, called the **Bocca** di Piazza (mouth of the square), the Venetian character **is** nearly destroyed, **first by the** frightful façade of San Moisè, which we **will pause at** another **time** to examine, and then by the modernizing of the shops as they near **the** piazza, and the mingling with the lower Venetian populace of lounging groups of English and Austrians. **We** will push fast through **them into** the shadow of the pillars at the end of the "**Bocca di Piazza,**" and then we forget them all; **for between those pillars there opens a great light, and, in** the midst **of it, as we** advance **slowly, the vast** tower **of St.** Mark seems **to** lift **itself** visibly **forth from** the level field of chequered stones; and, on each side, the countless arches prolong themselves into ranged symmetry, **as if the** rugged and irregular houses that pressed together

---

The paragraph, ll. **112–137** begins **in the same** tone of detailed description, prosaic **though** rich. Point **out where** the tone changes to prose-poetry, and point out the words **and** phrases in the latter part which are especially heightened and **poetic.** Compare Rhet. p. 65, and explain what it is in the object described that elevates the style.

above us in the dark alley had been struck back into sudden obedience and lovely order, and all their rude casements and broken walls had been transformed into arches charged with goodly sculpture, and fluted shafts of delicate stone.

And well may they fall back, for beyond those troops of ordered arches there rises a vision out of the earth, and all the great square seems to have opened from it in a kind of awe, that we may see it far away;—a multitude of pillars and white domes, clustered into a long low pyramid of colored light; a treasure-heap, it seems, partly of gold, and partly of opal and mother-of-pearl, hollowed beneath into five great vaulted porches, ceiled with fair mosaic, and beset with sculpture of alabaster, clear as amber and delicate as ivory,—sculpture fantastic and involved, of palm leaves and lilies, and grapes and pomegranates, and birds clinging and fluttering among the branches, all twined together into an endless network of buds and plumes; and, in the midst of it, the solemn forms of angels, sceptred, and robed to the feet, and leaning to each other across the gates, their figures indistinct among the gleaming of the golden ground through the leaves beside them, interrupted

---

The gorgeously descriptive paragraph, ll. **138–180**, may be more closely analyzed. Mention the most vividly descriptive epithets. Note the epithets formed from nouns, ll. **131, 136, 145, 151, 152, 163**; does this mode of formation belong more distinctively to prose or poetry? Note further the compounds, ll. **143, 144, 156, 158, 160, 179**: some of these are equally well adapted to poetry and prose, some belong only to prose-poetry or poetry,—discriminate them. Show further what details would not naturally occur in a piece designed merely to give information, that is, what details are especially poetic and imaginative. Finally, read the paragraph carefully aloud, and report what you find of rhythm so regular as to be metre, as for instance, ll. **155, 156**. Report what-

and dim, like the morning light as it faded back among the branches of Eden, when first its gates were angel-guarded long ago. And round the walls of the porches there are set pillars of variegated stones, jasper and porphyry, and deep-green serpentine spotted with flakes of snow, and marbles, that half refuse and half yield to the sunshine, Cleopatra-like, "their bluest veins to kiss"—the shadow, as it steals back from them, revealing line after line of azure undulation, as a receding tide leaves the waved sand; their capitals rich with interwoven tracery, rooted knots of herbage, and drifting leaves of acanthus and vine, and mystical signs, all beginning and ending in the Cross; and above them, in the broad archivolts, a continuous chain of language and of life—angels, and the signs of heaven, and the labors of men, each in its appointed season upon the earth; and above these, another range of glittering pinnacles, mixed with white arches edged with scarlet flowers, —a confusion of delight, amidst which the breasts of the Greek horses are seen blazing in their breadth of golden strength, and the St. Mark's Lion, lifted on a blue field covered with stars, until at last, as if in ecstasy, the crests of the arches break into a marble foam, and toss themselves far into the blue sky in flashes and wreaths of sculptured spray, as if the breakers on the Lido shore had been frost-bound before they fell, and the sea-nymphs had inlaid them with coral and amethyst.

Between that grim cathedral of England and this, what an interval! There is a type of it in the very birds that haunt them; for, instead of the restless crowd, hoarse-

---

ever else you find that is distinctively poetic, as word-painting, alliteration, bold figure, inversion, and so forth; in short, endeavor to get a *feeling* of the beauty of the style, and to trace it to its causes.

voiced and sable-winged, drifting on the bleak upper air, the St. Mark's porches are full of doves, that nestle among the marble foliage, and mingle the soft iridescence of their living plumes, changing at every motion, with the tints, hardly less lovely, that have stood unchanged for seven hundred years.

And what effect has this splendor on those who pass beneath it? You may walk from sunrise to sunset, to and fro, before the gateway of St. Mark's, and you will not see an eye lifted to it, nor a countenance brightened by it. Priest and layman, soldier and civilian, rich and poor, pass by it alike regardlessly. Up to the very recesses of the porches, the meanest tradesmen of the city push their counters; nay, the foundations of its pillars are themselves the seats — not "of them that sell doves" for sacrifice, but of the venders of toys and caricatures. Round the whole square in front of the church there is almost a continuous line of cafés, where the idle Venetians of the middle classes lounge, and read empty journals; in its centre the Austrian bands play during the time of vespers, their martial music jarring with the organ notes, — the march drowning the miserere, and the sullen crowd thickening round them, — a crowd, which, if it had its will, would stiletto every soldier that pipes to it. And in the recesses of the porches, all day long, knots of men of the lowest classes, unemployed and listless, lie basking in the sun like lizards; and unregarded children, — every heavy glance of their young eyes full of desperation and stony depravity, and their throats hoarse with cursing, — gamble, and fight,

---

Point out the epithets and compounds of the paragraph, ll. **181-189**. Compare this paragraph with the next, ll. **190-216**; do you find bold poetic devices in the latter? **Note the** character of the description,

and snarl, and sleep, hour after hour, clashing their bruised centesimi upon the marble ledges of the **church** porch. **And the** images of Christ and His angels look down upon 215 it continually.

[Before describing the interior, "that we may not enter the church out of the midst of the horror of this," Ruskin devotes two pages, here omitted, to describing the Baptistery, with the tomb therein, of the Doge Andrea Dandolo.]

Through the heavy door whose bronze **network** closes the place of his rest, let us enter the church itself. **It is** lost in still deeper twilight, to which the eye must **be** accustomed for some moments before the form of the build- 220 ing can be traced; and then there opens **before us a vast cave, hewn** out into the **form of a** Cross, and divided into **shadowy aisles by** many **pillars.** Round **the** domes **of its** roof the light **enters only** through narrow apertures like large stars; and here and there a ray or two **from some far** 225 away casement wanders into the darkness, and casts a narrow phosphoric stream upon the waves of marble that **heave and fall** in **a thousand colors** along the floor. What else there is of light is **from torches, or** silver lamps, burning ceaselessly **in the recesses of the chapels;** the roof 230 sheeted with gold, and the **polished walls covered with** alabaster, give back **at** every curve and angle **some feeble** gleaming to the flames; and the glories round the heads **of** the sculptured saints flash out upon us as we pass them, **and** sink again into the gloom. Under foot and over head, 235

---

ll. **206–214**, which deals with a different **kind** of object from the preceding; do **you find words whose sound** corresponds with **the sense?** Cf. Rhet. pp. 61, 168.

In the same way as pointed out before, note where and **how** the language becomes more heightened in paragraph, ll. **217–259**, and estimate

a continual succession of crowded imagery, one picture passing into another, as in a dream; forms beautiful and terrible mixed together; dragons and serpents, and ravening beasts of prey, and graceful birds that in the midst of them drink from running fountains and feed from vases of crystal; the passions and the pleasures of human life symbolized together, and the mystery of its redemption; for the mazes of interwoven lines and changeful pictures lead always at last to the Cross, lifted and carved in every place and upon every stone; sometimes with the serpent of eternity wrapt round it, sometimes with doves beneath its arms, and sweet herbage growing forth from its feet; but conspicuous most of all on the great rood that crosses the church before the altar, raised in bright blazonry against the shadow of the apse. And although in the recesses of the aisle and chapels, when the mist of the incense hangs heavily, we may see continually a figure traced in faint lines upon their marble, a woman standing with her eyes raised to heaven, and the inscription above her, "Mother of God," she is not here the presiding deity. It is the Cross that is first seen, and always, burning in the centre of the temple; and every dome and hollow of its roof has the figure of Christ in the utmost height of it, raised in power, or returning in judgment.

Nor is this interior without effect on the minds of the people. At every hour of the day there are groups collected before the various shrines, and solitary worshippers scattered through the darker places of the church, evidently in prayer both deep and reverent, and, for the most

---

how the object, in its richness or its beauty, calls for it. Rewrite, in merely matter-of-fact language, and retaining only such details as are needed for plain information, the description of the interior.

part, profoundly sorrowful. The devotees at the greater 265
number of the renowned shrines of Romanism may be
seen murmuring their appointed prayers with wandering
eyes and unengaged gestures; but the step of the stranger
does not disturb those who kneel on the pavement of St.
Mark's; and hardly a moment passes, from early morning 270
to sunset, in which we may not see some half-veiled figure
enter beneath the Arabian porch, cast itself into long
abasement on the floor of the temple, and then rising
slowly with more confirmed step, and with a passionate
kiss and clasp of the arms given to the feet of the crucifix, 275
by which the lamps burn always in the northern aisle,
leave the church, as if comforted.

From STONES OF VENICE, Vol. II.

On the foregoing passage, ll. **138-180**, Mr. Joseph Payne (Studies in English Prose, p. 429) remarks: " It would be difficult — nay, more than difficult — impossible — to match the above passage by any other of a similar kind in the English language. To call it 'poetical prose' is to degrade it to the level of much that is simply intolerable to read, and of which it is easy — too easy — to find specimens everywhere. When this wonderful passage has been read over half a dozen times, it will be more admired than at first. As a description of the actual building — open to the observation of all, on the Piazza at Venice — it is difficult to call it true; but it is more difficult to call it false. It is the idealized St. Mark's, as seen through the mist of time in the clear light of its first creation — and, indeed, further back still, in the artist's mind that conceived it — that the writer has placed before us; but we must yield ourselves up to the magic of his inspiration, before we can see what he shows us. The sacrifice, however, if it be one, is well worth making."

VI.

JAMES RUSSELL LOWELL.

THE POETRY OF ST. PETER'S, ROME.

"Lowell's [prose] is clear enough to those familiar with the choicest literature. In critical exploits that bring out his resources, he is not a writer for dullards, and to read him enjoyably is a point in evidence of a liberal education. His manner, in fact, is Protean, adjusted to his topic, and has a flexibility that well expresses his racy wit and freshness." — E. C. STEDMAN.

IT is very common for people to say that they are disappointed in the first sight of St. Peter's; and one hears much the same about Niagara. I cannot help thinking that the fault is in themselves, and that if the church and
5 the cataract were in the habit of giving away their thoughts

---

This Selection and the one following are studied as illustrating Figures of Speech, and the suggestiveness of figurative style; and presuppose a knowledge of the Rhetoric as far as page 107. See also what is said about **Allusion**, Rhetoric, pages 298, 299, and **Analogy**, page 395.

The most striking characteristic of Lowell's style is its suggestiveness, due to its abundance of allusion, figurative expression, and the ceaseless play of fancy round every important thought. Let us endeavor here to note, in some of the most striking cases, how one thing is made more significant or telling by being compared, directly or indirectly, with another, or by being expressed in terms of another.

Lines 1–9. The opening statement about St. Peter's is illustrated by a comparison with what? What are the exact things compared? Is this a simile? See Rhet. p. 89, 1. — **5. Giving away their thoughts,** —

with that rash generosity which characterizes tourists, they might perhaps say of their visitors, "Well, if you are those men of whom we have heard so much, we are a little disappointed, to tell the truth!" The refined tourist expects somewhat too much when he takes it for granted that St. Peter's will at once decorate him with the order of imagination, just as Victoria knights an alderman when he presents an address. Or perhaps he has been getting up a little architecture on the road from Florence, and is discomfited because he does not know whether he *ought* to be pleased or not, which is very much as if he should wait to be told whether it was fresh water or salt which makes the exhaustless grace of Niagara's emerald curve, before he benignly consented to approve. It would be wiser, perhaps, for him to consider whether, if Michael Angelo had had the building of *him*, his own personal style would not have been more impressive.

It is not to be doubted that minds are of as many different orders as cathedrals, and that the Gothic imagination is vexed and discommoded in the vain endeavor to flatten

---

the act of talking is here expressed in language suitable to what? What figures does this involve? See Rhet. pp. 90–94. — How do these figures illustrate what is said in ll. 3, 4? — 11. **Decorate him with the order,** — allusion to what custom? Express it literally. — 12. **Just as, etc.** Is this a figurative or an unfigurative comparison? — 13. **Getting up,** — is this idiom applicable to all styles? Why in taste here? — 16. **Which is very much as if, etc.** How does this comparison differ from simple simile? See Rhet. p. 395. — What call for the essential epithet of l. 18, and what hidden antithesis (see Rhet. p. 103, 2) does the description sharpen? — 19. **Benignly consented,** — this elaborate expression hints at what character of the tourist? — 21. **Personal style,** — this manner of expression regards the person for the moment as what?

23, 24. **Different orders,** — a technical term belonging to what art, and involving what metaphor? — 25. **Discommoded,** — what is the

its pinnacles, and fit itself into the round Roman arches.
But if it be impossible for a man to like everything, it is
quite possible for him to avoid being driven mad by what
does not please him; nay, it is the imperative duty of a
30 wise man to find out what that secret is which makes a
thing pleasing to another. In approaching St. Peter's, one
must take his Protestant shoes off his feet and leave them
behind him in the Piazza Rusticucci. Otherwise the great
Basilica, with those outstretching colonnades of Bramante,
35 will seem to be a bloated spider lying in wait for him, the
poor Reformed fly. As he lifts the heavy leathern flapper
over the door, and is discharged into the interior by its
impetuous recoil, let him disburden his mind altogether of
stone and mortar, and think only that he is standing before
40 the throne of a dynasty which, even in its decay, is the
most powerful the world ever saw. Mason-work is all very
well in itself, but it has nothing to do with the affair at
present in hand.

---

more usual word? See Webster's Dict. — **25. Flatten its pinnacles,**
— what essential character of Gothic architecture furnishes suggestiveness to this passage? — It is to be noted how freely figure is here
superinduced upon figure without confusion. To speak of the Gothic
imagination as an order of architecture is what figure? To speak of
this order further as vexed and discommoded in endeavoring involves
what further figure? — **32. Protestant shoes off his feet,** — for the
allusion here, see Exodus iii. 5. Express this idea literally. What
useful implication does the allusion supply? — **33-36.** What peculiarity
of the ground plan of St. Peter's, with its approaches, furnishes the
suggestion for the simile of these lines? Point out how simile and
metaphor are combined in this sentence. Cf. Rhet. p. 92, 3. — **37. Discharged,** — to what kind of action is this verb applicable, and what
metaphor does it here involve? — **39. Stone and mortar,** — what
figure? See Rhet. p. 88. Does this naming of part of the idea by
these words set off the antithesis more effectively, — and what antithesis?

Suppose that a man in pouring down a glass of claret could drink the South of France; that he could so disintegrate the wine by the force of imagination as to taste in it all the clustered beauty and bloom of the grape, all the dance and song and sunburnt jollity of the vintage. Or suppose that in eating bread he could transubstantiate it with the tender blade of spring, the gleam-flitted corn-ocean of summer, the royal autumn with its golden beard, and the merry funerals of harvest. This is what the great poets do for us, we cannot tell how, with their fatally-chosen words, crowding the happy veins of language again with all the life and meaning and music that had been dribbling away from them since Adam. And this is what the Roman Church does for religion, feeding the soul not with the

---

Read the whole paragraph, ll. **44-99**, and determine exactly what is the main literal thought that the writer intends to express and illustrate. Having determined this, look now at the main figures by which it is set off. Two figures, ll. 45-48, and ll. 48-52, prepare the way. Would you call these simile or analogy? You notice what an imaginative heightening there is in the language, ll. 46-52, and ll. 54-56; what call is there to set off this part of the idea with such beauty? — **45. Disintegrate,** — a technical term drawn from what science? — **47-48.** The use of the general terms for particular involves what figure? — What poetic element do you discern in l. **48**? — **49. Transubstantiate,** — from what department or sphere of thought is this term borrowed? Cf. Rhet. p. 40, bottom. — **Tender blade** is used for what, and what figure is involved? — **50, 51.** Point out the poetic words and manners of expression in these lines. — In what **figure is the royal autumn** represented? — **53.** Give the meaning that lies in the words fatally-chosen. — **54. Crowding the happy veins,** — language is viewed for the moment as what? — What force in the epithet happy? — **55. Dribbling,** — why this word instead of running or escaping? **56-67.** Having prepared for his main thought by two figures and a parallel case, the writer in these lines gives his main thought in three figurative statements; state what figures they are, and analyze them. Under

essential religious sentiment, not **with a drop** or two of the tincture of worship, but **making** us feel **one** by one all those original elements of which worship **is** composed ; not bringing the end to us, but making us **pass over** and feel beneath our feet all the golden rounds of the **ladder by** which the climbing generations have reached that end ; not handing us dryly a dead and extinguished Q. E. D., but letting it rather declare itself by the glory with which it interfuses the incense-clouds of wonder and aspiration and beauty in which it is veiled. The secret of her power is typified **in** the mystery of the Real Presence. She is the only church that has been loyal to the heart and soul of man, that has clung to her faith in **the** imagination, and that would not give over her symbols and images and sacred vessels to the perilous **keeping of the iconoclast** Understanding. She has never **lost sight of the truth** that the product human **nature is composed of the sum** of flesh and spirit, and has **accordingly regarded** both this world and the **next** as the **constituents of that** other world which **we** possess **by faith.** She knows that poor Panza, the body, has his kitchen-longings and visions, as well as Quixote, the soul, his ethereal, and has wit enough to supply **him** with **the** visible, tangible raw material of imagination. She

---

what guise is the Roman church represented in each? — **58.** What is the significance of **essential,** and how is it distinguished from tincture? — **64.** For what do the letters **Q. E. D.** stand? — Point out the antithesis involved in each of the figures, ll. **58–67.** — **69, 70.** With what are heart and soul and **imagination** set in contrast? — **72.** Derivation of iconoclast? Under what figure does it represent understanding? — Under what mathematical figure does the writer speak, ll. **74, 75?** — In the allusion, ll. **77, 78,** on what characters and relations of **Panza and** Quixote does the suggestiveness of the figure depend? — **80. Raw material,** — a term drawn from what part of **the** vocabulary? — Point

is the only poet among the churches, and, while Protestantism is unrolling a pocket surveyor's-plan, takes her votary to the pinnacle of her temple, and shows him meadow, upland, and tillage, cloudy heaps of forest clasped with the river's jewelled arm, hillsides white with the perpetual snow of flocks, and, beyond all, the interminable heave of the unknown ocean. Her empire may be traced upon the map by the boundaries of races; the understanding is her great foe; and it is the people whose vocabulary was incomplete till they had invented the arch-word Humbug that defies her. With that leaden bullet John Bull can bring down Sentiment when she flies her highest. And the more the pity for John Bull. One of these days some one whose eyes are sharp enough will read in the *Times* a standing advertisement, — " Lost, strayed, or stolen from the farm-yard of the subscriber the valuable horse Pegasus. Probably has on him part of a new plough harness, as that is also missing. A suitable reward, etc. J. BULL."

Protestantism reverses the poetical process I have spoken of above, and gives not even the bread of life, but instead of it the alcohol, or distilled intellectual result. This was very well so long as Protestantism continued to protest; for enthusiasm sublimates the understanding into imagina-

---

out the antithesis between Protestantism and Romanism in ll. **81-87**, and explain why in the latter member of it the writer should use such poetic expression. Point out what is especially poetic. — **91.** How does the introduction of the word **Humbug** set out the thought? — Under what figure is **Humbug** then treated? — Express the thought ll. **91-99** in literal language. — Who is **John Bull**, and with what character is he represented in ll. **95-99**? — Explain what is meant by **Pegasus**.

102. Alcohol, — what characteristic makes this antithetic to bread? Under what figure is Protestantism represented? — Explain the tech-

105 tion. But now that she **also has** become an establishment, she begins to perceive that **she made a** blunder in trusting herself to the **intellect** alone. **She is** beginning to feel her way back again, as one notices in Puseyism and other such hints. One is put upon reflection when he sees
110 burly Englishmen, who dine on beef and porter every **day,** marching proudly through St. Peter's on Palm Sunday, with those frightfully artificial palm branches in their hands. Romanism wisely provides for the childish in men.
115 Therefore I say again that one must lay aside his Protestantism in order to have a true feeling of St. Peter's. **Here in Rome is the laboratory of that mysterious enchantress, who** has known so well how to adapt herself to all the wants, or, if you will, the weaknesses, **of human** nature,
120 making the retirement of the convent-cell a merit to the solitary, the scourge or the **fast a** piety to the ascetic, the enjoyment **of pomp and music and incense a** religious act **in the sensual,** and furnishing **for the** very soul **itself a** *confidante* in that ear of the dumb confessional, where it
125 may securely disburden itself of its sins and sorrows. And

---

nicalism, l. **104.** — What figure involved in ll. **105, 107?** — **108. Feel her way,** — this expression **views** Protestantism under what **guise?** To what ancient legend is **it an** allusion? **Puseyism, a** movement toward Romanism, **which took place about the middle of this century** in the Church of **England.** — **110.** How does it help the expression to mention the **fact** that these Englishmen **dine** on beef and porter? — What antithesis is here involved, and to what reflection does it give rise?

Of what figurative expression in l. 32 is l. **115** sq. **a** repetition? — **117.** Under what figure is the Roman church represented here? How does this figure utilize what has been said? — **124.** *Confidante,* — what justifies the use of this foreign term here? What does the epithet **dumb** add to the expression? — **125. Disburden itself,** —

the dome of St. Peter's is the magic circle within which
she works her most potent incantations. I confess that I
could not enter it alone without a kind of awe.

From FIRESIDE TRAVELS.

---

under what figure is the soul here recognized? — **126. What is** a magic
circle, and what architectural feature of St. Peter's is taken **advantage**
of here to point the figure?

Are the figures of the foregoing predominantly ornamental, or **does**
the subtilty of the idea that they aid in conveying make them useful?
Is the idea with which the Selection deals an idea of the fancy or of the
reason; that is, is it predominantly poetic **or** prosaic? How do the
figurative expressions correspond with this **character?**

VII.

THOMAS CARLYLE.

COLERIDGE AS A TALKER.

"Carlyle's greatest distinction has yet to be referred to — his endowment, namely, as a writer. He was a good and in many ways a wise man; but his goodness was not without spots, and his wisdom was not always sufficient to save him from serious error. But his literary faculty, if not perfect — very few are perfect — was extraordinary and magnificent in the extreme. His supreme gift is his penetrating imagination, of seeing as it were into the heart of things in a moment, and reproducing them in words which it is impossible to forget." — J. COTTER MORISON.

COLERIDGE sat on the brow of Highgate Hill, in those years, looking down on London and its smoke-tumult, like

---

The study of this Selection will furnish good occasion to note how the management of figures, especially simile and metaphor, may be made the means of imparting a certain spirit to the passage, humorous or other, as pointed out in Rhet. pp. 90, 91. In this respect we shall find Carlyle more inclined to humorous and intense figures, while Lowell's figures incline more to the imaginative and poetic. Though also Lowell is by no means devoid of humorous suggestion; note, for instance, the spirit of the figure, Lowell, ll. 35, 36, of the word "discharged," l. 37, and of the antithesis, l. 82.

Besides the figures of the Selection, some of Carlyle's peculiarities in the use of words need also to be noted.

Line 1. Note the peculiar figurative effect given to this first sentence by the verb **sat**, instead of the more literal verb *dwelt*. What figure does this involve? See Rhet. p. 88. — **2. Smoke-tumult,** — an example of Carlyle's peculiar freedom in compounding words (cf. Rhet. p. 36, rule 6) due perhaps to the influence of German style. — **Like a**

a sage **escaped from the** inanity of life's battle; attracting towards him the thoughts of innumerable brave souls still engaged there. . . . Here for hours would Coleridge talk, concerning all conceivable or inconceivable things; and liked nothing better than to have an intelligent, or failing that, even a silent and patient human listener. He distinguished himself to all that ever heard him as at least the most surprising talker extant in this world, — and to some small minority, by no means to all, as the most excellent.

The good man, he was now getting old, towards sixty perhaps; and gave you the idea of a life that had been full of sufferings; a life heavy-laden, half-vanquished, still swimming painfully in seas of manifold physical and other bewilderment. Brow and head were round, and of massive weight, but the face was flabby and irresolute. The **deep** eyes, of a light hazel, were as full of sorrow as of inspiration; confused pain looked mildly from them, as in a kind of mild astonishment. **The** whole figure and air, good and

---

sage, — why is not this **a simile?** — **3. Inanity,** — Carlyle has certain favorite **words of frequent recurrence, of which** this is one. It it an example also of a *kind* of **word of which he** is fond, namely, **the** abstract noun. — **Life's battle,** — a possessive **more** natural to poetry; **is it the** poetic feeling, or some other motive, that leads to **its use here?** — **What** significance does this figure gather from the suggestiveness of *Highgate Hill* and *smoke-tumult?* In what parts of the idea, **then, is a simile involved? and what part is** metaphor? — **5. A page,** here omitted, describes **his thought,** manner of life, **and residence. — 6. All conceivable or inconceivable things,** — what **figure?** Rhet. p. 99. What useful office has this figure in describing his conversation? — **10. Extant,** — another **of** Carlyle's favorite **words.** What is its derivation?

What Carlylisms in l. **15?** — **16.** Under what figure is Coleridge's **life** represented? In the **kind of** action with which his life **is associated, is** there any disparaging spirit in the figure? — Is there a personification

amiable **otherwise, might** be called flabby and irresolute;
expressive of weakness under possibility of strength. He
hung loosely on his limbs, with knees bent, and stooping
attitude; **in** walking, he **rather** shuffled than decisively
stept; and a lady once remarked, he never could fix which
side of the garden walk would suit him best, but continually
shifted, **in** corkscrew fashion, and kept trying both. A
heavy-laden, high-aspiring and surely much-suffering man.
His **voice,** naturally soft and good, had contracted itself
into **a** plaintive **snuffle and** singsong; he spoke **as if**
preaching, — you would have said, preaching earnestly
and also hopelessly the weightiest things. I still recollect
his "object" **and** "subject," terms of continual recurrence
in the Kantean **province;** and how he sang and snuffled
them **into** "om-m-mject" **and** "sum-m-mject," with a kind
of solemn shake or **quaver, as** he rolled **along.** No talk,
in his century or in any other, could be **more surprising.**

Sterling, who assiduously **attended him, with** profound
reverence, and was often with him **by** himself, for a good
many months, gives a record of their first colloquy. Their
colloquies were numerous, and he had taken note of many;
but they are all gone to the fire, except this first, which
Mr. Hare has printed, — unluckily without **date.** It contains **a number of ingenious,** true and **half-true observations, and is of course a faithful epitome of the** things

---

in l. **20?—28.** What simile, and what the sign of likeness? — Cf. Rhet.
p. 89, top. — **29.** Point out Carlylisms. — **31.** Connection between
sound and sense in this line? — **35. Kantean province,** — that is, the
province of Kant's philosophy, with its peculiar philosophical terms. —
37. As he rolled along, — what characteristic of his talk does this
figure vivify?

41. Colloquy, — why is this word more fitting here than *conversa-*

said; but it **gives small idea of** Coleridge's way of talking;
— this one feature is perhaps the most recognizable, "Our
interview lasted for three hours, during which he talked
two hours and three quarters." Nothing could be more
copious than his talk; and furthermore it was always,
virtually or literally, of the nature of a monologue; suffering no interruption, however reverent; hastily putting
aside all foreign additions, annotations, or most ingenuous
desires for elucidation, as well-meant superfluities which
would never do. Besides, it was talk not flowing any-
whither like a river, but spreading every-whither in inextricable currents and regurgitations like a lake or sea;
terribly deficient in definite goal or aim, nay often in logical intelligibility; *what* you were to believe or do, on any
earthly or heavenly thing, obstinately refusing to appear
from it. So that, most times, you felt logically lost;
swamped near to drowning in this tide of ingenious vocables, spreading out boundless as if to submerge the world.

---

tion? — **52. Virtually or literally,** — trace, by the derivations, how
these **words** get their antithesis **to each other.** — **52. Suffering no interruption,** — of what is this predicated, and what figure is involved?
Does the figure aid the directness of expression? — **55. Superfluities,**
— the pluralizing of the abstract noun is a Carlylism **which has been**
much imitated. — **56.** What idiom in this line, and how **translated into**
more formal speech? — **56, 57.** What Carlylese compounds in these
lines? — Trace the simile, ll. **57-64,** and mention what parts of the object compared are significant. — Is any advantage gained, in exactness,
or amount of meaning, or sonority, by the use of the Latin derivatives,
inextricable, regurgitations, intelligibility, vocables, ll. **57, 58,
60, 63?** — **59. Terribly,** — what call for so strong a word? — **61. Obstinately refusing,** — by what figure is the vividness of this clause
increased? — **62-64.** What expressions here lower the dignity of the
figure, and what opinion concerning Coleridge's **conversation is thus
betrayed?** Cf. Rhet. p. 90, 3.

To sit as a passive bucket and be pumped into, whether
you consent or not, can in the long-run be exhilarating to
no creature; how eloquent soever the flood of utterance
that is descending. But **if it** be withal a confused unintelligible flood of utterance, threatening to submerge all
known landmarks of thought, and drown the world and
you! — I have heard Coleridge talk, with eager musical
energy, two stricken hours, his face radiant and moist,
and communicate **no** meaning whatsoever to any individual
of his hearers, — certain **of** whom, **I** for one, still kept
eagerly listening in hope; the most had long before given
up, and **formed** (if the room were large enough) secondary
humming groups of their own. He began anywhere: you
put some question to him, made some suggestive observation: instead of answering this, or decidedly setting out
towards answer of it, **he would** accumulate formidable
apparatus, logical **swim-bladders, transcendental life-pre-
servers** and other precautionary and **vehiculatory gear, for**
setting **out**; perhaps did at last get **under way**, — but was

---

65. By what means is this simile made humorous? Are this sentence and the next inconsistent with the figure already used, ll. 57–64? What idea do they add to the preceding? — **67. How eloquent soever,** — the separation of words compounded with *soever* is a not infrequent Carlylism. — **71–73.** The adjectives in these lines are good exam- ples of what is said, Rhet. p. 34, rule 4, on the vital associations of words. Consider what significance they gather from their collocation. — **72. Stricken,** — has this epithet an effect, merely from the fact that it is present, and apart from its meaning? — **73. Individual,** — why better than *person?* — **79. Setting out,** — under what figure is he represented as answering? — **80–83.** Study the humor of this figure. How does it depend on the dignity, **or lack of** dignity, of the object associated? — In ll. **81, 82** are examples **of** Carlyle's fondness for long and unusual words. — **84.** What modification of the figure begins here? How **is its** humor maintained?

swiftly solicited, turned aside by the glance of some radiant new game on this hand or that, into new courses; and ever into new; and before long into all the universe, where it was uncertain what game you **would** catch, or whether any.

His talk, alas, **was** distinguished, like himself, by irresolution: it disliked **to be** troubled with conditions, abstinences, definite fulfilments;—loved **to** wander **at** its own sweet will, and make its auditor and his claims **and** humble wishes a mere passive bucket for itself! He had knowledge about many things and topics, much curious reading; but generally all topics led him, after a pass or two, into the high **seas of** theosophic philosophy, the hazy infinitude of Kantean transcendentalism, with **its** "sum-m-mjects" and "om-m-mjects." Sad enough; for with such indolent impatience of the claims and ignorances of others, he had not the least talent for explaining this or anything unknown to them; and you swam and fluttered in the mistiest wide unintelligible deluge of things, for most part **in a rather** profitless uncomfortable manner.

Glorious islets, too, I have seen rise out of the haze; but they were few, and soon swallowed in the general

---

90. **Disliked,**—the same figure here used of his talk as in l. 52, which compare.—91. **Wander at its own sweet will,**—a quotation, in part, from Wordsworth, Sonnet on Westminster Bridge.— 95. **A pass or two,**—figure taken from what?—96. Are the figures suggested by **high seas** and **hazy infinitude** intended to make concrete, or just the opposite? Sometimes indeed figurative language may be, as it were, inverted. Note the **same of the figure in** l. 101.— **Swam and fluttered,**—does this convey, or indeed intend or need to convey, a self-consistent image of the hearer's progress?

104. **Glorious islets,**—what picture **does** this present of Coleridge's conversation? Observe that this figure suggests a picture of

element again. Balmy sunny islets, islets of the blest and
the intelligible: — on which occasions those secondary humming groups would all cease humming, and hang breathless upon the eloquent words; till once your islet got
wrapt in the mist again, and they could recommence
humming. Eloquent artistically expressive words you
always had; piercing radiances of a most subtle insight
came at intervals; tones of noble pious sympathy, recognizable as pious though strangely colored, were never
wanting long: but in general you could not call this aimless, cloud-capt, cloud-based, lawlessly meandering human
discourse of reason by the name of "excellent talk," but
only of "surprising"; and were reminded bitterly of Hazlitt's account of it: "Excellent talker, very, — if you let
him start from no premises and come to no conclusion."
Coleridge was not without what talkers call wit, and there
were touches of prickly sarcasm in him, contemptuous
enough of the world and its idols and popular dignitaries;
he had traits even of poetic humor: but in general he
seemed deficient in laughter; or indeed in sympathy for
concrete human things either on the sunny or on the
stormy side. One right peal of concrete laughter at some

---

great beauty, while generally some grotesque or disparaging element
has been intermixed. What call is there for this figure to be so beautiful? — **106. The blest and the intelligible,** — note the felicity of
making these synonymous; in what does it consist? — What Carlylism,
already pointed out, in l. **112**? — Can you construct a self-consistent
figure from l. **116**? What mixtures of previous figures are there, and
why the mixture? — **119.** Analyze the figure of the quotation from
Hazlitt according to Rhet. p. **104.** Under which class of examples at
the bottom of the page does it come? — **122.** What figurative suggestion in the epithet? — **127. Right,** — how does the use of this word
here answer to its primary meaning? — **Concrete,** — what antithesis

convicted flesh-and-blood absurdity, one burst of noble indignation at some injustice or depravity, rubbing elbows with us on this solid Earth, how strange would it have been in that Kantean haze-world, and how infinitely cheering amid its vacant air-castles and dim-melting ghosts and shadows! None such ever came. His life had been an abstract thinking and dreaming, idealistic, passed amid the ghosts of defunct bodies and of unborn ones. The moaning singsong of that theosophico-metaphysical monotony left on you, at last, a very dreary feeling.

From THE LIFE OF STERLING.

---

does this imply and derive suggestiveness from? How is the antithesis benefited by the compound epithet, l. **128**? — Trace the antithesis further in ll. **129-132**. Point out the Carlylisms. What is the use of the idiom **rubbing elbows**? — **130**. **Solid**, — what good does the epithet do?

Recall now the picturing power of the figures, and consider how they go to exemplify what is said of Carlyle's style in the note prefixed to this Selection.

STUDY OF FIGURES IN PREVIOUS SELECTIONS.

LET us now go back and notice, in the Selections that have preceded these last two, some of the figures that are most striking and that accomplish the most for the writer's purpose.

Bunyan: Pages 1-6. — The Selection from Bunyan is *all* figure; that is, it is a section from his allegory, "The Pilgrim's Progress," which under the story of a journey portrays the Christian life; see Rhet. pp. 94-96. As a story, it has interest in itself; but upon this is also superinduced a second interest, the interest of the abstract idea, the inner experience, which it illustrates. At all the main points of the story we are reminded that it has a double meaning. In the selection before us the connexion between figure and literal is revealed mainly by two means: by the proper names selected, and by allusions to or quotations from Scripture. Let us trace the allegory in some of its principal points.

The name of the hero, Christian, and the name of the place, The Valley of Humiliation, indicate that the part of the story now before us refers to a stage of his experience where the Christian is cast down by trials and doubts, and subject to spiritual conflicts. With this idea in mind, analysis of the allegory is easy. — **4. Apollyon.** For the origin of this name see Rev. ix. 11. What is its derivation? — **15.** What expression in this line from **Job xli. 15**, and to what is it applied in the original? — **21, 22.** How do these names of places connect the allegory with what it illustrates? — **31.** How does the quotation from Romans vi. 23 preserve the allegory? — **39.** How does Bunyan use Isa. xxxv. 8 to explain the meaning of the road in which Christian is travelling? — **46.** What does Bunyan get here from Eph. vi. 16, and how does it help us interpret the allegory? — **51.** In a sidenote Bunyan thus explains his allegory here: "Christian wounded in his understanding, faith, and conversation." — **63.** How is the expression here influenced by 2 Cor. i. 8, and to what does the original refer? — **78.** For this rather awkward parenthesis, see **Rev. xiii. 11.** Introduced in order to identify Christian's enemy more closely with the adversary there mentioned. — **82. Two-edged,** — this epithet, taken from Heb. iv. **12,** identifies Christian's sword, allegorically, with what? — **87. The lion.** Bunyan goes out of his way to use this word: he wants to incorporate the suggestiveness of 1 Sam. xvii. 37 into his allegory. To what does the original **refer?** — **98. Tree of Life,** — see Rev. xxii. 2. What characteristic of the Tree of Life is used here? — Endeavor now to relate, in literal language, the story of Christian's fight with Apollyon.

De Quincey: Pages 8–16. — In ll. **13-26** is suggested a **manner of** regarding murder, as a performance to be criticised rather than as a horror to be shunned, which was sixteen years **afterward worked out at** length in his essay on "Murder Considered as One of the Fine Arts." What figure of speech does this whole conception involve? See Rhet. p. 100, and compare especially example at top of p. 101. Trace now, in ll. **15, 16, 19, 21, 22,** the words that accord, in figurative suggestiveness, with this conception. — **55-58.** The germs of what metaphors can you trace here? Are **they unjustifiably mixed?** — **105-123.** In these lines De Quincey **labors to express a highly abstract and** metaphysical idea; trace and explain the metaphors **and similes in which he** makes it palpable. — **133-143.** In what **figure is this paragraph written?** See Rhet. p. 98. What emotion gives rise to it, and what has he revealed in **the previous exposition to justify such emotion?** — Point out the similes in **this paragraph, and trace how** they illustrate the idea.

Burke: Pages 18-23. — Under what figure, ll. **1-7,** does Burke describe the Queen of France? — **7-9.** In what emotional **figure is this** sentence written? See Rhet. p. 97. Put it in unemotional language. — **16.** What bold personification **here, and how does it affect** the intensity **of the idea?** Express it literally. — **49.** Of the metaphor here Abbott ("How to Write Clearly," p. 37) says, "This metaphor is not recommended for imitation." — **58-64.** Trace the **figure suggested and** detailed in these lines. — **65-67.** Explain by Rhet. p. 105.

Thackeray: Pages 24-35. — Compare the interrogations in ll. 12 and 14. What answer does the first imply? What the second? Test the two by Rhet. p. 97, and determine which is a figure of speech. — **15** sq. What **figure here?** — **23.** What double meaning in the word **habits?** Trace the allegory that Thackeray here uses. — **25.** Compare this exclamation with the **one in Burke, l. 7, and note the** difference of emotion that gave rise to it. — **39.** To what well-known ancient philosopher is allusion **here made,** and what added clause increases its humor? — **50-67.** These lines **are** almost **wholly in** exclamation; what emotion gives rise to and justifies the figure? — **120**. What humorous figure suggested in a single word, in this line? — **131**. The emotion passes spontaneously here into what figure? — **215-217**. In what figure does Thackeray describe the working of **his mind**, and what gives it a humorous turn?

Ruskin: Pages 36-47. — Why is not the comparison in l. **46** a simile? See Rhet. p. 89, 1. — Compare the similes, ll. **94** and **210** with **the simile**, l. 155 sq. Between them is all the difference between prose and poetry. Consider what there is in the objects illustrated to make the difference. — **128-141**. Trace how much of the poetic suggestiveness here is due to an implied personification. — **167**. Trace the metonymy in this line, and **explain what makes it metonymy** (Rhet. p. 88). — **175-180**. Into what figure does the writer break in these lines? — **181**. Does the beauty of the preceding justify the exclamation here? — **190**. Is this interrogation a figure of speech?

VIII.

THOMAS HENRY HUXLEY.

A LIBERAL EDUCATION.

"It may be fairly said that **the able** English biologist **has no equal as an** expounder, both to scientific and popular audiences, of matters difficult to comprehend. Nor perhaps is it too much to say that no one **before** ever wrote with such marvellous clearness, united with equal literary finish. Clearness of **writing, though of course always** esteemed, has never been valued **so highly as by** our generation. Formerly an embellishment, it has now become a prime requisite, since so much of our reading has for its purpose to acquaint ourselves with the progress in special fields of knowledge, which we can enter only with a guide and interpreter." — C. S. MINOT.

LET us ask **ourselves, what is** education? **Above** all **things, what is our** ideal of a thoroughly **liberal** education?

The two Selections that follow will be studied mainly for the illustrations they furnish of Fundamental Processes; and presuppose a knowledge of the Rhetoric as far as page 171.

The present Selection is taken from "an **address to the South London Working Men's College, delivered on the 4th of** January, **1868.**" Explain what type of diction the object and occasion lead you to expect, and **what** are its desirable characteristics; see Rhet. p. 79. Note the **familiarity of tone, as seen in** conversational expletives and contractions; e.g. ll. **6, 11, 44, 97.** A more pervasive and significant feature is the simplicity of **word and phrase, the careful** adaptation of expression to ordinary and unlearned **minds, which the** occasion evidently led **the** author to seek.

Lines 1-3. The **question asked in** l. 1 is immediately repeated with **variations.** Show how the repetition illustrates Rhet. p. 163, 78; how

— of that education which, if we could begin life again, we would give ourselves — of that education which, if we could mould the fates to our own will, we would give our children. Well, I know not what may be your conceptions upon this matter, but I will tell you mine, and I hope I shall find that our views are not very discrepant.

Suppose it were perfectly certain that the life and fortune of every one of us would, one day or other, depend upon his winning or losing a game at chess. Don't you think that we should all consider it to be a primary duty to learn at least the names and the moves of the pieces; to have a notion of a gambit, and a keen eye for all the means of giving and getting out of check? Do you not think that we should look with a disapprobation amounting to scorn, upon the father who allowed his son, or the

---

the opening of the second sentence illustrates p. 139, 40; and how the whole repetition illustrates p. 151, 60. — **3, 4.** Explain position of if-clauses by p. 147, 52, and try the effect of putting them after the verb. As it is, what part of the sentence has the stress? — **4, 5. Would give.** Explain *would* with first person, by p. 114, 8. In the same way explain **I will**, l. 7, and discriminate from **I shall**, l. 7. — The first clause of sentence, ll. **6–8**, is of what nature, as explained by Rhet. p. 151, 59?

Why **would**, in l. **10**, and **should**, ll. **12, 16**? Does either auxiliary indicate more than simple futurity? — **10. One day or other,** — observe the position of this time-phrase, buried in the sentence, so as to do its work but have as little stress as possible. To feel the difference of emphasis, try putting it at the beginning or at the end. — **11.** Don't, — note how this is slightly varied in the repetition, l. 15, and compare Rhet. p. 162, 76. — **14. Gambit,** — observe that when the writer introduces a technicalism he has already said enough, in general terms, so that a reader can understand its bearings, whether the word itself is understood or not. — **16.** Why such full way of expressing this, instead of simply saying "look with scorn"? See Rhet. p. 151. — **17, 18. Father who . . . state which,** — are these relatives coördinating or restrictive? See Rhet. p. 127. Try how *that* would sound, and see if

state which allowed its members, to grow up without knowing a pawn from a knight?

Yet it is a very plain and elementary truth, that the life, the fortune, and the happiness of every one of us, and, more or less, of those who are connected with us, do depend upon our knowing something of the rules of a game infinitely more difficult and complicated than chess. It is a game which has been played for untold ages, every man and woman of us being one of the two players in a game of his or her own. The chess-board is the world, the pieces are the phenomena of the universe, the rules of the game are what we call the laws of Nature. The player on the other side is hidden from us. We know that his play is always fair, just, and patient. But also we know, to our cost, that he never overlooks a mistake, or makes the smallest allowance for ignorance. To the man who plays well, the highest stakes are paid, with that sort of over-

---

there is anything in the previous part of the sentence against using it. See Rhet. p. 129, examples, 1.

20. Yet. This word sets off its sentence in adversative relation (see Rhet. p. 142) to something preceding; to what is it thus adversative? — Study the amplitude (see Rhet. p. 151) of the statements in this paragraph; e.g. why not say " of all," in ll. 21, 22, and what is gained by fuller statement? how condense, grammatically, "It is a game which has been played," l. 25? It is evidently the writer's intention, by introducing many modifying and intensifying elements, to make the sentence ll. 20-24 move slowly; try to state its substance in more rapid style; see Rhet. p. 157. — **22. Do depend,** — why is the emphatic form of the verb used? See Rhet. p. 163, 78. — **25. Which.** What other relative would more closely discriminate the relation of the relative clause to the antecedent? See Rhet. p. 127. Is there any reason against the use of it here? — **27. His or her own,** — note here Huxley's usage, where some crude writers would say *their*. — **31. But also.** To what is the *but* adversative, and how is its adversative relation

₃₅ flowing generosity with which the strong shows delight in strength. And one who plays ill is checkmated — without haste, but without remorse.

My metaphor will remind some of you of the famous picture in which Retzsch has depicted Satan playing at
₄₀ chess with man for his soul. Substitute for the mocking fiend in that picture, a calm, strong angel who is playing for love, as we say, and would rather lose than win — and I should accept it as an image of human life.

Well, what I mean by Education is learning the rules
₄₅ of this mighty game. In other words, education is the instruction of the intellect in the laws of Nature, under which name I include not merely things and their forces, but men and their ways; and the fashioning of the affections and of the will into an earnest and loving desire to
₅₀ move in harmony with those laws. For me, education means neither more nor less than this. Anything which professes to call itself education must be tried by this standard, and if it fails to stand the test, I will not call it

---

modified? See Rhet. p. 142, 45. — Trace also the reason of using but in l. **37.** — How is the sentence ll. **33–36** suspended? See Rhet. p. 148, 53.

Of what is the imperative construction l. **40** a condensation? See Rhet. p. 156, 68, example 4. — Why would you call the adjectives in l. **41** epithets? — **43. I should accept,** — what tense, as relative to this, is implied in the condensed conditional clause preceding? See Rhet. p. 112, 5.

44. What means of suspense in this sentence, and what is effected by it? See Rhet. p. 149, 55. — **47.** How is the antecedent defined in this line, and what would be the implication without the defining word? See Rhet. p. 126, 23. — What illustration in this line and the next, of Rhet. p. 164, 80? — **51.** Why would the relative *that* be preferable to *which* here? — **53. Standard, stand.** See Rhet. p. 168, 86; and try, by reading aloud, whether the different stress of the words

education, whatever may be the force of authority, or of numbers, upon the other side.

It is important to remember that, in strictness, there is no such thing as an uneducated man. Take an extreme case. Suppose that an adult man, in the full vigor of his faculties, could be suddenly placed in the world, as Adam is said to have been, and then left to do as he best might. How long would he be left uneducated? Not five minutes. Nature would begin to teach him, through the eye, the ear, the touch, the properties of objects. Pain and pleasure would be at his elbow telling him to do this and avoid that; and by slow degrees the man would receive an education, which, if narrow, would be thorough, real, and adequate to his circumstances, though there would be no extras and very few accomplishments.

And if to this solitary man entered a second Adam, or, better still, an Eve, a new and greater world, that of social and moral phenomena, would be revealed. Joys and woes, compared with which all others might seem but faint shadows, would spring from the new relations. Happiness and sorrow would take the place of the coarser monitors,

---

tends to obviate the jingle. — **53. I will.** What implication in using *will* instead of *shall?* — Observe how copiously this **sentence is punctuated**, and how the movement is retarded thereby. **What call for** retarded movement here?

62, 63. What ambiguity in this sentence, and how obviated? — **63.** By what figurative means is the concreteness of the sentence increased? — **66. If narrow,** — is the word *if* the most accurate that could be used for expressing **this condition?** See Rhet. p. 140, 42. Compare also the condition, l. 68, for difference in implication. — **67.** The language used here fits what **figurative suggestion?**

69–71. How is this sentence suspended, and what element **is thereby** put into a prominent place? Do the two succeeding sentences need any inversion of **structure,** in order to be adjusted to this? Compare

₇₅ pleasure and **pain**; but conduct would still be shaped by **the observation of the natural** consequences of actions; **or,** in other words, by the laws of the nature **of man.**

To **every one** of us the world was once **as** fresh and new as to Adam. And then, long before we were susceptible ₈₀ of any other mode of instruction, Nature took **us in hand,** and every minute **of** waking life brought **its** educational influence, shaping our actions into rough accordance with **Nature's** laws, **so that we** might not be ended untimely by too gross disobedience. Nor should **I** speak of this process ₈₅ **of education as** past, for any **one,** be he as old as he may. For **every man, the** world is as fresh **as** it was at the first day, and **as full of** untold novelties for him who has the eyes to see them. And **Nature is still** continuing her patient education **of us** in that great university, the uni- ₉₀ verse, of which **we are all** members — Nature **having no** Test-Acts.

Those who take **honors in Nature's university,** who learn the laws which **govern men and** things and obey them, are

---

Rhet. p. 166. — **75. By the observation of.** If we should say " By observing " we could obviate one of the *ofs* in this sentence; but a stronger reason leads us to put a noun here instead of a participle; see if you can discover it from 1. 77, and Rhet. p. 164, 79.

Study the suspense of sentences, ll. **78-84,** and state what desirable emphasis is gained thereby. — **83. Untimely,** — what advantage given to the adverb by this position? See Rhet. p. 119, 16. — **84.** Explain the use of **nor** by Rhet. p. 144, 49. — **86.** Explain the inverted order of this sentence by Rhet. p. 166, and point out the ideas brought together thereby. — **88. And** beginning a sentence ought not to be very usual; but Huxley uses it occasionally with **grace, as a** means of cumulative statement; see also l. 117. — **89.** What metaphor here suggested?

92-98. The extension of the metaphor through this paragraph makes it approach what figure? See Rhet. p. 94, and compare Thackeray, ll. 24-36. Point **out the words that are** polarized by the figure;

the really great and successful men in this world. The great mass of mankind are the "Poll," who pick up just enough to get through without much discredit. Those who won't learn at all are plucked; and then you can't come up again. Nature's pluck means extermination.

Thus the question of compulsory education is settled so far as Nature is concerned. Her bill on that question was framed and passed long ago. But, like all compulsory legislation, that of Nature is harsh and wasteful in its operation. Ignorance is visited as sharply as wilful disobedience — incapacity meets with the same punishment as crime. Nature's discipline is not even a word and a blow, and the blow first; but the blow without the word. It is left you to find out why your ears are boxed.

The object of what we commonly call education — that education in which man intervenes and which I shall distinguish as artificial education — is to make good these defects in Nature's methods; to prepare the child to receive Nature's education, neither incapably nor ignorantly, nor with wilful disobedience; and to understand the preliminary symptoms of her displeasure, without waiting for the box on the ear. In short, all artificial

---

point out also university provincialisms; see Rhet. p. 39, 9. Does the figurative sense justify the use here? Does the audience? — What idiom in l. 96?

100. A new metaphor is entered upon here; what in preceding sentence suggests it? — **106.** What ellipsis condenses this sentence?

108–110. Note how meagre is the punctuation in the parenthesis, and contrast ll. 53–55. Is there a reason for making this rapid? — **109. And which** ought not to be used except as the second of two relative clauses beginning with *which*. Is it correctly used here? — **I shall,** — what implication of *shall*, by Rhet. p. 114, 8? — **112.** Explain and justify the position of the adverbs. — **Neither . . . nor . . . nor,**

education ought to be an anticipation of natural education. And a liberal education is an artificial education, which has not only prepared a man to escape the great evils of disobedience to natural laws, but has trained him to ap-
120 preciate and to seize upon the rewards, which Nature scatters with as free a hand as her penalties.

That man, I think, has had a liberal education, who has been so trained in youth that his body is the ready servant of his will, and does with ease and pleasure all the work
125 that, as a mechanism, it is capable of; whose intellect is a clear, cold, logic engine, with all its parts of equal strength, and in smooth working order; ready, like a steam engine, to be turned to any kind of work, and spin the gossamers as well as forge the anchors of the mind; whose mind is
130 stored with a knowledge of the great and fundamental truths of Nature and of the laws of her operations; one who, no stunted ascetic, is full of life and fire, but whose passions are trained to come to heel by a vigorous will, the servant of a tender conscience; who has learned to love
135 all beauty, whether of Nature or of art, to hate all vileness, and to respect others as himself.

Such an one, and no other, I conceive, has had a liberal education; for he is, as completely as a man can be, in

---

— are the three correlatives correct? See Rhet. p. 137, 36. — **115.** What antithesis in this sentence? — **118, 119. Not only . . . but,** — are these correlated correctly, by Rhet. p. 137, 37?

125. That is undoubtedly the correct relative; but what consideration might justify using *which* here? See Rhet. p. 129, examples, 2. — **126.** Note the felicity of the epithets, and explain how they illustrate Rhet. p. 34, rule 4. — **127-129.** Under what figure is the mind represented, and how is the figure carried out? — **132. No stunted ascetic,** — explain the strength of this negative by Rhet. 144, 48. — **133.** What curious idiom here, and what figure does it involve?

harmony with Nature. He will make the best of her, and she of him. They will get on together rarely; she as his [140] ever beneficent mother; he as her mouth-piece, her conscious self, her minister and interpreter.

From LAY SERMONS, ADDRESSES, AND REVIEWS.

---

140. What colloquial usage here in the adverb?

IX.

JOHN HENRY, CARDINAL NEWMAN.

I. ACCURACY OF MIND.

"There is no living writer who has attained to such supreme mastery over the English tongue. It is to him an instrument of which he knows all the mysterious capabilities, all the hidden sweetness, all the latent power; and it responds with marvellous precision to his every touch, the boldest or the slightest." — W. S. LILLY.

IT has often been observed that, when the eyes of the infant first open upon the world, the reflected rays of light which strike them from the myriad of surrounding objects

---

These two Selections are taken, as was the preceding, from lectures; but whereas the other was delivered to workingmen, these were delivered to students of a university. We naturally look, therefore, for greater freedom in the use of learned language, as suited to the more educated audience; and we see indications of it in the Latin quotations, ll. 100, 121-127, and in occasional learned words, as for instance, "ecumenical," l. 152, "the two-fold Logos," l. 110, "otiose," l. 130, to say nothing of the comparatively abstruse nature of the thought.

The first Selection is from the beginning, the second from the end, of a public discourse. It will be observed that the second, in accordance with the momentum derived from the previous thought that it sums up and culminates, is considerably heightened in diction, which fact is observable mainly in its more rolling and stately rhythm. Read, for instance, the paragraphs, ll. **128-145**, and ll. **155-173**, aloud.

Line **1**. What office does the prospective *it* fulfil? See Rhet. p. 133. — How otherwise is the main assertion of the sentence delayed? See Rhet. p. 147, 52. — **3**. **Which**, — what relative would better express the nature of the clause? Cf. Rhet. p. 128. Is there any reason against

present to him no image, but a medley of colors and
shadows. They do not form into a whole; they do not rise
into foregrounds and melt into distances; they do not
divide into groups; they do not coalesce into unities; they
do not combine into persons; but each particular hue and
tint stands by itself, wedged in amid a thousand others
upon the vast and flat mosaic, having no intelligence, and
conveying no story, any more than the wrong side of some
rich tapestry. The little babe stretches out his arms and
fingers, as if to grasp or to fathom the many-colored vision;
and thus he gradually learns the connexion of part with
part, separates what moves from what is stationary, watches
the coming and going of figures, masters the idea of shape
and of perspective, calls in the information conveyed
through the other senses to assist him in his mental process, and thus gradually converts a kaleidoscope into a
picture. The first view was the more splendid, the second
the more real; the former more poetical, the latter more

---

its use here? — Derivation of **myriad**? For this particular audience
would this word increase the concreteness of the passage? — **4-12**. Study
the two kinds of negatives in these lines and compare their strength,
according to Rhet. p. 144, 48. — In the same lines, show what clauses
and words are antithetic to each other. — Three figures are used to
convey and illustrate the idea; show how it **grows in** suggestiveness,
through the metaphor, l. **10**, the simile, l. **11**, and the metaphor, l. **19**.
How is the **last figure prepared for in** the intervening lines? — **10, 11**.
Point out the repetition **of manner of** expression, according to Rhet. p.
164, 79. — **14. And thus,** — is this **connective** accurately used, according
to Rhet. p. 143, 47? — **16. Of shape and of perspective,** — observe
how scrupulous a careful writer like Newman **is** to repeat **connectives,**
where a slovenly writer would omit them; compare also ll. 23-25, 38.
On the other hand, when rapidity is needed (Cf. **Rhet.** p. 157) the connective is omitted; see, e.g., ll. 101, 111. — **20-22**. Point out the
means of retrospective reference in this sentence, and explain by Rhet.

philosophical. Alas! what are we doing all through life, both as a necessity and as a duty, but unlearning the world's poetry, and attaining to its prose! This is our education, as boys and as men, in the action of life, and in the closet or library; in our affections, in our aims, in our hopes, and in our memories. And in like manner it is the education of our intellect; I say, that one main portion of intellectual education, of the labors of both school and university, is to remove the original dimness of the mind's eye; to strengthen and perfect its vision; to enable it to look out into the world right forward, steadily and truly; to give the mind clearness, accuracy, precision; to enable it to use words aright, to understand what it says, to conceive justly what it thinks about, to abstract, compare, analyze, divide, define, and reason, correctly. There is a particular science which takes these matters in hand, and it is called logic; but it is not by logic, certainly not by logic alone, that the faculty I speak of is acquired. The infant does not learn to spell and read the hues upon his

---

p. 124, 21. Is the reference clear enough? — 22-24. What figure predominates, exclamation or interrogation? See the punctuation. — 24-27. Point out balance in sentence. Cf. Rhet. p. 164. — 27. And, — compare what is said, Huxley, l. 88. It will be observed that this case of *and* introducing a sentence is similar to that, in that the sentence so introduced merely continues and cumulates the idea of the preceding. So also in l. 91 below. — 27-36. Study how this sentence illustrates Rhet. p. 30, rule 2. Note that the various repetitions begin with figurative and pass into literal, the latter being thus a kind of interpretation of the former. — 36. On what word does the there prospective (Rhet. p. 133) enable the writer to lay stress? — 38. What is effected by the inverted construction in this sentence? See Rhet. p. 166. — 39. I speak of, — why is the relative omitted? See Rhet. p. 159, 71. Try the effect of expressing it. — What, in principle, is the statement, ll. 39-42? See Rhet. p. 89, examples, 2. — Condense

retina by any scientific rule; nor does the student learn
accuracy of thought by any manual or treatise. The instruction given him, of whatever kind, if it be really instruction, is mainly, or at least pre-eminently, this, — a discipline
in accuracy of mind.

Boys are always more or less inaccurate, and too many,
or rather the majority, remain boys all their lives. When,
for instance, I hear speakers at public meetings declaiming
about "large and enlightened views," or about "freedom
of conscience," or about "the Gospel," or any other popular subject of the day, I am far from denying that some
among them know what they are talking about; but it
would be satisfactory, in a particular case, to be sure of the
fact; for it seems to me that those household words may
stand in a man's mind for a something or other, very glorious indeed, but very misty, pretty much like the idea of
"civilization" which floats before the mental vision of a
Turk, — that is, if, when he interrupts his smoking to utter
the word, he condescends to reflect whether it has any
meaning at all. Again, a critic in a periodical dashes off,
perhaps, his praises of a new work, as "talented, original,
replete with intense interest, irresistible in argument, and,
in the best sense of the word, a very readable book";—

---

the sentence, ll. **42–45**, to its lowest terms, and **explain** how it illustrates Rhet. p. 151, 60.

47. Or rather the majority, — **this** self-correction exemplifies a
frequent means of amplitude; see reference, previous note. — **Remain
boys,** — a softer way of saying what? See Rhet. p. **154,** 64. — **47. When,**
— see Rhet. 147, 52. — **51. I am far from denying,** — this phrase in
the beginning of the sentence leads us to expect **what kind** of clause
following? See Rhet. p. 138, 38. — **53. The fact,** — why not *it?* See
Rhet. p. 132, 28. — **57. Which,** — see note, l. 3. — **59. Condescends
to reflect,** — is this circumlocution justifiable? **See Rhet. p. 153, and**

and the more he has of them the greater he is; but I ascribe to him, as his characteristic gift, in a large sense the faculty of Expression. He is master of the two-fold Logos, the thought and the word, distinct, but inseparable from each other. He may, if so be, elaborate his compositions, or he may pour out his improvisations, but in either case he has but one aim, which he keeps steadily before him, and is conscientious and single-minded in fulfilling. That aim is to give forth what he has within him; and from his very earnestness it comes to pass that, whatever be the splendor of his diction or the harmony of his periods, he has with him the charm of an incommunicable simplicity. Whatever be his subject, high or low, he treats it suitably and for its own sake. If he is a poet, "nil molitur ineptè." If he is an orator, then too he speaks, not only "distinctè" and "splendidè," but also "aptè." His page is the lucid mirror of his mind and life —

"Quo fit, ut omnis
Votivâ pateat veluti descripta tabellâ
Vita senis."

He writes passionately, because he feels keenly; forcibly, because he conceives vividly; he sees too clearly to

---

sentence softened? Cf. Rhet. p. 144, 49. — What antecedent does such recognize, and how? See Rhet. p. 133, 30. — **107.** Give the rationale of this inverted clause; Rhet. p. 166, 83. — **109, 110. Ascribe . . . faculty,** — compare what is said in note to ll. 92, 93. — **116. That aim,** — how does this illustrate Rhet. p. 126, 23? — **117-123.** Point out the sentence structures balanced against each other, as defined, Rhet. p. 164, 80. — **124. Lucid,** — instead of this word, Newman originally wrote *clear*, and changed to this in a subsequent edition. Would Rhet. p. 168, 86 explain the revision?

128, 129. Explain order of adverbs, according to Rhet. p. 119, 16. — **128-135.** Point out the balancing and grouping of clauses, accord-

be vague; he is too serious to be otiose; he can analyze 130
his subject, and therefore he is rich; he embraces it as a
whole and in its parts, and therefore he is consistent; he
has a firm hold of it, and therefore he is luminous. When
his imagination **wells up, it** overflows in ornament; when
his **heart is touched, it thrills** along his verse. He always 135
has the right word for the right idea, and never a word too
much. If he is brief, it is because few words suffice; **when
he is** lavish of them, still each word **has its mark, and** aids,
not embarrasses, the vigorous march of his elocution. He
expresses what all feel, but all cannot say; and **his** sayings 140
pass into proverbs among his people, and his phrases become household words and idioms of their daily speech,
which is tesselated with the rich fragments of his language,
as we see in foreign lands the marbles of Roman grandeur
worked into the walls and pavements of modern palaces. 145

Such preëminently is Shakespeare among ourselves;
such preëminently Virgil among the Latins; such in their
degree are all those writers who in every nation go by the

---

ing to Rhet. p. 164, 79. — **130. Otiose,** — derive, and name a synonymous expression. — **134, 135. Wells up, overflows, thrills along,** — what is the figurative suggestion in each of these verbs? Observe how the style is vivified by them; compare also the verb, l. 101. Such figurative suggestions, expressed by single **words, are** called *tropes.* — **139.** How is the negative here condensed? Compare the negatives in ll. 5–8. Is there anything in the elevated diction of the passage to cause the condensation? Compare Rhet. pp. 50, 71. — **140. All cannot say,** — what alternative form of the negative would tend less to ambiguity? What reason, however, greater than the slight ambiguity, for choosing this order? See Rhet. p. 164, 79. — **143.** What trope in this line, and how explained afterward? — **144. The marbles of Roman grandeur,** — what figure is this?

146, 147. Such, such. — How does the sentence structure here illustrate Rhet. p. 166, 82? — Point out the balancing in order of ad-

name of Classics. To particular nations they are necessarily attached from the circumstance of the variety of tongues, and the peculiarities of each; but so far they have a catholic and ecumenical character, that what they express is common to the whole race of man, and they alone are able to express it.

If then the power of speech is a gift as great as any that can be named, — if the origin of language is by many philosophers even considered to be nothing short of divine, — if by means of words the secrets of the heart are brought to light, pain of soul is relieved, hidden grief is carried off, sympathy conveyed, counsel imparted, experience recorded, and wisdom perpetuated, — if by great authors the many are drawn up into unity, national character is fixed, a people speaks, the past and the future, the East and the West are brought into communication with each other, — if such men are, in a word, the spokesmen and prophets of the human family, — it will not answer to make light of Literature or to neglect its study; rather we may be sure that, in proportion as we master it in whatever language, and imbibe its spirit, we shall ourselves become in our own measure

---

verbs. — **147.** What illustration here of Rhet. p. 159, 71? — **149.** Explain the inverted construction of this sentence. — **151. So far** fulfils, in the sentence structure, a somewhat unusual office; what is it? — **152. Catholic, ecumenical,** — derive, and express in other words.

155 sq. Explain the structure by Rhet. p. 147, 52. — **157.** Point out amplitude here, and show what word gains in emphasis by it. — **161-164.** Observe how in the accumulation of details here, which gives a motive for rapidity, the connectives are omitted; see Rhet. p. 159, 71. — **164.** What office does the if-clause in this line fulfil in the sentence? See Rhet. p. 160, 73. How is this indicated here? — **166.** How does the prospective **it** aid the grouping of clauses afterward? — **Will not answer,** — See Rhet. p. 46, 14. For a parallel idiom with nearly the

the ministers of like benefits to others, be they many or few, be they in the obscurer or the more distinguished walks of life, — who are united to us by social ties, and are within the sphere of our personal influence.

From LECTURES ON UNIVERSITY SUBJECTS.

---

same meaning, see Selection from Carlyle, l. 56. — **167.** Note the suspense, **and** how it aids the grouping of the succeeding part of the sentence. — **170, 171. Be they,** — condensed for what? Is this condensed conditional clause suitable to all kinds of prose? Cf. Rhet. p. 71. It is interesting to note that in the original edition of this lecture these conditions were expressed in the full form, and that the author's sense of style led him to condense them afterward.

STUDY OF FUNDAMENTAL PROCESSES IN PREVIOUS SELECTIONS.

A FEW of the more noteworthy illustrations of Fundamental Processes in the previous Selections will here be pointed out.

Bunyan: Pages 1-6. — **Lines 6-9.** Point out the ambiguity in the retrospective reference of this sentence, according to Rhet. p. 123 sq., and reconstruct the sentence. — **10.** How does this clause illustrate Rhet. p. 127, 24? Bunyan almost always reports a speaker's words, and sometimes, as here, thoughts, in the speaker's person, — a custom due, perhaps, to his vivid imagination, which put him, as it were, in each speaker's place. The dialogue form, illustrated farther on in this Selection, is due to the same cause. — **10.** How is the conditional clause condensed? — **13.** Use of **now**; see Rhet. p. 139. — Bunyan uses the rather indefinite connective **so** (cf. Rhet. p. 143, 47) a good deal; see examples also in ll. 85, 102. — **29.** What illustration in this line, of Rhet. p. 138, 38? — **44.** What inversion here for adjustment, and what is the relation of the ideas so adjusted? See Rhet. p. 166, 83. — **48.** Observe that Bunyan uses **then** at the beginning very often (see also ll. 4, 34, 41, 59, 62, 97); and with such stress as sometimes to cause inversion of the structure. — **75. That,** — is this connective alone sufficient for an illative (or ecbatic) now? Cf. Rhet. p. 143. — **100. Immediately,** — compare order of adverb here with *nimbly*, l. 67, and explain the difference in stress by Rhet. p. 119, 16.

De Quincey: Pages 8-16. — **Line 2. This,** — also in l. 37. Explain by Rhet. p. 135, 32. — **5.** The effect, — to begin the sentence with *it* would produce no real ambiguity; but try it and see if euphony would be violated; see Rhet. p. 168, 86. — **42. An instinct which,** — how does this illustrate Rhet. p. 126, 23? — **51.** *Him*, — what law prevents ambiguity of reference here? See Rhet. p. 125, 22. — **63.** What use of **his** here? See Rhet. p. 135, 32, examples. — **70. Of necessity,** — why not *necessarily?* Rhet. p. 167, 85. — **71.** What is the antecedent of **this**? Cf. Rhet. p. 132, 28, examples. — **89-103.** Observe how, in the suspension of this sentence, the first if-clause prepares, not for the final *dénouement*, but for the second if-clause. — **124. Hence it is,** — explain the kind of conjunctional relation (Rhet. p. 143), and how it is emphasized (Rhet. p. 133). — **142. Had seen,** — what curious relation of tenses to each other in this sentence? Cf. Rhet. p. 112, 5.

Burke: Pages 18-23. — **Line 3.** What condensed structure here, and due to what? Cf. Rhet. p. 71. — **6. Just began,** — is the relation of tense to the preceding exact? What ought it to be? See Rhet. p. 112, 5. — **9-15.** Explain the repetitions in this sentence by Rhet. p. 161, 74. Also in ll. 20, 26, 38-47.

Thackeray: Pages 24-35. — **Line 15. But bettering, etc.** An inexactness somewhat like a double negative (cf. Rhet. p. 145). How correct it from Rhet. p. 131, II. 5? — **58-64.** What condensed constructions in this sentence? See Rhet. p. 159, 71. — **75-79.** What different means of suspense in this sentence? — **89. Only,** — is the position right? See Rhet. p. 119, 17. — **90.** What grouping of ideas by inversion? — **93. Or if not papa,** — what slight inaccuracy in this sentence, analogous to misrelated participle? Cf. Rhet. p. 115, 10. — **104. And in which,** — how is this inaccurate? See note on Huxley, l. 109. How does this use differ from l. 142 below? How can this sentence be corrected? — **118, 124.** What difference in stress in the repetition of the phrase **what a night, etc.?** See Rhet. p. 163, 78. — **127 sq.** What illustration of Rhet. p. 113, 7, and what adverb, l. 125, begins to prepare for it? — **128.** Note grouping of similar ideas by attraction. — **136.** What illustration of Rhet. p. 137, 37? Note how the usual way of expressing the correlation is varied. — **141. A day which came,** — *that* would be the exacter relative here; why is *which* better nevertheless? Cf. Rhet. p. 164, 79. — **173. Will warm 'em,** — what inexactness in tense-relation here? — **189-212.** Observe the studied monotony in conjunctional relation, and see note there. — **224 sq.** Explain construction by Rhet. p. 159, 71.

Ruskin: Pages 36-47. — **Line 147.** Point out illustration of Rhet. p. 117, 14, and give its rationale. — **172.** What illustration of Rhet. p. 158, examples, 5? — **195.** Note the order of the adverb (Rhet. p. 119, 16), and see if there is anything in the preceding to give it such stress. — **216.** Note again the fine effect produced by the order of the adverb. — **221.** What advantage of grouping effected by the prospective **there**? — **227.** Example of a rapid relative. Try the effect of the other relative here. — **237.** See note, l. 147. — **260.** What illustration of Rhet. p. 144, 49?

Lowell: Pages 48-55. — Line 4. The church and the cataract, — how does the use of these words illustrate Rhet. p. 162, 76? — **21, 22.** What, in the first member of the sentence, determines putting these tenses so far in the past? See Rhet. p. 112, 5. — **23. Doubted that.** Many writers would say "doubted *but* that," and some would use the vulgarism "but *what*." Both are incorrect; this is the exact usage. — **27. If it be impossible,** — is this a real condition of what follows? See Rhet. p. 140, 42, and express the condition exactly. — **29. Nay,** — office of this connective? See Newman, l. 65, note. — **33. The great Basilica, with those outstretching columns of Bramante,** — of what are these terms a repetition, and what good does such a repetition do? See Rhet. p. 31; 163, 78. — **41.** Mason-work illustrates what aspect of repetition? Compare l. 39, and see Rhet. p. 162, 76, examples, 1. — **63.** What illustration of Rhet. p. 158, examples, 2? Express the full implication. — **79. Ethereal,** — point out how this illustrates Rhet. p. 159, 71, examples, 2. — **91. That leaden bullet,** — compare l. 33, note. — **97.** Subject omitted in imitation of advertisement style.

Carlyle: Pages 56-63. — Line 11. Illustration of Rhet. p. 144, 48. — **15.** See Ruskin, l. 147, note. — **65-67.** How is the negative delayed in this sentence? — **68-71.** What is there incomplete in this sentence? Cf. Rhet. p. 147, 52. Does the exclamation-point do anything toward filling the ellipsis? — **73.** How is the negative intensified? — **102.** Note the unusual accumulation of adjectives. Also ll. 111, 116. — **104.** What means of emphasis is employed here? See Rhet. p. 166, 82.

X.

NATHANIEL HAWTHORNE.

THE CUSTOM-HOUSE INSPECTOR.

"Hawthorne not only writes English, but the sweetest, simplest, and clearest English that ever has been made the vehicle of equal depth, variety, and subtilty of thought and emotion. His mind is reflected in his style as a face is reflected in a mirror; and the latter does not give back its image with less appearance of effort than the former. His excellence consists not so much in using common words, as in making common words express uncommon things." — E. P. WHIPPLE.

THE father of the Custom-House — the patriarch, not only of this little squad of officials, but, I am bold to say, of the respectable body of tide-waiters all over the United States — was a certain permanent Inspector. He might

---

This Selection and the one following will be studied with special reference to Sentence Structure; and presuppose a knowledge of the Rhetoric as far as page 192.

The subject-matter of the present Selection, being mainly descriptive, leads to a comparatively simple type of sentence for the most part; shown especially in the relation of sentence-members to each other, which is never complex, but generally a relation of simple sequence. See Rhet. p. 177, 2.

Lines 1-4. Observe that the subject of remark, the rhetorical subject, is placed last, and what precedes is really its predicate. Explain how this affects the stress of the sentence, by Rhet. p. 180, 2; and what type of sentence it gives rise to, by Rhet. p. 188. By what means is the delay of the subject increased? — **4.** Where do you find the subject of the second sentence; and what grouping does this position effect,

truly be termed a legitimate son of the revenue system, dyed in the wool, or, rather, born in the purple; since his sire, a Revolutionary colonel, and formerly collector of the port, had created an office for him, and appointed him to fill it, at a period of the early ages which few living men can now remember. This Inspector, when I first knew him, was a man of fourscore years, or thereabouts, and certainly one of the most wonderful specimens of wintergreen that you would be likely to discover in a lifetime's search. With his florid cheek, his compact figure, smartly arrayed in a bright-buttoned blue coat, his brisk and vigorous step, and his hale and hearty aspect, altogether he seemed — not young, indeed — but a kind of new contrivance of Mother Nature in the shape of man, whom age and infirmity had no business to touch. His voice and laugh, which perpetually reëchoed through the Custom-House, had nothing of the tremulous quaver and cackle of an old man's utterance; they came strutting out of his

---

as related to preceding sentence? Compare Rhet. p. 183, 3. — What type does this second sentence exemplify? See Rhet. p. 188, and 190, 1. — **6. Dyed in the wool, etc.** This, which is a common proverbial expression, is introduced as the basis for the next suggestion, then immediately corrected for an expression more to the author's purpose. What is the allusion in **born in the purple?** — **7. Sire,** — a rather pretentious word for *father* (cf. Rhet. p. 45, 13); what makes it in taste here? — **10. This Inspector,** — what reason in previous sentence for resuming this subject with such emphasis? — Why is not the when-clause placed first? — **12. Winter-green,** — as used here, this may be called a polarized word. How is it modified from its ordinary meaning? — **14-19.** What is the type of this sentence? Rhet. p. 188. How does putting these descriptive details first help the latter part of the sentence? — **17.** How does the parenthesis aid in anticipating the important assertion of the sentence? — **19.** How does the type of this sentence differ from that of the preceding? — **22.** How is the clause set

lungs, like the crow of a cock, or the blast of a clarion.
Looking at him merely as an animal,—and there was very
little else to look at,—he was a most satisfactory object,
from the thorough healthfulness and wholesomeness of his
system, and his capacity, at that extreme age, to enjoy all,
or nearly all, the delights which he had ever aimed at, or
conceived of. The careless security of his life in the
Custom-House, on a regular income, and with but slight
and infrequent apprehensions of removal, had no doubt
contributed to make time pass lightly over him. The
original and more potent causes, however, lay in the rare
perfection of his animal nature, the moderate proportion
of intellect, and the very trifling admixture of moral and
spiritual ingredients; these latter qualities, indeed, being
in barely enough measure to keep the old gentleman from
walking on all-fours. He possessed no power of thought,
no depth of feeling, no troublesome sensibilities; nothing,
in short, but a few commonplace instincts, which, aided by
the cheerful temper that grew inevitably out of his physical

---

off by semicolon related to the **previous, and** is there anything in the
latter to prepare for it? See **Rhet.** p. 177, 2. — Point out the trope in
this line. For definition of *trope*, see Newman, ll. 134, 135, note. Note
how this trope illustrates Rhet. p. 169, 87. — **24–29.** Point out how
much of this sentence is periodic, and how much loose; see Rhet.
p. 190, 2. — The participle at the beginning is used a little vaguely, no
subject being expressed; cf. Rhet. p. 115, 10. Such use of the participle is said to be one of the few **ways** in which De Quincey was careless.
— **32.** Analyze the adversative relation between this sentence and preceding; see Rhet. p. 143, 46, and point out what ideas are in contrast.
— **33–36.** What illustration here of Rhet. p. 106, **1**? **36.** What relation of this clause to preceding permits it to remain in the sentence? —
36. Indeed, — what influence has this word on its clause? See Rhet.
p. 139, 40. Note the different office of *indeed*, in l. 17, for which latter,
see Rhet. p. 138, 38. — How is the clause l. **39** made cumulative? —

well-being, did duty very respectably, and to general acceptance, in lieu of a heart. He had been the husband of three wives, all long since dead; the father of twenty children, most of whom, at every age of childhood or maturity, had likewise returned to dust. Here, one would suppose, might have been sorrow enough to imbue the sunniest disposition, through and through, with a sable tinge. Not so with our old Inspector! One brief sigh sufficed to carry off the entire burden of these dismal reminiscences. The next moment, he was as ready for sport as any unbreeched infant; far readier than the Collector's junior clerk, who, at nineteen years, was much the elder and graver man of the two.

I used to watch and study this patriarchal personage with, I think, livelier curiosity, than any other form of humanity there presented to my notice. He was, in truth, a rare phenomenon; so perfect, in one point of view; so

---

42. Did duty,—note the adverbial modifiers of this predicate, and their grouping, before and after; which have the greater stress? See Rhet. p. 119, 16, and p. 181, 4.—**44.** What condensation here, according to Rhet. p. 159, examples, 2?—Explain how this sentence is loose. —**46. Returned to dust,**—how illustrative of Rhet. p. 162, 76?— **Here,**—what is the antecedent, and what kind of reference? See Rhet. p. 133, 30.—**48. Sable tinge,**—is this rather fine expression in taste, according to the implications of the preceding?—**48-50.** Two short sentences; is there anything in the subject-matter to make them better short? See Rhet. p. 186, 1.—**50. The next moment,**—what is there in the preceding to attract this time-phrase to the beginning?

55. The subject of remark is not kept at the beginning of the sentence here; but observe that its prominence is still maintained by the new designation chosen for it.—**57.** But observe also that the pronoun representing it is brought to the forefront of the next sentence; after which it is presumably prominent enough before the reader's mind, so that in the succeeding sentences of the paragraph it need not be so em-

shallow, so delusive, so impalpable, such an absolute nonentity, in every other. My conclusion was that he had no soul, no heart, no mind; nothing, as I have already said, but instincts; and yet, withal, so cunningly had the few materials of his character been put together, that there was no painful perception of deficiency, but, on my part, an entire contentment with what I found in him. It might be difficult — and it was so — to conceive how he should exist hereafter, so earthly and sensuous did he seem; but surely his existence here, admitting that it was to terminate with his last breath, had been not unkindly given; with no higher moral responsibilities than the beasts of the field, but with a larger scope of enjoyment than theirs, and with all their blessed immunity from the dreariness and duskiness of age.

One point, in which he had vastly the advantage over his four-footed brethren, was his ability to recollect the good dinners which it had made no small portion of the

---

phasized. — **59.** What figure here? See Rhet. p. 105. — **60-65.** Show the relation to each other of the members set off by semicolons. — **62.** How is the adversative emphasized? Cf. Rhet. p. 143, 46. — **62, 67.** Note the different relative stress of **so cunningly, etc., and so earthly, etc.**: the one suspended, the other loose. Try the effect of putting these clauses in the same relative positions in their sentences, and test it by reading aloud. — **67, 68. Exist hereafter . . . existence here.** Is there anything in the respective orders that these antithetic expressions take in their clauses, to help the reader in grouping them together? — **69. Not unkindly,** — how illustrative of Rhet. p. 145, 50? — The added clause here is loose; does its thought belong to the same unity as the preceding, and is it important enough to pay for adding? Cf. Rhet. p. 150, 58.

74-77. On what idea of the sentence is the emphasis, and how is stress gained for it? — **76. No small,** — explain by Rhet. p. 145, 51. — For what does **it**, prospective, stand, and what stress is gained by it?

happiness of his life to eat. His gourmandism was a highly agreeable trait; and to hear him talk of roast-meat was as appetizing as a pickle or an oyster. As he possessed no higher attribute, and neither sacrificed nor vitiated any spiritual endowment by devoting all his energies and ingenuities to subserve the delight and profit of his maw, it always pleased and satisfied me to hear him expatiate on fish, poultry, and butcher's meat, and the most eligible methods of preparing them for the table. His reminiscences of good cheer, however ancient the date of the actual banquet, seemed to bring the savor of pig or turkey under one's very nostrils. There were flavors on his palate, that had lingered there not less than sixty or seventy years, and were still apparently as fresh as that of the mutton-chop which he had just devoured for his breakfast. I have heard him smack his lips over dinners, every guest at which, except himself, had long been food for worms. It was marvellous to observe how the ghosts of bygone meals were continually rising up before him; not in anger or retribution, but as if grateful for his former appreciation, and

---

— **77.** Note what similar ideas are grouped, at the end of this sentence and the beginning of the next. — **83. Pleased and satisfied me,** — that the writer should let such a thing please and satisfy him requires justification; accordingly, what office has the suspensive part of this sentence? Cf. Rhet. p. 188. — **82. Maw,** — what justification is there for using this rather coarse word for *stomach?* — **86, 87. Ancient; banquet; savor,** — there is a touch of fineness in these words (cf. Rhet. p. 45, 13); does the importance that feasting occupies in the old man's mind justify the use of them? Notice what is said about Hawthorne, Rhet. p. 46. — **91. Devoured,** — compare l. 82, note. — **92. Every guest,** — how is stress given to these words? — **93. Food for worms,** — for the sake of what antithesis is this expression used? — **93. It,** prospective, gains stress for *marvellous;* but note further how it

seeking to resuscitate an endless series of enjoyment, at once shadowy and sensual. A tender-loin of beef, a hind-quarter of veal, a spare-rib of pork, a particular chicken, or a remarkably praiseworthy turkey, which had perhaps adorned his board in the days of the elder Adams, would be remembered; while all the subsequent experience of our race, and all the events that brightened or darkened his individual career, had gone over him with as little permanent effect as the passing breeze. The chief tragic event of the old man's life, so far as I could judge, was his mishap with a certain goose which lived and died some twenty or forty years ago; a goose of most promising figure, but which, at table, proved so inveterately tough that the carving-knife would make no impression on its carcass, and it could only be divided with an axe and handsaw.

But it is time to quit this sketch; on which, however, I should be glad to dwell at considerably more length, because, of all men whom I have ever known, this indi-

---

groups ideas with reference to next sentence. Try effect of putting *marvellous to observe* last. — **97. Resuscitate,** — for this word a vulgarism, much in use but not an established word, is *resurrect*. — **At once,** — this expression implies what relation between the words that follow it? — **98–105.** Note how subjects are accumulated at the beginning; are the ideas at the end of previous sentence left in readiness for this series of details? — How are the members of this sentence balanced? — **104.** To have said *would be forgotten* in the second clause, though a balanced expression to *would be remembered*, would nevertheless be insignificant; how is this lack of distinction obviated? Cf. Rhet. p. 151. — **105.** The predicate of this sentence is placed first; what, in preceding, attracts it to that position? — **108. A goose,** — how illustrative of Rhet. p. 126, 23? — **111.** Is **only** in the right position? See Rhet. p. 119, 17.

115. Individual, — this word is often used incorrectly for *person;*

vidual was **fittest to be a** Custom-House officer. Most persons, owing to causes which I may not have space to hint at, suffer moral detriment from this peculiar mode of life. The old Inspector was incapable of it, and, were he to continue in office to the end of time, would be just as good as he was then, and sit down to dinner with just as good an appetite.

From THE CUSTOM-HOUSE.
Introductory to THE SCARLET LETTER.

---

is it correctly used here? See its derivation. —**116. Was fittest,**— how is stress gained for this predicate? —**116. Most persons,** — what antithetic idea in previous sentence makes it natural for this to stand first in this sentence? —**119.** How does the beginning of this sentence balance with the beginning of the preceding? —**Were he,** — condensed for what? — The suspense, by means of the condition, enables the writer to end his sketch with a prominent idea.

XI.

MATTHEW ARNOLD.

THE LITERARY SPIRIT OF THE ENGLISH AND OF THE FRENCH COMPARED.

"This great world was brought to perceive [by the publication of 'Essays in Criticism'], or to take for granted, in default of percipient power, that here was a critic, not only of rare technical ability, but one possessed of original and fertilizing conceptions on the subject of the critic's art, and the master, above all, of a style which, whatever fault might be found with it on other grounds, had become in his hands an instrument of marvellous delicacy and power." — H. D. TRAILL.

"One of the two or three best English prose writers of his day." — HENRY JAMES.

"IN France," says M. Sainte-Beuve, "the first consideration for us is not whether we are amused and pleased by a work of art or mind, nor is it whether we are touched by it. What we seek above all to learn is, whether *we were*

The present Selection will be studied as illustrating not only the construction of sentences, individually, but also the way in which sentences are adapted to one another, and the offices that they severally fulfil, as looking to the building up of paragraphs. In preparation for this study, therefore, learn what is said of Explicit Reference, Rhet. pp. 202-206.

Lines 1-3. — The first sentence consists merely of two negative statements, introduced to make preparation for the principal assertion, and illustrating, in a broad way, Rhet. p. 151, 59. The principal assertion, because it is important, is relegated to a sentence by itself; it might have been joined to the first sentence, without disturbing unity (Cf. Rhet. p. 177, 2), but it is better as it is. — **4. What we seek above all to learn,** — a repetition of what? Note that the repetition

right in being amused with it, and in applauding it, and in being moved by it." Those are very remarkable words, and they are, I believe, in the main quite true. A Frenchman has, to a considerable degree, what one may call a conscience in intellectual matters; he has an active belief that there is a right and a wrong in them, that he is bound to honor and obey the right, that he is disgraced by cleaving to the wrong. All the world has, or professes to have, this conscience in moral matters. The word *conscience* has become almost confined, in popular use, to the moral sphere,

---

defines the subject more closely for the writer's purpose, and that both original and repetition are only preliminary and preparatory to the real subject of remark. What then *is* the subject of remark here, for which such distinction has been accumulated? How is it further made distinctive? — **6.** A short transitional sentence, leading us to expect what character of remark in next sentence? — **7. Quite true,** — how is this assertion guarded in the sentence? — **Quite,** — from what Americanism is this, in meaning, to be distinguished? See Bunyan, l. 56, note. — **7-12.** On what word is the chief stress in this sentence, and how is it prepared for and guarded, according to Rhet. p. 151, 59? — The sentence consists of two members, separated by a semicolon; what is the relation of the second member to the first? — **12, 13.** Compare the order of this sentence with the first member of the previous sentence. What ideas are in balance and antithesis? Note that by such balance this sentence goes out on "this conscience in moral matters," which thus has the stress, ready to be taken up and defined in next sentence. See Rhet. p. 182, 1. Note also that, if the order were reversed, and written, "This conscience in moral matters all the world has, or professes to have," the sentence would be well adapted in stress to the preceding, but it would not be so ready for the following; we should rather expect something more to be said about "all the world," rather than about "conscience in moral matters." Try it and see. — **13-21.** This sentence, as you read it, seems lacking in unity; the member ll. 17-20 does not seem closely enough related to come under Rhet. p. 177, **2.** But remember, the whole sentence is but subordinate, dealing with the converse of the real subject; and to put its matter in more

because this lively susceptibility of feeling is, in the moral
sphere, so far more common than in the intellectual sphere;
the livelier, in the **moral** sphere, this susceptibility is, the
greater becomes a man's readiness to admit a high standard
of action, an ideal authoritatively correcting his everyday
moral habits; here, such willing admission of authority is
due to sensitiveness of conscience. And a like deference
to a standard higher than one's own habitual standard in
intellectual matters, a like respectful recognition of a
superior ideal, is caused, in the intellectual sphere, by
sensitiveness of intelligence. Those whose intelligence is
quickest, openest, most sensitive, are readiest with this
deference; those whose intelligence is less delicate and
sensitive are less disposed to it. Well, now we are on the
road to see why the French have their Academy and we
have nothing of the kind.

---

than one sentence would make it too prominent; see Rhet. p. 176, 2.
The goal of the sentence is "sensitiveness of conscience," which the
writer **wishes to** reach in order to have it ready for "sensitiveness of
intelligence," the balancing goal of the next sentence. **In order to do**
this some defining material has to be crowded in, which cannot be dispensed with; see, for instance, how necessary are ll. 17-20 to the proper
understanding of ll. 22-24. — The **triple recurrence of the words the
moral sphere**, in ll. **14, 15, 17,** is an instance of Matthew Arnold's
perfect fearlessness in repetition; but note how the phrase has a different
relative position in its clause, at each repetition; and compare Rhet.
p. 163, 78. — **21-25.** This sentence, with its goal "sensitiveness of
intelligence," is balanced with, not the whole of the preceding sentence,
but its last member; which latter had to be prepared for by all that
preceded. — **25-28.** This sentence really summarizes for the writer's
purpose all that has gone before in the paragraph. For structure, what
is its type? See Rhet. p. 191. — **28-30.** This sentence refers to the
main subject of the essay, "The Literary Influence of Academies," a
subject with which in this Study we have only subordinately to do.

The foregoing paragraph has been analyzed in full, in order to show

What are the essential characteristics of the spirit of our nation? Not, certainly, an open and clear mind, not a quick and flexible intelligence. Our greatest admirers would not claim for us that we have these in a pre-eminent
35 degree; they might say that we had **more of** them than our detracters gave us credit for; but they would not assert them to be our essential characteristics. They would rather allege, as our chief spiritual characteristics, energy and honesty; and, if we are judged favorably and positively,
40 not invidiously and negatively, our chief characteristics are, no doubt, these:—energy and honesty, not an open and clear mind, not a quick and flexible intelligence. Openness

how delicately, by a skilful writer, sentences are adjusted to one another. The student can carry on such study for himself, and with practical profit **too**; **for it is** just such problems **of** adjustment that he must continually solve in his own writing, if he becomes skilled in expression.

32. Not, certainly. Explain **structure of** this sentence by Rhet. p. 174. — Note position of **certainly**. Has it more stress, or less, than if it were at the beginning? See Rhet. p. 181, 4. — **An open and clear mind, etc.** Where has the writer already collected material for these expressions? By what added words do they grow in this repetition? — **33-37.** Study in this sentence the skilful management of **they, these,** and **them,** with different antecedents. The pronoun **whose** antecedent is our **greatest admirers** is always in what case, and in what position in its clause? The pronouns with the **other** antecedent are how placed and in what case? Which are kept uniformly subordinate, and how? Cf. Rhet. p. 125, 22. — Report the relation of the three sentence-members to each other; and compare Rhet. p. 178, examples, 3. — **37-42.** Point **out, in** this sentence, the parts that are repetitionary of what precedes; report what repetitions vary from preceding, in expression or stress (cf. Rhet. p. 163, 78), and what iterate the same words, according to Rhet. p. 162, 75. Note how the author has gradually been crystallizing his thought to certain exactly defined expressions, which henceforth he uses without variation. — **41.** Note that the negative phrases here, though a repetition, make a fine con-

of mind and flexibility of intelligence were very signal characteristics of the Athenian people in ancient times; everybody will feel that. Openness of mind and flexibility of intelligence are remarkable characteristics of the French people in modern times; at any rate, they strikingly characterize them as compared with us; I think everybody, or almost everybody, will feel that. I will not now ask what more the Athenian or the French spirit has than this, nor what shortcomings either of them may have as a set-off against this; all I want now to point out is that they have this, and that we have it in a much lesser degree.

Let me remark, however, that not only in the moral sphere, but also in the intellectual and spiritual sphere, energy and honesty are most important and fruitful qualities; that, for instance, of what we call genius energy is the most essential part. So, by assigning to a nation energy and honesty as its chief spiritual characteristics, — by refusing to it, as at all eminent characteristics, openness of mind and flexibility of intelligence, — we do not by any

---

trasted suggestion for opening of next sentence. — **42–45 and 45–49.** Study these two sentences together; report wherein they are alike in construction, and wherein their assertions are varied in degree. — **49–53.** By what means does the author define his limits of assertion more closely here, and to exactly what narrow topic does he steer the paragraph at the end? How is this related to the assertion of the beginning?

54. However, — what inference from the preceding does this adversative arrest and correct? How does this correction affect the order of the present sentence, — **that is,** what element does it attract to the beginning? — **Not only . . . but also,** — see if these agree with Rhet. p. 137, 37. — **57.** How is the clause after the semicolon balanced in order with the preceding? Compare Rhet. p. 191. This latter clause is thus in inverted structure (cf. Rhet. p. 165); to what idea is stress thereby given? — **58–61.** Compare ll. 37–42 preceding, and show how the idea is subordinated in repetition. — **61. We do not by any**

means, as some people might at first suppose, relegate its importance and its power of manifesting itself with effect from the intellectual to the moral sphere. We only indi-
65 cate its probable special line of successful activity in the intellectual sphere, and, it is true, certain imperfections and failings to which, in this sphere, it will always be subject. Genius is mainly an affair of energy, and poetry is mainly an affair of genius; therefore, a nation whose spirit
70 is characterized by energy may well be eminent in poetry; —and we have Shakspeare. Again, the highest reach of science is, one may say, an inventive power, a faculty of divination, akin to the highest power exercised in poetry; therefore, a nation whose spirit is characterized by energy
75 may well be eminent in science;—and we have Newton. Shakspeare and Newton: in the intellectual sphere there can be no higher names. And what that energy, which is the life of genius, above everything demands and insists upon, is freedom; entire independence of all authority,
80 prescription, and routine,—the fullest room to expand as

---

means,—see Rhet. p. 144, 48. What call to intensify the negative? See next clause, and note l. 54.—Note that this negative and its corresponding positive assertion are so important that they occupy different sentences, though grammatically they might have been put in one. This, then, is an exception to Rhet. p. 176, 2.— **66. It is true,**—a concessive, without corresponding correlative; cf. Rhet. p. 138, 38.— **67. In this sphere,**—how do the position and stress of this idea differ from those of its former appearance, l. 65?— **68.** Compare line 57, whose idea is here resumed and amplified.— **68-77.** Study these three sentences together: how the first two are balanced with each other, and how in each the clauses are related (cf. Rhet. p. 177, 2); and how the third summarizes the ideas of the others. In the last-named sentence, what inverted order, and what stress in consequence?— **77. What,**—this word stands prospectively for what word? and by what amplitude is that word further prepared for?— **79.** What office has the part of the

it will. Therefore, a nation whose chief spiritual characteristic is energy, will not be very apt to set up, in intellectual matters, a fixed standard, an authority, like an academy. By this it certainly escapes certain real inconveniences and dangers, and it can, at the same time, as we 85 have seen, reach undeniably splendid heights in poetry and science. On the other hand, some of the requisites of intellectual work are specially the affair of quickness of mind and flexibility of intelligence. The form, the method of evolution, the precision, the proportions, the relations 90 of the parts to the whole, in an intellectual work, depend mainly upon them. And these are the elements of an **intellectual** work which are really most communicable **from it,** which can most be learned and adopted from it, which have, therefore, the greatest effect upon the intellectual per- 95

---

sentence after the semicolon? — **81. Therefore, etc.** See Rhet. p. 143. The illatives corresponding to this, ll. 69, 74, have occupied **clauses** in their sentences; this has a sentence to itself. Find the rea**son of** the greater prominence here in the title of the essay from which this Selection **is taken. — 84. By this,** — that is, by not setting up a fixed standard. **The reference of this is** a little vague, — too vague? See Rhet. p. 132, 28, and 133, 30. — **Certainly,** — what kind of correlate **do we naturally expect to this?** See Rhet. p. 138, 38. — **87. On the other hand,** — a strong adversative, **which not only sets** this sentence over against the preceding, but the coming **part of the** paragraph over against what has been said. Having spoken of energy and its results, the author is here to speak of quickness and flexibility **and** their results. — From this adversative to l. **106,** study the explicit reference, bearing in mind that the point to which the author is steering **is the thought of** academies and their establishment. — **87. Some of the requisites,** — this implication that there *are* requisites, without a specification **of** them, leads us to expect what in the next sentence? Accordingly, does the next sentence need to be introduced by a connective? See Rhet. p. 206, 4, (2). — Does the sentence beginning l. **92** change the direction of the thought? Why then the co-ordinating con-

authority tend to embarrass energy and inventive genius, academies may be said to be obstructive to energy and inventive genius, and, to this extent, to the human spirit's general advance. But then this evil is so much compensated by the propagation, on a large scale, of the mental aptitudes and demands which an open mind and a flexible intelligence naturally engender, genius itself, in the long run, so greatly finds its account in this propagation, and bodies like the French Academy have such power for promoting it, that the general advance of the human spirit is perhaps, on the whole, rather furthered than impeded by their existence.

How much greater is our nation in poetry than prose! how much better, in general, do the productions of its spirit show in the qualities of genius than in the qualities of intelligence! One may constantly remark this in the work of individuals; how much more striking, in general, does

---

opening a new stage of the subject, is not connected with preceding by any explicit reference; nor is what follows put into a paragraph by itself, being in its importance but a corollary of the preceding, and not requiring so much prominence.—**225-229.** In these sentences study the repetitions, of connectives and other elements, by which the progress of the thought is made clear. How is so far as, etc., repeated later in the sentence? What repetitions or identical terms in this sentence?—In the next sentence (ll. 225–229) the latter part, introduced by that, l. 228, is prepared for by three clauses; point out the equivalent particles by which these clauses are introduced.—**226. This propagation, —how illustrative** of Rhet. p. 106, 29?—Note the slight variation in repetition, between l. 226 and l. 228.

The rest of the Selection, instead of being studied out so fully, will be merely accompanied with an occasional question and reference to the Rhetoric, which latter the student will look out as a basis for a study of his own.—**231.** Rhet. p. 97. What produces the emotion?—**232, 233. How much better . . . than.**—Rhet. p. 198. What ellipsis after than?—**234. This,** Rhet. p. 191, 18.—**235.** Rhet. p. 192, 21.—

any Englishman, — of some vigor of mind, but by no means a poet, — seem in his verse than in his prose! His verse partly suffers from his not being really a poet, partly, no doubt, from the very same defects which impair his prose, and he cannot express himself with thorough success in it. But how much more powerful a personage does he appear in it, by dint of feeling, and of originality and movement of ideas, than when he is writing prose! With a Frenchman of like stamp, it is just the reverse: set him to write poetry, he is limited, artificial, and impotent; set him to write prose, he is free, natural, and effective. The power of French literature is in its prose writers, the power of English literature is in its poets. Nay, many of the celebrated French poets depend wholly for their fame upon the qualities of intelligence which they exhibit, — qualities which are the distinctive support of prose; many of the celebrated English prose-writers depend wholly for their fame upon the qualities of genius and imagination which they exhibit, — qualities which are the distinctive support of poetry. But, as I have said, the qualities of genius are less transferable than the qualities of intelligence; less can be immediately learned and appropriated from their product; they are less direct and stringent intellectual agencies, though they may be more beautiful and divine. Shakspeare and our great Elizabethan group were certainly more gifted writers than Corneille and his group; but what was

---

127. Why **verse** here, instead of *poetry*, as in l. 121?—**128.** No doubt,—Rhet. p. 138, 38.—**132.** See Bunyan, l. 94 and note.—**133.** Rhet. p. 166, 83 and 205, 3.—**134, 135.** Rhet. p. 157, examples, 4.—Also Rhet. p. 102.—**136.** Rhet. p. 191.—**138. Nay, etc.**, Rhet. p. 139, 40. Trace balance of this sentence; also antithetic ideas.—**145 sq.** Analyze unity of sentence by Rhet. 177. 2.—**149. Though,**

the sequel to this great literature, this literature of genius,
as we may call it, stretching from Marlow to Milton?
What did it lead up to in English literature? To our provincial and second-rate literature of the eighteenth century. 155
What, on the other hand, was the sequel to the literature
of the French "great century," to this literature of intelligence, as, by comparison with our Elizabethan literature,
we may call it; what did it lead up to? To the French
literature of the eighteenth century, one of the most power- 160
ful and pervasive intellectual agencies that have ever ex-
isted, — the greatest European force of the eighteenth
century. In science, again, we had Newton, a genius of
the very highest order, a type of genius in science, if ever
there was one. On the continent, as a sort of counterpart 165
to Newton, there was Leibnitz; a man, it seems to me
(though on these matters I speak under correction), of
much less creative energy of genius, much less power of
divination than Newton, but rather a man of admirable
intelligence, a type of intelligence in science, if ever there 170
was one. Well, and what did they each directly lead up
to in science? What was the intellectual generation that
sprang from each of them? I only repeat what the men
of science have themselves pointed out. The man of
genius was continued by the English analysts of the eigh- 175
teenth century, comparatively powerless and obscure fol-
lowers of the renowned master. The man of intelligence
was continued by successors like Bernouilli, Euler, La-

---

etc., Rhet. p. 141, 43. — **154.** Rhet. p. 174. — **163-171.** What balancing elements in these two sentences? — Note that in speaking of men
of science, in contrast to men of literature, the writer asks his question
all in one (l. 171), by way of condensation, instead of devoting a question to each side, as in ll. 154, 156. — **174, 177.** Rhet. p. 158, exam-

grange, and Laplace, the greatest names in modern mathematics.

What I want the reader to see is, that the question as to the utility of academies to the intellectual life of a nation is not settled when we say, for instance, "Oh, we have never had an academy, and yet we have, confessedly, a very great literature." It still remains to be asked: "What sort of a great literature? a literature great in the special qualities of genius, or great in the special qualities of intelligence?" If in the former, it is by no means sure that either our literature, or the general intellectual life of our nation, has got already, without academies, all that academies can give. Both the one and the other may very well be somewhat wanting in those qualities of intelligence out of a lively sense for which a body like the French Academy, as I have said, springs, and which such a body does a great deal to spread and confirm. Our literature, in spite of the genius manifested in it, may fall short in form, method, precision, proportions, arrangement, — all of them, I have said, things where intelligence proper comes in. It may be comparatively weak in prose, that branch of literature where intelligence proper is, so to speak, all in all. In this branch it may show many grave faults to which the want of a quick, flexible intelligence, and of the strict standard which such an intelligence tends to impose, makes it liable; it may be full of hap-

---

ples, 3. — **181. What I want, etc.,** — Rhet. p. 133, and 180, 2. — What is the subject of this sentence? — **186.** Rhet. p. 117, 14. Why the order? — **188.** Rhet. 124, 21. — **193. Out of a lively sense for which,** — an unusually intricate phrase. What is the antecedent of *which?* and what does the phrase modify grammatically? — **194. And which,** — compare, supplementary note on p. 87, to Thackeray, l. 104.

hazard, crudeness, provincialism, eccentricity, violence, 205
blundering. It may be a less stringent and effective intellectual agency, both upon our own nation and upon the world at large, than other literatures which show less genius, perhaps, but more intelligence.

The right conclusion certainly is that we should try, so 210 far as we can, to make up our shortcomings; and that to this end, instead of always fixing our thoughts upon the points in which our literature, and our intellectual life generally, are strong, we should, from time to time, fix them upon those in which they are weak, and so learn to 215 perceive clearly what we have to amend. What is our second great spiritual characteristic,—our honesty,— good for, if it is not good for this? But it will,—I am sure it will,—more and more, as time goes on, be found good for this. 220

From ESSAYS IN CRITICISM: *Essay on* THE LITERARY INFLUENCE OF ACADEMIES.

—**197** and **204-206**. Rhet. p. 156, 68. — **211**. To **this end**,— trace elements of suspension in this sentence. What part has the stress?
— **216, 220**. Trace the nucleus of this sentence, and point out the amplitude that gives its parts distinction.

STUDY OF SENTENCES IN PREVIOUS SELECTIONS.

LET us look at a few sentences in previous Selections, choosing especially such as reveal an author's prevailing type of structure, or such as illustrate usages not found in the last two Selections.

Bunyan: Pages 1–6. — Bunyan's sentences are very plain and simple. When they consist of more than one clause, the prevailing type of structure is illustrated in sentences ll. 1–4; 9–12; 23–25; 38–40; 43, 44; 55–58; 100–104. Each of these is loose (see Rhet. p. 188), consisting of a principal assertion, followed by its explanation connected by *for*. See Rhet. p. 177, 2. — **4. His name is Apollyon,** — this, by Rhet. p. 177, 2, is rather loosely connected with the main sentence; but would it do as a separate sentence? See Rhet. p. 176, 2. — How does the sentence ll. 13–17 illustrate Rhet. p. 178, 3? — How does sentence ll. **34–37** preserve the unity required in Rhet. p. 177, 2? Is there anything in Rhet. p. 206, 4, that justifies the absence of connectives? — Test the unity of sentences ll. **48–55** by Rhet. p. 178, 3. — **78. He spake like a dragon,** — this addition in the middle of the sentence quite disturbs its unity; see supplementary note, p. 64 preceding.

De Quincey: Pages 8–16. — De Quincey uses parentheses freely; see ll. 28, 29; 44; **51–54**; not for brevity (cf. Rhet. p. 159, examples, 6), but for explanation; and it will be noted that the parentheses are so constructed as to carry on the same grammatical structure. — **33–37.** Analyze sequence of clauses by Rhet. p. 178, 3. — **63–71.** Analyze sequence of clauses by Rhet. p. 177, 2. — De Quincey underlines (italicizes) freely; see ll. 9; 11; 51; 81, 82; 87. This is for emphasis (the italic word l. 14 has a very different explanation; what?); but does it transgress Rhet. p. 179, 1? that is, does the italicizing re-enforce or apologize for the position of the words? — Study how types of sentence-structure succeed one another ll. **84–113**. The two long sentences, ll. **84–88**, and **89–103**, are of what type? How is the type varied in succeeding sentences? See Rhet. p. 190, 1. Show how the long sentences exemplify Rhet. p. 186, 2, and the short sentences Rhet. p. 186, 1, in their subject-matter. — Observe that the sentence ll. 110-113 is really several short sentences; explain by Rhet. p. 178, 3. — Explain sentence ll. 124-132 by Rhet. p. 190, 2.

Burke: Pages 16-19. — Explain inversions of sentence-elements in ll. 3, 4, and show what stress is gained. See Rhet. p. 180, 2. — 9. Explain position of adverb, and its effect, by Rhet. p. 181, 4. — 20. Explain as in foregoing note. — 26. Point out pleonasm, and explain its use by Rhet. p. 174. On this expression Mr. Joseph Payne ("Studies in English Prose," p. 324) remarks, "The effect of employing this anticipatory clause, instead of commencing with the subject, is particularly fine. Put 'is gone' to the end, and you spoil the whole sentence." Why would the sentence thus be spoiled? — Explain how the sentences ll. 47-64 illustrate Rhet. p. 187, 3. Explain also how the short and the long sentences respectively exemplify the subject-matter natural to each kind, according to Rhet. p. 186, 1, 2.

Thackeray: Pages 24-35. — The series of short sentences, ll. 20-26 is not to be explained by Rhet. p. 186, 1; but explain how they answer to Rhet. p. 77, 1. So the prevailing type of sentence-structure is the colloquial. — 58-67. Point out how the narrative and descriptive elements influence the sentence-structure; see Rhet. p. 178, 3. — 105. How does this sentence show a mixture of types? See Rhet. p. 190, 2, also cf. Rhet. p. 149, 56. The stress of "we have our calendar" would be a little too great for this light subject-matter, if all the suspense came before. — Study the stress of adverbial phrases, ll. 128, 135, by Rhet. p. 181, 4. — 175. Explain ellipsis by Rhet. p. 174. — 178. What explanation of this sentence-structure, Rhet. p. 174? — In this story, ll. 183-212, examine the type of sentence by Rhet. p. 188. Are there any periodic sentences? and what type of sentence, by Rhet. p. 189, 1 and 2, is more natural to the subject-matter?

Ruskin: Pages 32-38. — Of the general style of Ruskin, as exemplified in his "Modern Painters," Peter Bayne wrote: "It recalled what had passed entirely out of English composition, the stately march and long-drawn cadence of Hooker and Taylor." These characteristics are especially conspicuous in the structure of the sentences, which are long, and which from the central nucleus of thought spread out into minute and sometimes quite remote details. Study the two long sentences, ll. 4-25, and ll. 25-47; report the framework of subject and predicate, and the relation of phrases, adverbial and other. Do the sentences, being descriptive, answer in subject-matter to what is natural in a long

sentence? See Rhet. p. 186, 2. Explain their unity by Rhet. p. 178, 3. — 68, 75. Explain the elliptical structure by Rhet. p. 175, examples, 3. — Trace the construction of sentences, ll. 138-180, reporting on their framework, and on the sequence of clauses and phrases.

Lowell: Pages 48-55. — Compare the stress of the when-clause, l. 10, with that of the if-clause, l. 20, and explain by Rhet. p. 181, 3. — Note that Lowell sets off with commas sometimes what other writers, perhaps with better justification, set off with a semicolon; why, for instance, should there be semicolons ll. **16, 75, 81**? Explain by Rhet. p. 177, 2. — On the other hand, the sentence ll. **87-91** contains a plurality of ideas not quite consistent with unity; is it justified by Rhet. p. 176, 2?

Carlyle: Pages 56-63. — **1. In those years.** The impulse would be natural in this opening sentence to put this time-phrase first. Carlyle, however, generally adopts the loose structure; besides, here undoubtedly he wishes to give the stress of the first place to the name Coleridge. — Carlyle often sets off by semicolons what others would set off by commas; see ll. 6, 14, 22, 35, 52, 53, 62, 67, 85, 125, and often. In a clause set off by a semicolon, we generally expect a complete grammatical structure, subject and predicate; these have not. — **13.** What is accomplished by the pleonasm? Rhet. p. 174. — **71.** An unusual ellipsis, the whole main sentence being understood, or left to emotion. A still bolder emotional ellipsis occurs at the end of Carlyle's fifth lecture on Heroes: " Richter says, in the Island of Sumatra there is a kind of ' Light-chafers,' large Fire-flies, which people stick upon spits, and illuminate the ways with at night. Persons of condition can thus travel with a pleasant radiance, which they much admire. Great honor to the Fire-flies! But — ! — " This is adduced more as a curiosity than as a model for imitation. — The use of the colon in sentence-members, as distinguished from the semicolon, is illustrated in several ways in this Selection. In ll. 77, 79, 90 it is used where we expect the succeeding to be a specification of what is given in general terms before; this is a common usage. In ll. 115, 124, it is used merely as a larger pause, the parts preceding and following being divided by semicolons. In l. 119, it introduces a quotation. These examples show the three main uses of the colon. — **104.** How is stress gained for the first part? See Rhet. p. 180, 2. — **106.** Explain construction by Rhet. p. 175, examples, 4. — What irregular construction is involved in sentence, ll. **127-133**?

Huxley: Pages 67-75. — Huxley employs sentences of moderate length and of simple construction, doubtless largely out of regard to his audience of workingmen. Lines 27-37 furnish a good example of this simplicity; note the type of sentence, there being only one approach to periodic structure (which sentence?) and the shortness of the sentences (the first sentence, ll. 27-29, being really three sentences). — **48.** A semicolon where we more naturally expect a comma; evidently to give the latter part of the sentence more distinction, and because the first part is already cut up into subordinate portions by commas. — **50.** What stress here, according to Rhet. p. 181, 4? — **63-68.** Report on grouping of subordinate clauses, and explain the stress of the last clause by Rhet. p. 181, 3. — **69-77.** Explain the combination of sentence-types here, by Rhet. p. 190, 1. — In sentences l. **85-88**, by what position of clause is the first sentence prepared, in dynamic stress, for the second? See Rhet. p. **182, 1.**

Newman: Pages 76-85. — The sentence ll. **5-12** is a good example of a structure common with Newman, — what may be called *cumulative* sentence-structure, consisting of a number of simple clauses with common bearing, building up by simple accretion a detailed idea. Explain its unity by Rhet. p. **178**, examples, 4 (which also is from Newman). — **20-22.** Of what type is this sentence, and how does its subject-matter make this type natural? See Rhet. p. 191. — **27-36.** Explain the structure of this sentence by note on ll. 5-12 preceding. — **36-39.** Explain by Rhet. p. 182, 1 the dynamic stress of the two clauses as related to each other. — **58.** Explain stress of the if-clause by Rhet. p. 181, 3. Observe that a when-clause is imbedded in the if-clause and has a different relative stress, — by what means obtained? — **65.** What ellipsis? Do you find warrant for it, Rhet. p. 175? — **128-145.** Explain how the variation of grouping and balance produce variety in dynamic stress, according to Rhet. p. 183, 3. Go through the sentence and mark where in each the stress is thrown.

XII.

THOMAS BABINGTON, LORD MACAULAY.

THE WORK OF THE IMAGINATION IN WRITING HISTORY.

"The care which Macaulay took to write before all things good and clear English, may be followed by writers who make no attempt to imitate his style, and who may be led by nature to some quite different style of their own. Many **styles** which are quite unlike one another, may all be equally good; but no **style** can **be** good which does not use pure and straightforward English. No style can be good where the reader has to read a sentence twice over to find out its meaning. In these ways the writings of Macaulay may be a direct model to writers and speakers whose natural taste, whose subject, or whose audience, may lead them to a style quite unlike his." — E. A. FREEMAN.

1. WHILE our historians are practising all the arts of controversy, they **miserably neglect the art** of narration, the art of interesting the affections and presenting pict-

---

This Selection will be devoted predominantly to the study of Paragraph structure, and to the larger groupings of thought therein involved; and presupposes a knowledge of the Rhetoric as far as page 214.

It will be observed that **Macaulay's sentences are comparatively poor in connectives, and that his paragraphs accordingly do** not seem very closely woven together. On the other hand, his sentences, having a common bearing as contributing to the proof of a strongly marked theme, **have less need of connectives** (see Rhet. p. 206); and the theme is generally the basis of a well articulated plan in the paragraph structure.

Paragraph 1. — This paragraph will be detailed in full, as **suggestion of how succeeding paragraphs** may be studied. — The first sentence **is a** transition (see Rhet. p. 282) from the previous line of thought.

ures to the imagination. That a writer may produce these effects without violating truth is sufficiently proved by many excellent biographical works. The immense popularity which well-written books of this kind have acquired deserves the serious consideration of historians. Voltaire's Charles the Twelfth, Marmontel's Memoirs, Boswell's Life of Johnson, Southey's account of Nelson, are perused with delight by the most frivolous and indolent. Whenever any tolerable book of the same description makes its appearance, the circulating libraries are mobbed; the book societies are in commotion; the new novel lies uncut; the magazines and newspapers fill their columns with extracts. In the meantime histories of great empires, written by men of eminent ability, lie unread on the shelves of ostentatious libraries.

2. The writers of history seem to entertain an aristocratical contempt for the writers of memoirs. They think it beneath the dignity of men who describe the revolutions

---

The author has been speaking of the present state of historical composition, which he says is devoted to discussing historical questions rather than to writing history proper. This **sentence now** enables him to introduce the subject of *historical narration*, which forms the subject not of this paragraph, strictly, but of the whole Selection. — The art **of** narration, — how is this subject defined in the same sentence? — The subject of the present paragraph follows in the second sentence: namely, "**that a** writer may produce these effects without violating truth." Trace how this proposition is proved, **in** the series of sentences without connectives. The one connective of the paragraph then follows, "in the **meantime**" (l. 16), a mild adversative (Rhet. p. 142), introducing the obverse. (For definition of this last term, see Rhet. p. 293, 3). **From** the foregoing indications write **out the** plan of this paragraph. See Rhet. pp. 198–202.

Par. 2. — Subject of this paragraph, and place of it? See Rhet. p. 196. Test the parallel construction, according to Rhet. p. 208. Of

of nations to dwell on the details which constitute the charm of biography. They have imposed on themselves a code of conventional decencies as absurd as that which has been the bane of the French drama. The most characteristic and interesting circumstances are omitted or softened down, because, as we are told, they are too trivial for the majesty of history. The majesty of history seems to resemble the majesty of the poor king of Spain, who died a martyr to ceremony, because the proper dignitaries were not at hand to render him assistance.

3. That history would be more amusing if this etiquette were relaxed will, we suppose, be acknowledged. But would it be less dignified or less useful? What do we mean when we say that one past event is important and another insignificant? No past event has any intrinsic importance. The knowledge of it is valuable only as it leads us to form just calculations with respect to the future. A history which does not serve this purpose, though it may be filled with battles, treaties, and commotions, is as use-

---

the first three sentences, what is the subject, and how is its prominence maintained? What change of construction in ll. **25-28**? What further in ll. **28-31**? Reconstruct the paragraph on the subject "the majesty of history," and keep that subject consistently prominent. Does the repetition of the phrase "the majesty of history," l. **28**, really aid the continuity of thought between this sentence and the preceding? How does the allusion at the end illustrate Rhet. p. 299?

Par. 3.—This paragraph and the next should be studied together, as dealing with the same subject. In how many sentences is the subject introduced? How repeated at the end of par. 4? Cf. Rhet. p. 198, examples, 3. The sentences ll. **34-42** illustrate a peculiar abruptness of Macaulay's, which consists in beginning with a thought comparatively remote, and bringing it by degrees toward his subject. The thought here dealt with is not closely connected with the paragraph; its connections have to be sought in the implications of the succeeding.

less as the series of turnpike tickets collected by Sir Matthew Mite.

4. Let us suppose that Lord Clarendon, instead of filling hundreds of folio pages with copies of state papers, in which the same assertions and contradictions are repeated till the reader is overpowered with weariness, had condescended to be the Boswell of the Long Parliament. Let us suppose that he had exhibited to us the wise and lofty self-government of Hampden, leading while he seemed to follow, and propounding unanswerable arguments in the strongest forms with the modest air of an inquirer anxious for information; the delusions which misled the noble spirit of Vane; the coarse fanaticism which concealed the yet loftier genius of Cromwell, destined to control a mutinous army and a factious people, to abase the flag of Holland, to arrest the victorious arms of Sweden, and to hold the balance firm between the rival monarchies of France and Spain. Let us suppose that he had made his Cavaliers and Roundheads talk in their own style; that he had reported some of the ribaldry of Rupert's pages, and some of the cant of Harrison and Fleetwood. Would not his work in that case have been more interesting? Would it not have been more accurate?

5. A history in which every particular incident may be true may on the whole be false. The circumstances which

---

Par. 4. — As the subject of this paragraph is already proposed in the foregoing, what kind of paragraph is this? See Rhet. p. 211. Show how this nature of the paragraph is shown in the structure and subject-matter of the sentences. Cf. Rhet. p. 186, 2. — In the last two sentences, ll. 61-63, which repeat the subject, what emphasis is given in the repetition? See Rhet. p. 97.

Par. 5. — This paragraph should be studied together with 6 and 7, the three being merely stages in the treatment of the same subject.

have most influence on the happiness of mankind, the changes of manners and morals, the transition of communities from poverty to wealth, from knowledge to ignorance, from ferocity to humanity — these are, for the most part, noiseless revolutions. Their progress is rarely indicated by what historians are pleased to call important events. They are not achieved by armies, or enacted by senates. They are sanctioned by no treaties, and recorded in no archives. They are carried on in every school, in every church, behind ten thousand counters, at ten thousand firesides. The upper current of society presents no certain criterion by which we can judge of the direction in which the under current flows. We read of defeats and victories. But we know that nations may be miserable amidst victories and prosperous amidst defeats. We read of the fall of wise ministers and of the rise of profligate favorites. But we must remember how small a proportion the good or evil effected by a single statesman can bear to the good or evil of a great social system.

6. Bishop Watson compares a geologist to a gnat mounted on an elephant, and laying down theories as to the whole internal structure of the vast animal, from the phenomena of the hide. The comparison is unjust to the geologists;

From a careful reading of the three, and especially from the suggestions in ll. 64, 65 and ll. 108-110, deduce the exact subject therein treated. With what *general* consideration, related to the subject, has Par. **5**, after the first sentence, to do? What then may be regarded as the subject of this paragraph? Explain the use of the short sentences, ll. **70-84**, by Rhet. p. 186, 1. — How are the last four sentences, ll. **78-84**, balanced with one another? See Rhet. p. 164, 80. Explain the relation of the adversative sentences to their foregoers by Rhet. 138, 38.

Par. **6**. — What is the office of the paragraph, and what stage in the subject does it set forth? How related to foregoing?

but it is very applicable to those historians who write as if the body politic were homogeneous, who look only on the surface of affairs, and never think of the mighty and various organization which lies deep below.

7. In the works of such writers as these, England, at the close of the Seven Years' War, is in the highest state of prosperity: at the close of the American War she is in a miserable and degraded condition; as if the people were not on the whole as rich, as well governed, and as well educated at the latter period as at the former. We have read books called Histories of England, under the reign of George the Second, in which the rise of Methodism is not even mentioned. A hundred years hence this breed of authors will, we hope, be extinct. If it should still exist, the late ministerial interregnum will be described in terms which will seem to imply that all government was at an end; that the social contract was annulled; and that the hand of every man was against his neighbor, until the wisdom and virtue of the new cabinet educed order out of the chaos of anarchy. We are quite certain that misconceptions as gross prevail at this moment respecting many important parts of our annals.

8. The effect of historical reading is analogous, in many respects, to that produced by foreign travel. The student, like the tourist, is transported into a new state of society.

Par. 7. — What kind of paragraph is this? See Rhet. p. 211. Observe that it accumulates material for the assertion of the last sentence, and that this last stands, to the assertion l. 64, in the relation of concrete to general. Turning now to l. 64 again, what figurative mode of expression gives it interest and stimulus? See Rhet. p. 102.

Par. 8. — Trace the analogy (see Rhet. p. 395) on its two sides, and write out the plan, according to following indications. (1) Analogy: (*a*) the tourist; (*b*) the student. (2) "But": (*a*) the tourist;

He sees **new** fashions. He hears new modes of expression. His mind is enlarged by contemplating the wide diversities of laws, of morals, and of manners. But men may travel far, and return with minds as contracted as if they had **never** stirred from their own market-town. In the **same** manner, men may know the dates of many battles and the genealogies of many royal houses, and yet be no wiser. Most people look at past times as princes look at foreign countries. **More than one** illustrious stranger has landed **on our island amidst the** shouts of a mob, has dined with the king, has hunted with the master of the stag-hounds, has seen the Guards reviewed, and a knight of the garter installed, has cantered along Regent Street, has visited St. Paul's, and noted down its dimensions; and has then departed, thinking that he has seen England. He has, in fact, seen a few public buildings, public men, and public ceremonies. **But of** the **vast** and complex system of society, of the fine shades **of** national character, of the practical **operation** of government and laws, he knows nothing. He who would understand these things rightly must not confine his observations to palaces and solemn days. He must see ordinary men as they appear in their ordinary business and in their ordinary pleasures. He must mingle in the crowds **of** the exchange and the coffee-house. He must obtain **admittance to the convivial table and the** domestic hearth. He must bear with vulgar expressions. He must not shrink from exploring even the retreats of

---

(*b*) **the** student. (3) "**As**": (*a*) the student; (*b*) the tourist. (4) "**Must**": (*a*) the tourist; (*b*) the student. (5) Conclusion. Are the comparisons of this paragraph similes? See Rhet. p. 89, 1.

The remainder of the Selection is to be studied together, being a portrayal of "**the** perfect historian," according **to** Macaulay's **idea.**

misery. He who wishes to understand the condition of
mankind in former ages must proceed on the same principle.   If he attends only to public transactions, to wars,
congresses, and debates, his studies will be as unprofitable
as the travels of those imperial, royal, and serene sovereigns
who form their judgment of our island from having gone
in state to a few fine sights, and from having held formal
conferences with a few great officers.

9. The perfect historian is he in whose work the character and spirit of an age is exhibited in miniature. He
relates no fact, he attributes no expression to his characters,
which is not authenticated by sufficient testimony. But
by judicious selection, rejection, and arrangement, he gives
to truth those attractions which have been usurped by fic-
tion. In his narrative a due subordination is observed:
some transactions are prominent; others retire. But the
scale on which he represents them is increased or dimin-
ished, not according to the dignity of the persons concerned
in them, but according to the degree in which they elucidate the condition of society and the nature of man. He
shows us the court, the camp, and the senate. But he
shows us also the nation. He considers no anecdote, no
peculiarity of manner, no familiar saying, as too insignificant for his notice which is not too insignificant to illustrate
the operation of laws, of religion, and of education, and to
mark the progress of the human mind. Men will not
merely be described, but will be made intimately known to
us. The changes of manners will be indicated, not merely

Par. 9. — This paragraph, after the subject-sentence, falls naturally into three stages and a conclusion. **Trace these** in a plan, and see how **all** of the three stages are balanced together according to Rhet. p 138, 38.

by a few general phrases or a few extracts from statistical documents, but by appropriate images presented in every line.

10. If a man, such as we are supposing, should write the history of England, he would assuredly not omit the battles, the sieges, the negotiations, the seditions, the ministerial changes. But with these he would intersperse the details which are the charm of historical romances. At Lincoln Cathedral there is a beautiful painted window, which was made by an apprentice out of the pieces of glass which had been rejected by his master. It is so far superior to every other in the church, that, according to the tradition, the vanquished artist killed himself from mortification. Sir Walter Scott, in the same manner, has used those fragments of truth which historians have scornfully thrown behind them in a manner which may well excite their envy. He has constructed out of their gleanings works which, even considered as histories, are scarcely less valuable than theirs. But a truly great historian would reclaim those materials which the novelist has appropriated. The history of the government, and the history of the people, would be exhibited in that mode in which alone they can be exhibited justly, in inseparable conjunction and intermixture. We should not then have to look for the wars and votes of the Puritans in Clarendon, and for their phraseology in Old Mortality; for one half of King James in Hume, and for the other half in the Fortunes of Nigel.

11. The early part of our imaginary history would be rich with coloring from romance, ballad, and chronicle.

Par. 10. — Write the plan of this paragraph, according to the following: 1. ll. **172-176**; 2. **176-187**; 3. **187-195**. Give names that shall indicate the *office* of each division.

We should find ourselves in the company of knights such as those of Froissart, and of pilgrims such as those who rode with Chaucer from the Tabard. Society would be shown from the highest to the lowest, — from the royal cloth of state to the den of the outlaw; from the throne of the legate, to the chimney-corner where the begging friar regaled himself. Palmers, minstrels, crusaders, — the stately monastery, with the good cheer in its refectory and the high-mass in its chapel, — the manor-house, with its hunting and hawking, — the tournament, with the heralds and ladies, the trumpets and the cloth of gold, — would give truth and life to the representation. We should perceive, in a thousand slight touches, the importance of the privileged burgher, and the fierce and haughty spirit which swelled under the collar of the degraded villain. The revival of letters would not merely be described in a few magnificent periods. We should discern, in innumerable particulars, the fermentation of mind, the eager appetite for knowledge, which distinguished the sixteenth from the fifteenth century. In the Reformation we should see, not merely a schism which changed the ecclesiastical constitution of England and the mutual relations of the European powers, but a moral war which raged in every family, which set the father against the son, and the son against the father, the mother against the daughter, and the daughter against the mother. Henry would be painted with the skill of Tacitus. We should have the change of his character from his profuse and joyous youth to his savage and imperious old age. We should perceive the gradual progress of selfish and tyrannical passions in a

---

Par. 11. — How is the nature of this paragraph, as to subject and sequence, explained by Rhet. p. 195 (also ib. examples, 2)? Trace

mind not naturally insensible or ungenerous; and to the last we should detect some remains of that open and noble temper which endeared him to a people whom he oppressed, struggling with the hardness of despotism and the irritability of disease. We should see Elizabeth in all her weakness and in all her strength, surrounded by the handsome favorites whom she never trusted, and the wise old statesmen whom she never dismissed, uniting in herself the most contradictory qualities of both her parents, — the coquetry, the caprice, the petty malice of Anne, — the haughty and resolute spirit of Henry. We have no hesitation in saying that a great artist might produce a portrait of this remarkable woman at least as striking as that in the novel of Kenilworth, without employing a single trait not authenticated by ample testimony. In the meantime, we should see arts cultivated, wealth accumulated, the conveniences of life improved. We should see the keeps, where nobles, insecure themselves, spread insecurity around them, gradually giving place to the halls of peaceful opulence, to the oriels of Longleat, and the stately pinnacles of Burleigh. We should see towns extended, deserts cultivated, the hamlets of fishermen turned into wealthy havens, the meal of the peasant improved, and his hut more commodiously furnished. We should see those opinions and feelings which produced the **great** struggle against the house of Stuart slowly growing up in the bosom of private families, before they manifested themselves in Parliamentary debates. Then would come the Civil War. Those skirmishes on which Clarendon dwells so minutely would be told, as Thucydides would have told

---

the stages of English history over which it courses. What kind of paragraph is it? **197.** What touch of poetic feeling? See Rhet. p. 51,

them, with perspicuous conciseness. They are merely connecting links. But the great characteristics of the age, the loyal enthusiasm of the brave English gentry, the fierce licentiousness of the swearing, dicing, drunken reprobates, **whose excesses** disgraced the royal cause, — the austerity of the Presbyterian Sabbaths in the city, the extravagance of the independent preachers in the camp, the precise garb, the severe countenance, the petty scruples, the affected accent, the absurd names and phrases which marked the Puritans, — the valor, the policy, the public spirit, which lurked beneath these ungraceful disguises, — the dreams of **the** raving Fifth-monarchy-man, the dreams, scarcely less wild, of the philosophic republican, — all these **would enter** into the representation, and render it at once more exact and more striking.

12. **The** instruction derived from history thus written would be of a **vivid** and practical character. It would be received by the imagination as well as by the reason. It would be not merely traced on the mind, but branded into it. **Many** truths, too, would be learned, which can be learned in no other manner. As the history of states is generally written, the greatest and most momentous revolutions seem to come upon them like supernatural inflictions, without warning or cause. But the fact is, that such revolutions are almost always the consequences of moral changes, which have gradually passed on the mass of the community, and which ordinarily proceed far before their progress is indicated by any public measure. An intimate knowledge

---

examples, 2. — How does the last sentence illustrate Rhet. p. 209? — 270. **All these**, — explain by Rhet. p. 160, 73.

Par. 12. — In this paragraph trace (1) The definitive part, indicated in its short sentences; cf. Rhet. p. 186, 1. (2) General truth

of the domestic history of nations is therefore absolutely necessary to the prognosis of political events. A narrative, defective in this respect, is as useless as a medical treatise which should pass by all the symptoms attendant on the early stage of a disease and mention only what occurs when the patient is beyond the reach of remedies.

13. A historian, such as we have been attempting to describe, would indeed be an intellectual prodigy. In his mind, powers scarcely compatible with each other must be tempered into an exquisite harmony. We shall sooner see another Shakspeare or another Homer. The highest excellence to which any single faculty can be brought would be less surprising than such a happy and delicate combination of qualities. Yet the contemplation of imaginary models is not an unpleasant or useless employment of the mind. It cannot indeed produce perfection; but it pro-

---

of the paragraph, in obverse (see Rhet. p. 293, 3), positive assertion, and illative conclusion (cf. Rhet. p. 143). (3) Illustration by comparison.

Par. 13. — What is illustrated from this paragraph, Rhet. p. 209? As the same paragraph is cited again, Rhet. p. 281, it need not be studied farther here.

Two or three remarks on Macaulay's style, apart from paragraph structure, may here be made.

1. As to diction, ll. **106, 221-223** will illustrate, what is a striking feature throughout Macaulay's writings, the spontaneousness with which he moulds expression according to Biblical diction. Macaulay was a great student of the Bible. In one of his letters he wrote, "A person who professes to be a critic in the delicacies of the English language, ought to have the Bible at his fingers' ends."

2. The short, abrupt character of many of Macaulay's sentences is due largely to punctuation. He generally expresses in two sentences what most writers would express in one with a semicolon between the clauses; see how this is exemplified in ll. **32-38**; **78-80**; **80-84**; **150-155**; **155-160**; **160-162**.

duces improvement, and nourishes that generous and liberal fastidiousness which **is not** inconsistent with the strongest sensibility **to merit, and** which, while it exalts **our** conceptions **of** the **art,** does not render **us** unjust to the artist.   305

From ESSAY ON HISTORY.

---

3. A very noticeable feature of Macaulay's style is the abundance of illustration, especially by comparison and simile, introduced formally with the object of clearness.   See ends of paragraphs **2, 3,** and **12,** and ll. **85–92, 176–187.**

STUDY OF PARAGRAPHS IN PREVIOUS SELECTIONS.

The sense for rounded and symmetrical paragraph structure is comparatively modern in the history of English prose; and even now there are few eminent prose writers whose style in this particular can profitably be studied as a model. Macaulay, as we have seen, was especially good at constructing paragraphs on a definite plan, with all its parts conspicuously marked and arranged; but in other respects he was poor: his paragraphs are somewhat hard, mechanical, inflexible, and the paucity of connectives and sentence-adjustments leaves the style very meagre in delicate shadings and fine relations between ideas. We need therefore to compare with others; and doubtless we shall find in them points of excellence, though in the important matter of plan they may be poor.

We will select paragraphs from a few of the selections for examination.

De Quincey: Pages 8–16. — In the matter of explicit reference De Quincey is the opposite of Macaulay, being indeed very, sometimes almost excessively, minute, in words, phrases, and sentence-adjustments, for reference. — To find how this, and his paragraph-structure in general, may be illustrated, take lines **10-62**. How is it connected with the preceding paragraph? With what thought does it begin, and to what thought is it conducted? Trace now how each sentence is connected with its foregoer, explaining by Rhet. pp. 202–206. — **17-26**. How does this passage illustrate Rhet. p. 207? By what connective is it introduced? How is return made to the main subject, l. 26? See Rhet. p. 139, list. — **37**. Where do you find the connective here, and of what nature is it? — **49**. How does the means of explicit reference here used illustrate Rhet. p. 133, 30? — **54**. What influence operates to invert the order of this sentence? Trace the influence both before and after. — Observe that part of this paragraph is narrative, furnishing the preparation, and part expository, furnishing the conclusion. Point out where its character divides.

Burke: Pages **18-23.** — In the second paragraph (ll. 32-51), note what is the subject, and what place it occupies. Is the subject given in identical words as in preceding paragraph, or in a definition? — Point out how the subject of remark is kept prominent throughout, according to Rhet. p. 208. By what grammatical device is it emphasized? See Rhet. p. 133. Why may it be less distinguished in last sentence?

What favorite structure of Burke's, as pointed out Rhet. p. 209, do you note in the fifth paragraph (ll. **77-99**)? How much of the paragraph does the last sentence summarize? How is the early part of the paragraph related to the latter?

Ruskin: Pages **36-47.** — Read the third paragraph (ll. **63-111**), and report what is its subject, and where found. How is this kind of paragraph described, Rhet. p. 195? Point out the connectives in the paragraph; of what kind are they, and founded on what relation? Cf. Rhet. p. 273, 1.

Point out the subject in paragraph seven (ll. **190-216**), and report in how many ways it is expressed. What right have the succeeding sentences in the paragraph, according to Rhet. p. 199, — that is, what is their relation to the subject? — The short sentence at the end, though not summarizing (Rhet. p. 209), makes a beautiful ending, by its poetic suggestiveness, so contrasted with what precedes.

Huxley: Pages **67-75.** — In place of notes on any of the paragraphs of this Selection, the remark may here be made that all of these paragraphs, with their perfectly clear and definite structure, are well adapted for use as an exercise in analysis, especially by those who would make a beginning in the independent study of paragraph structure.

Newman: Pages **76-85.** — The first paragraph (ll. **1-45**) consists broadly of two parts; point out where the first part ends and the second begins. Which is the principal part, and which ancillary? — What is the general subject of remark in the first part? How changed in the second? In what sentence does the paragraph put its most important matter? To what goal is the thought conducted? Compare the last sentence with the first, — how are they related?

Matthew Arnold: Pages **97-109.** — Study the plan of the fourth paragraph (ll. **121-180**), according to the following indications of structure: 1. ll. **121-124.** 2. ll. **124-133.** 3. ll. **133-136.** 4. ll. **136-144.** 5. ll. **145-149.** 6. ll. **149-163.** 7. ll. **163-180.** Taking these indications, draw up a tabular plan, which shall show how the thought progresses, what is principal, what summarizing, what illustrative.

II.

STUDIES IN INVENTION.

HOW THESE STUDIES ARE CONNECTED WITH THE RHETORIC.

ON ORDERING OF MATERIAL: RHETORIC, TO PAGE 300. — Morley, p. 133; Addison, p. 141; Helps, p. 147.

ON DESCRIPTION: RHETORIC, TO PAGE 353. — Blackmore, p. 156; Stanley, p. 161; Green, p. 169; Notes on Description in Previous Selections, p. 185.

ON NARRATION: RHETORIC, TO PAGE 382. — Hughes, p. 187; Shorthouse, p. 198; Scott, p. 206.

ON EXPOSITION: RHETORIC, TO PAGE 406. — Mill, p. 225; Ruskin, p. 233; Notes on Exposition in Previous Selections, p. 253.

ON ARGUMENTATION: **RHETORIC, TO PAGE 446.** — Tyndall, p. 255; Macaulay, p. 266.

ON PERSUASION (ORATORY): RHETORIC, TO PAGE 474. — Curtis, p. 275.

XIII.

JOHN MORLEY.

PROGRESSIVE TENDENCIES OF THE AGE OF BURKE.

1. HISTORY has strictly only to do with individual men as the originals, the furtherers, the opponents, or the representatives of some of those thousand diverse forces which, uniting in one vast sweep, bear along the successive generations of men as upon the broad wings of sea-winds to new and more fertile shores. No modern epoch has witnessed the beginnings of so many of these important movements as that which is covered by Burke's parliamentary life. In every order of activity a fresh and gigantic impulse was given, the tide of national life widened and swelled under

---

This Selection, and the two that follow, are studied as exemplifying the general processes in the ordering of material, namely the theme, the plan, and amplification; and presuppose a knowledge of the Rhetoric as far as page 300.

This Selection from Morley, although taken from the middle of a chapter, deals with a distinct subject of its own, and presents all the essential characteristics of a complete essay in miniature.

Let us first inquire into the expression of the theme; see Rhet. p. 248 sqq. The heading put over this Selection was not taken from Morley, but deduced from study of the selection itself. Point out in the essay the grounds for choosing the word *tendencies* in the theme. Why would not *characteristics* be fitting? Why add the adjective *progressive* to the term tendencies? Would it be exact to say "*the* progressive tendencies," — and why? Is the expression "the age of

the influence of new and flushed tributaries, the springs and sources were unsealed of modern ideas, modern systems, and of ideas and systems that are still to be developed.

2. In the Spiritual order, for instance, when Burke was
15 achieving his first successes in the House of Commons (1766), Wesley and Whitefield were strenuously traversing

---

Burke" exactly commensurate with the time contemplated by the essay? If not, why is it used in the heading? Try the effect of making the heading the exact theme; would it make a good title? See Rhet. p. 258. Is the theme anywhere expressed in so many words, and does it need to be? See Rhet. p. 254. How does the statement of the theme, as above evolved, fulfil the requisites, Rhet. pp. 254-256?

As this Selection is part of a chapter, the introduction is a transition. The writer has been speaking of Burke as an individual, and here he is to speak of the characteristics of Burke's age. How does the opening sentence, ll. **1-6**, fulfil the characteristics of a transition, as given, Rhet. p. 282, — that is, what aspect of the preceding idea does it retain, how does it connect with the idea which is the subject of this essay, and what is the connecting link? Point out now, in this first paragraph, how the theme is (1) introduced generally; (2) particularized to one period, and (3) defined and described in that period. Test this introduction by Rhet. p. 267, 1. How are the first and third steps amplified? See Rhet. p. 295, 2.

As to its main ideas, this little essay falls into three divisions. Deduce the first main division from paragraphs **1-5**; the second from paragraphs **6** and **7**; the third from paragraph **8**; and set them down in tabular form. How express in the skeleton (Rhet. p. 264) the subdivisions of the first main division, paragraphs **2-5**? In the same way set down the two subdivisions represented in paragraphs **6, 7**; and the two represented in paragraph **8**. What consideration, drawn from ll. **138-146**, forms the conclusion? How does the conclusion answer to Rhet. p. 280?

Let us now see how the amplification helps along the current of the thought.

Par. 2. — Is there a significance in mentioning this particular fact about Burke, ll. **15, 16**, as related to the subject of the paragraph? What call for the somewhat imaginative type of style, ll. **18-24**, as set-

the length and breadth of the land, quickening the deep-hidden sensibilities, and filling with lofty and divine visions the once blind souls of men and women who had labored blankly, as brute beasts labor, down in coal mines, in factories, over furnaces and forges, in dank fields, on barren, remote moors, and who till then had known no glimpses of a wider and more joyful life than the life of a starved and ever-benumbed sense.

3. In the Industrial order a development of no less momentous importance dates from the same time. In the year in which Burke published his "Thoughts on the Present Discontents" (1770), Hargreaves took out his patent for the spinning-jenny, the year before that is the date of Arkwright's patent, and nine years later Samuel Crompton invented that wonderful machine, the mule, which endures as a marvel of ingenuity even in our own ingenious times. The improvement of means of transport proceeded at an equal pace with improvements in means of production. For while Burke was pondering his maiden speech (1766), Brindley was beginning the Grand Trunk Canal from the Trent to the Mersey, and Watt was busy on the third model of the steam-engine.

4. In the Speculative and Scientific order, while Burke and the Rockingham party were marking their abhorrence

---

ting forth this particular kind of thought? See Rhet. p. 289, 3. What kind of epithet is **brute**, l. **20**? See Rhet. p. 56. Would it be adapted to all kinds of prose? What means of amplification predominates in this second paragraph? See Rhet. p. 295, 1.

Par. 3. — Trace the connection, whether antithetic or illustrative, between the fact mentioned, ll. **27, 28**, and the thought of the paragraph. What means of amplification is employed **here**? See Rhet. p. 290, 1.

Par. 4. — Note that the fact here connected with the thought of the paragraph has to do with theories of the policy of government, just as the paragraph has to do with theories of wealth and philosophy. Point

and despair at the American policy of Lord North and the Court by a partial secession from Parliament (1776), the "Wealth of Nations" was given to the world, and the foundations laid of economic science. Nor should we overlook
45 the important fact that the tremendously powerful solvents supplied by Hume forty years before, were at this time as potent for destruction in one set of opinions as Adam Smith's book was for construction in another set. Thus Burke's contemporaries saw the Wesleyan revival of Chris-
50 tian belief. They saw the rise of a philosophy which directly and indirectly has done more to weaken and narrow that belief than Wesley or Butler, or anybody else did, to restore it. They saw those triumphs of mechanical invention and engineering science which were destined
55 to revolutionize modern life. And, above all, they saw established those theoretic principles of commerce which, overthrowing the old notions of the mercantile system, were to add a thousandfold to the material comfort of mankind, and to prove an indispensable, though rough and
60 temporary means, of propagating the idea of the brotherhood of nations.

5. Fourthly, and finally, in the Political order. The year which saw the "Wealth of Nations" (1776), saw also the Declaration of American Independence. The year before
65 Burke wrote the Letter to the Sheriffs of Bristol, Franklin

---

out the antithetic facts, regarding constructive and destructive influences, and how each general fact is based on particular events. In the latter part of the paragraph, how are preceding ideas summarized to illustrate the thought?

Par. 5. — The ideas of this paragraph are first given in amplified form and then summarized in a brief statement. Point out how this is, and to what "two great events" the political facts are reduced. The facts mentioned, ll. **63–65**, are related to each other, perhaps, as abstract to

was consoling Jefferson by the story of John Thompson the hatter, for the changes made by their colleagues in Jefferson's draft of the Declaration, and shortly afterwards they all agreed upon that ever memorable announcement, "We, therefore, the representatives of the United States of America, in general congress assembled, appealing to the Supreme Judge of the world for the rectitude of our intentions, do in the name and by the authority of the good people of these colonies, solemnly publish and declare that these united colonies are, and of right ought to be, Free and Independent States." Thirteen years later, "the evening sun of July" shone over the blood-stained ruin of the Bastille. The foundation of the new republic and the uprooting of the old monarchy were the two great events in the political order. Each is an achievement that in its relation to ourselves and some generations of our descendants, can have no rival in importance save the other.

6. Though for the purposes of analysis and clear classification it is essential that we should speak of each of these impulses as single and distinct, it is highly important that we should recognize their common direction. Each of

---

concrete. Burke's letter to the Sheriffs of Bristol explained and justified his attitude of conciliation toward America; while Franklin's story to Jefferson was an incident in the American debate which resulted in independence. For the story, see Sparks's "Life of Franklin," p. 407.

The four paragraphs together, **2–5**, which are here treated as subdivisions, may be regarded as amplification of the first main thought; what means of amplification do they exemplify? See Rhet. p. 290, 1.

Note the relation between paragraphs **6** and **7**. The former gives in brief the thought which the latter amplifies. Of what kind, then, is the seventh paragraph? See Rhet. **p. 211.**

Par. 6. — How does the amplification of the latter part of the paragraph illustrate Rhet. p. 291, 3? Can you point out also a case of amplification by obverse? See Rhet. p. 293, 3.

them is one element in the history of the country, but all
the elements receive a common suffusion, which we are
content vaguely to call the spirit of the times. Every age
has its strong setting current of ideas. Those movements
only retain a permanent interest which are in harmony
with this current. Isolated fragments of antipathetic
effort, spasmodic outbreaks of counter endeavor, pass away
and are lost. It is the composition and fusion of main
forces which arrest the eye of the historian.

7. It is not necessary for me to show in detail how the
spirit of the Wesleyan reformation fitted in with the characteristic movements of the time. It is enough to commemorate the aid given to industrial development by
the increase of thrift, sobriety, diligence, and those other
moral virtues, a disposition to which was borne into the
heart along with the newly-awakened spirit of religious
fervor. The development of democratic principles was
just as powerfully, though less palpably and visibly, helped
forward by the Christian revival in the eighteenth century,
as it has been by every system which calls the individual
to think, and makes him responsible, at the peril of his soul,
for the results of his thinking. In England, moreover,
dissent from the Established Church has always been more
or less democratic, because the Church is the emblem and
ally of authority. The way in which the discoveries of
Adam Smith fitted in with the great mechanical inventions
that were made at the same time is too obvious to need

Par. 7. — Notice how the amplification in this paragraph takes the unity of idea in the preceding, and works it out toward the *two* thoughts which are the subject of the next paragraph. Thus, what two influences were exerted by the Wesleyan reformation (ll. **98–111**)? What was the influence of the industrial movement (ll. **111–132**)? Note now to what two main influences these details have tended.

dwelling upon. To perceive clearly, first, that manufactures enrich, not impoverish a country, and second, that manufactures thrive better where there are the fewest restrictions on the free interchange of commodities — first, to assert the power of manufactures in increasing the national wealth, and second, to establish the conditions under which this power can rise to the greatest height of efficiency — this was the natural accompaniment in theory to the inventions of Arkwright and Crompton and Watt in practice. Still less need I devote any words to establish the underlying connection which subsists between a vigorous industrial movement and the impulse towards the abolition of privilege. Any ordinary House of Commons politician knows that the artisans are, as a class, the resolute enemies of Privilege, though perhaps barely resolute enough. The vigorous growth of manufactures is indirectly as fatal to favored orders, as the foundation of the American Republic and the French Revolution were directly.

8. These, then, were the two prime characteristics which sum up the tendencies of Burke's age: an enormous development of industry, and the first germs of a substitution of the government of a whole people by itself for the exploded and tottering system of government by privileged orders. The seeds thus sown have come up with unequal rapidity, yet their maturity will not improbably be contemporaneous. The organization of Labor and the

---

Par. 8. — The thought of this paragraph is not amplified, being the summary of previous thoughts. How does this illustrate Rhet. p. 287? The difference between amplified and unamplified thought is well illustrated by comparing the preceding paragraph with this, and noting how what seems there mixed together without order assumes definite form and articulation here.

overthrow of Privilege are tasks which **we** may expect to see perfected at the same time, because most of the conditions that lie about the root of the one are also at the foundation of the other. When we can grapple with the moral confusion that reigns in one field, the obstacles in the other will no longer discourage or baffle us.

From EDMUND BURKE: A HISTORICAL STUDY.

What *additional* thought — that is, what thought not suggested in the body of the essay — does this conclusion contain?

XIV.

JOSEPH ADDISON.

LUCIDUS ORDO.

AMONG my daily papers which I bestow on the public, there are some which are written with regularity and method, and others that run out into the wildness of those

---

"It was said of Socrates, that he brought philosophy down from heaven, to inhabit among men; and I shall be ambitious to have it said of me, that I have brought philosophy **out of closets and** libraries, schools and colleges, to dwell in clubs and assemblies, at tea-tables **and** in coffee-houses." Such, in his own words, was Addison's general aim in writing the papers of the Spectator, from which the present Selection is taken. Being intended for ordinary readers, therefore, we expect this paper to be not strenuous or severe in its thought, or minute and exhaustive in its **range**, but plain, interesting, popular; perhaps indeed its plan and amplification will be a little over easy, because, representing some of the earliest attempts at popularizing instruction, it may overrate its task and talk *down* to its readers. If, however, it betrays tendencies to this fault, we may remember that the fault is in the right direction.

The only clew that Addison furnishes to the theme of his paper is the motto from Horace, "Light-giving method," or, "Method is light-giving," here used **as a** title. Read the whole paper and see if you can **formulate the theme more** closely, with some indication, in the way it is stated, of manner of treatment. Do you find any single sentence, or passage, that includes the **theme as** exactly **as, for** instance, ll. 8-13, of the foregoing selection, suggest *its* **theme?**

If the motto justly suggests **the** subject, how does the first paragraph make approach to it? This first paragraph really treats of *two* contrasted **ideas**; do both belong strictly to the theme, or is one merely an ob-

compositions which go by the names of essays. **As for the first**, I have the whole scheme of the discourse in my mind before **I set pen** to paper. In the other kind of writing, it is sufficient that I have several thoughts on a subject, without troubling myself to range them in such order that they may seem to grow out of one another, and be disposed under the proper heads. Seneca and Montaigne are patterns for writing in this last kind, as Tully and Aristotle excel in the other. When I read an author of genius who writes without method, I fancy myself in a wood that abounds with a great many noble objects, rising among one another in the greatest confusion and disorder. When I read a methodical discourse, I am in a regular plantation, and can place myself in its several centres, **so as to take a** view of all the lines and walks that are **struck from them.** You may ramble in the one a **whole** day together, and every moment discover something or other that is new to you; but when you have done, you will have but a confused, imperfect notion of the place. In the other, your eye commands the whole prospect, and gives you such an idea of it as is not easily worn out of the memory.

---

verse amplification of the other? — **4. Which go by the names of essays**, — in Addison's time the term essay was not so extended as it is now; see Rhet. pp. 403, 404. The first sentence, ll. **1-4**, lays down the subject of the paragraph, which the rest of it amplifies. How do ll. **10-12** illustrate Rhet. p. 291, 2 (top of page)? What means of amplification is employed in the rest of the paragraph? Rhet. p. 295, 2. Do you think of these figures as predominantly ornamental? Which of the three uses of amplification, mentioned Rhet. pp. 288, 289, seems to be mainly subserved in thus opening the idea of this paragraph? — **12. An author of genius**, — the qualification needs to be noted, in view of what is said ll. 26, 27. An author with neither genius nor method is wholly excluded from the treatment. — **14. A great many,** — explain by Rhet. p. 46, 14.

Irregularity and want of method are only supportable in men of great learning or genius, who are often too full to be exact, and therefore choose to throw down their pearls in heaps before the reader, rather than be at the pains of stringing them.

Method is of advantage to a work, both in respect to the writer and the reader. In regard to the first, it is a great help to his invention. When a man has planned his discourse, he finds a great many thoughts rising out of every head, that do not offer themselves upon the general survey of a subject. His thoughts are at the same time more intelligible, and better discover their drift and meaning, when they are placed in their proper lights and follow one another in a regular series, than when they are thrown together without order and connexion. There is always an obscurity in confusion, and the same sentence that

---

The paragraph, ll. **25–29**, gives only one side of the thought,— namely, defines where alone want of method is "supportable"; — this leaves what implication open as to where method is necessary? Which side of the thought really belongs to the present theme,— the expressed or the implied? Express in a proposition the implied idea, and note how it aids the development of the thought. **25.** Is **only** rightly placed? See Rhet. p. 119, 17. — **27. Choose to throw down their pearls,** etc. See if you can state this so briefly and effectually in literal language.

30 sq. Comparing the beginning of this paragraph with the beginning of the next, what two main divisions of the subject are suggested? **Put them** down as headings. Does the order of these opening sentences, as they now stand, give these main divisions proper distinction? Change the sentences by Rhet. p. 181, 4, so as to adjust them better to their office and to each other. — What subdivisions does the sentence, ll. **31, 32,** suggest? Point out what part of the paragraph each subdivision occupies. Why is the second so much shorter than the first? How does the amplification, ll. **32–46**, illustrate Rhet. p. 290, 1? How **many** distinct particulars do you discover in it? Discriminate, and set

would have enlightened the reader in one part of a discourse perplexes him in another. For the same reason likewise every thought in a methodical discourse shows itself in its greatest beauty, as the several figures in a
45 piece of painting receive new grace from their disposition in the picture. The advantages of a reader from a methodical discourse are correspondent with those of the writer. He comprehends everything easily, takes it in with pleasure, and retains it long.

50 Method is not less requisite in ordinary conversation than in writing, provided a man would talk to make himself understood. I, who hear a thousand coffee-house debates every day, am very sensible of this want of method in the thoughts of my honest countrymen. There is not
55 one dispute in ten which is managed in those schools of politics, where, after the three first sentences, the question is not entirely lost. Our disputants put me in mind of the cuttle-fish, that when he is unable to extricate himself, blackens all the water about him till he becomes invisible.
60 The man who does not know how to methodize his thoughts has always, to borrow a phrase from the dispensary, "a barren superfluity" of words; the fruit is lost amidst the exuberance of leaves.

Tom Puzzle is one of the most eminent immethodical

---

down as briefly as possible. Do the particulars, ll. **48, 49,** correspond with the particulars in the previous part of the paragraph?

Is the next paragraph as susceptible of being arranged in subdivisions as the one just studied? — **53. This want of method,** — is the reference of the pronoun exact? Does the amplification in this paragraph deal with the subject or its obverse? Point out by what means and accessories (see Rhet. p. 297) the thought is developed. How is the significance of the phrase quoted from the dispensary brought out by figure?

disputants of any that has fallen under my observation. 65
Tom has read enough to make him very impertinent; his
knowledge is sufficient to raise doubts, but not to clear
them. It is a pity that he has so much learning, or that
he has not a great deal more. With these qualifications
Tom sets up for a free-thinker, finds a great many things 70
to blame in the constitution of his country, and gives
shrewd intimations that he does not believe another
world. In short, Puzzle is an atheist as much as his parts
will give him leave. He has got about half a dozen commonplace topics, into which he never fails to turn the con- 75
versation, whatever was the occasion of it. Though the
matter in debate be about Douay or Denain, it is ten to one
but half his discourse runs upon the unreasonableness of
bigotry and priestcraft. This makes Mr. Puzzle the admiration of all those who have less sense than himself, and 80
the contempt of those who have more. There is none in
town whom Tom dreads so much as my friend Will Dry.
Will, who is acquainted with Tom's logic, when he finds
him running off the question, cuts him short with a "What
then? We allow all this to be true, but what is it to our 85
present purpose?" I have known Tom eloquent half an

Lines **64-94** are an amplifying paragraph; what means of amplification are here represented? See Rhet. pp. 291, 2; 296, 3. The most of the paragraph is devoted to amplifying what side of the thought? With which of two characters does the writer leave the advantage, and how? Is there a formal conclusion to the essay as a whole? Does the manner of treatment require it? Is the figure at the end luminous enough to stand in lieu of a summarizing conclusion? — **65. Any that has fallen,** — point out the inexactness here. — **68. It is a pity,** etc. One is reminded of what Lord Bacon says, in his essay on Atheism: "It is true that a little philosophy inclineth man's mind to atheism; but depth in philosophy bringeth men's minds about to religion." — **81. There is none,** — a slight inexactness, by present stand-

hour together, and triumphing, as he thought, in the superiority of the argument, when he has been nonplussed on a sudden by Mr. Dry's desiring him to tell the company
90 what it was that he endeavored to prove. **In short, Dry is a man of a clear, methodical head, but few words, and gains the same advantage over Puzzle that a small body of regular troops would gain over a numberless undisciplined militia.**

From THE SPECTATOR [No. 476].

---

ards, — none used with a singular verb. — **88. Nonplussed,** — what is the derivation of this word?

From the indications brought to light in the notes, draw out the whole plan of the essay in tabular form.

XV.

SIR ARTHUR HELPS.

ON THE ART OF LIVING WITH OTHERS.

THE Iliad for war; the Odyssey for wandering: but where is the great domestic epic? Yet it is but commonplace to say, that passions may rage round a tea-table, which would not have misbecome men dashing at one

---

The present Selection exemplifies, in a modern and more familiar manner, the kind of essay of which Lord Bacon is the greatest representative: a series of semi-detached observations on a large and weighty subject, not obviously exhaustive of its theme, nor conspicuously maintaining a progressive and consecutive order, yet none the less truly organized, according to that instinctive sequence which a logical mind naturally obeys, and presenting, by the same instinct of completeness, the really important points relating to the subject, though in outline rather than in amplified fulness. Let us study principally the indications of that logically moving mind.

The divisions here marked by Roman numerals are represented in the original by larger spaces between the paragraphs. This method of Roman numeration is much used nowadays to mark main divisions that are real but not obtrusive, — divisions interpreted by the general body of the thought, rather than by sharply defining propositions.

What beginning does the first paragraph make toward suggesting the theme? What importance and what lack, regarding it, are brought to light? How is the domestic theme set off against themes dealing (1) with greater relations, (2) with narrower relations? Notice some of the things conveyed by suggestion (cf. Rhet. p. 300). The question l. 1, But where, etc., implies what answer? Rhet. p. 97. How is this taken for granted in the connective of the next sentence? — 3. May rage,

another in **war** chariots; and evolutions of patience and temper **are** performed at the fireside, worthy to be compared with the Retreat of the **Ten Thousand**. Men have worshipped some fantastic being for living alone in a wilderness; but social martyrdoms place no saints upon the calendar.

We may blind ourselves to it if we like, **but** the hatreds and disgusts **that there are** behind friendship, relationship, service, and, indeed, proximity of all kinds, is **one of** the darkest spots upon earth. The various relations of life, **which** bring people together, cannot, as we know, be perfectly fulfilled except in a state where there will, perhaps, be no occasion for any of them. It is no harm, however, to endeavor to see whether there **are** any methods which may make these **relations in the least degree more** harmonious now.

I.

In the first **place, if people are** to live happily together, they must not fancy, because they are thrown together now, that all their lives have been exactly similar up to the present time, that they started exactly alike, and that they

---

5. **Evolutions . . . are performed,** — what figurative suggestion in these expressions and what their fitness here? — 8. **Fantastic being,** — how does this epithet betray the author's estimate of the subject mentioned? How does the figurative suggestion of the second member of the antithesis (l. 9) agree with that of the first?

The second paragraph suggests what limitations of the subject, as expressed in the title? To what point, then, is the subject steered in the last sentence (ll. **17-20**), — that is, how much and how little does the author undertake to treat? In thus bringing to light these three things: importance of subject, lack, and limitations, how does the Introduction answer to the rationale, Rhet. p. 267?

21. **In the first place,** — point out how the first consideration is expressed (1) negatively, (2) positively. What reason is apparent in

are to be for the future of the same mind. A thorough conviction of the difference of men is the great thing to be assured of in social knowledge: it is to life what Newton's law is to astronomy. Sometimes men have a knowledge of it with regard to the world in general: they do not expect the outer world to agree with them in all points, but are vexed at not being able to drive their own tastes and opinions into those they live with. Diversities distress them. They will not see that there are many forms of virtue and wisdom. Yet we might as well say, "Why all these stars; why this difference; why not all one star?"

Many of the rules for people living together in peace, follow from the above. For instance, not to interfere unreasonably with others, not to ridicule their tastes, not to question and requestion their resolves, not to indulge in perpetual comment on their proceedings, and to delight in their having other pursuits than ours, are all based upon a thorough perception of the simple fact, that they are not we.

---

ll. **25-28** for choosing just this as the opening consideration? How do ll. **28-35** show that it is a consideration of especial importance in the case of the present subject?—Point out how ll. **22-25** illustrate Rhet. p. 162, 76. Expound the analogy suggested ll. **33-35**.

The sentence, ll. **36, 37**, indicates that the subdivisions of this main thought are to be of what kind, and how related to it? On which of the three Laws of Association, Rhet. pp. 273-275, is this sequence based? Why are so many of the Rules lumped together, in the rest of the paragraph? See Rhet. p. 286. The words **for instance**, l. **37**, indicate what as regards the exhaustiveness of these rules?

Study now the successive paragraphs in this main division I. (as far as l. **103**), and set down the rules therein contained. Is the paragraph, ll. **77-83**, of equal rank with its preceding, that is, does it contain a distinct and correlate thought, or is it subordinate?

Taking now the distinct subdivisions (rules) as thus brought to light,

Another rule for living happily with others, is to avoid
having stock subjects of disputation. It mostly happens,
when people live much together, that they come to have
certain set topics, around which, from frequent dispute,
there is such a growth of angry words, mortified vanity and
the like, that the original subject of difference becomes a
standing subject for quarrel; and there is a tendency in all
minor disputes to drift down to it.

Again, if people wish to live well together, they must
not hold too much to logic, and suppose that everything
is to be settled by sufficient reason. Dr. Johnson saw
this clearly with regard to married people, when he said,
" wretched would be the pair above all names of wretched-
ness, who should be doomed to adjust by reason every
morning, all the minute detail of a domestic day." But
the application should be much more general than he made
it. There is no time for such reasonings, and nothing that
is worth them. And when we recollect how two lawyers,

---

let us endeavor to see how they fulfil the requisites of construction mentioned, Rhet. pp. 262, 263, — especially sequence and climax. The first
rule (l. **44**) relates to what is very palpable and pronounced — disputation. The second (ll. **52-54**) is not so pronounced, but correspondingly more inward — demands for logical reasons of action. On this
same line trace the connection of the next rule (l. **67**) with this. How
is the next (l. **84**) a more inward thing? Finally, how does the last
rule (l. **92**) come home to genuine heart-conduct, as compared with the
first? We are prepared now to see that there is a regular gradation
or sequence in the rules, and that they form a real climax. What is the
law of the climax?

The amplification is mostly in the way of giving in extended form
what the rule, or key-sentence, gives in brief. Show how this is the
case in ll. **45-51**.

How does the use of quotation as accessory, ll. **56-58**, correspond to
the directions, Rhet. p. 297? What is done to the quotation by way of
fitting it to the subject in hand? See Rhet. p. 288, 1. Why does it

or two politicians, can **go on** contending, and that there is
no end of one-sided reasoning on any subject, we shall not
be sure that such contention is the best mode for arriving
at truth. But certainly it is not the **way** to arrive at good
temper.

If you would be loved as a companion, avoid **unnecessary**
criticism upon those **with** whom you live. The number of
people who have taken out judges' **patents** for themselves
is very large in any society. Now it would be hard for a
man to live with another who was always criticising his
actions, even if it were kindly and just criticism. It would
be like living between the glasses **of a** microscope. But
these self-elected judges, like their prototypes, are very
apt to have the persons they judge brought before them
in the guise of culprits.

One of the most provoking forms of the criticism above
alluded to, is that which may be called, criticism **over the
shoulder.** "Had I been consulted," "had you listened **to
me,**" "but you always will," and such short scraps of sen-
tences may remind **many of us of dissertations** which we
have suffered and inflicted, **and of which we cannot** call to
mind any soothing effect.

Another rule is, not to let familiarity swallow up all

---

need to be so adapted? — **64. Such contention** is apparently differ-
enced from the *disputation* of the preceding paragraph, in being governed merely by logic instead of by rancor (cf. ll. 49–51); so it is in
this line that this rule **advances** on the previous one.

Line **71** will indicate how the next paragraph advances still in the
same direction. — **69. Taken** out judges' **patents,** — from what is
this figure taken, and what does it mean? — How is "kindly and just
criticism" made to apply to the subject **in hand** (ll. 77, 78)?

78. Criticism over the shoulder, — explain the suggestiveness of
the expression. — If the other paragraphs represent rules, this may be
called a corollary, — why?

courtesy. Many of us have a habit of saying to those with whom we live such things as we say about strangers behind their backs. There is no place, however, where real politeness **is** of more value than where we mostly think it would be superfluous. You **may** say more truth, or rather speak out more plainly, to your associates, but not less courteously, than you do to strangers.

Again, we must not expect more from the society of our friends and companions than it can give; and especially **must** not expect contrary things. It is somewhat arrogant to talk of travelling over other minds (mind being, for what we know, infinite) : but still we become familiar with the upper views, tastes and tempers of our associates. And it is hardly in man to estimate justly what is familiar to him. In travelling along at night, as Hazlitt says, we catch a glimpse into cheerful looking rooms with light blazing in them, and we conclude, involuntarily, how happy the inmates must be. Yet there is Heaven and Hell in those rooms, the same Heaven and Hell that we have known in others.

II.

There are two great classes of promoters of social happiness, cheerful people, and people who have some reticence.

How is the sentence, ll. **89-91**, related to the lesson of the preceding paragraph? What part of *criticism* does it retain? How do you reconcile "speaking out more plainly" with "not less courteously"?

The next paragraph, ll. **92–103**, has not to do with outer conduct and courtesy at all; it is wholly inward, dealing with what we are to expect. — What accessory of amplification is used, ll. **98–103**, to illustrate the assertion preceding? How does it apply to the general subject?

Evidently the first main division, which is much the longest, **has** contained the most important considerations relating to the subject;

The latter are more secure benefits to society even **than
the former. They are non-conductors** of all the heats and
animosities around them. **To have peace in a** house, or a
family, or **any social circle,** the members of it must beware
of passing on hasty and uncharitable speeches; which, the 110
whole **of the** context seldom being told, is often not conveying, but creating, mischief. They must be very good
people to avoid doing this; for let human nature say what
it will, it likes sometimes to **look on at** a quarrel: and that,
not altogether from ill-nature, **but** from a love of excite- 115
ment — for the same reason that Charles the Second **liked**
to attend the debates in the Lords, **because they were** "**as
good as a play.**"

III.

We **come now to the** consideration **of temper, which**
might **have** been expected **to be treated first.** But to cut off 120
the means and causes **of bad temper, is,** perhaps, of as much
importance **as any direct** dealing with the temper itself.
Besides, **it is probable that** in small social circles there is

---

the succeeding ones are in some degree incidental and supplementary,
though still distinct and co-ordinate divisions.

Some indication of their relation to the first division and to each
other is furnished in III. ll. **119-122.** They show, for one thing (l. 120),
that the author had distinctly in mind what he should put first and what
afterward, with the reasons for his chosen order. How does this illustrate what Dr. Johnson says, Rhet. p. 262? **He has** chosen to put
means and causes (l. 121) before the treatment of temper. How does
division I. "**cut off the means**" of bad temper? How does division II.
"cut off the causes"? If this is the order in the author's mind, what
is the prevailing law of association, **thus far,** between the main divisions?
See Rhet. pp. 273-275.

Of the two classes of "**promoters of social happiness**" mentioned,
ll. **104-118,** the first class is merely mentioned, the second amplified.
Why this difference **of treatment?** What felicitous figure is used to

more suffering from unkindness than ill-temper. Anger is a thing that those who live under us suffer more from than those who live with us. But all the forms of ill-humor and sour-sensitiveness, which especially belong to equal intimacy (though indeed they are common to all) are best to be met by impassiveness. When two sensitive persons are shut up together, they go on vexing each other with a reproductive irritability. But sensitive and hard people get on well together. The supply of temper is not altogether out of the usual laws of supply and demand.

IV.

Intimate friends and relations should be careful when they go out into the world together, or admit others to their own circle, that they do not make a bad use of the knowledge which they have gained of each other by their intimacy. Nothing is more common than this, and did it not mostly proceed from mere carelessness, it would be superlatively ungenerous. You seldom need wait for the

---

characterize the second class? — What is the antecedent of **which**, l. **110**? — How does the illustration, ll. **113–118**, apply to the subject?

One reason has already been given for assigning a subordinate position to " the consideration of temper "; but there is also another reason (l. 123), — what is it? How far does the second reason extend, and where does the real consideration of temper begin? Notice how the author fixes at once upon the one aspect of temper which is of cardinal importance to consider, and lets secondary aspects go. How does the last sentence (l. **132**) illustrate what precedes? Explain its office in the paragraph by Rhet. p. 209, and its amplifying office by Rhet. p. 291, 3.

The succeeding divisions seem to be more purely supplementary or incidental than divisions II., III.; but may the words **mere carelessness**, l. **139**, explain the relation of IV. to the preceding, which treats of temper?

written life of a man to hear about his weaknesses, or what are supposed to be such, if you know his intimate friends or meet him in company with them.

V.

Lastly, in conciliating those we live with, it is most surely done, not by consulting their interests, nor by giving way to their opinions, so much as by not offending their tastes. The most refined part of us lies in this region of taste which is perhaps a result of our whole being rather than a part of our nature, and at any rate is the region of our most subtle sympathies and antipathies.

It may be said that if the great principles of Christianity were attended to, all such rules, suggestions and observations as the above would be needless. True enough! Great principles are at the bottom of all things; but to apply them to daily life, many little rules, precautions, and insights are needed. Such things hold a middle place between real life and principles, as form does between matter and spirit : moulding the one and expressing the other. *From* FRIENDS IN COUNCIL.

---

144. Lastly, — this word is another indication of sequence from a beginning to a culmination in the author's mind; though as we have traced it we find it somewhat subtle. Perhaps it could not easily be otherwise in such a purely abstract subject. The relation of this division is not very close; but may not its general relation to the whole subject, and its importance as culminating the treatment be indicated in l. **146**? Does it not deserve its position, also, as indicating the finest touches in the "art of living with others"?

What consideration forms the conclusion, and how is it applied to the subject in hand? Trace how " the great principles of Christianity " are apparent in the various main thoughts and rules that make up the body of the essay.

XVI.

RICHARD DODDRIDGE BLACKMORE.

DESCRIPTION OF GLEN DOONE.

I. FROM THE CLIFF ABOVE THE SIDE.

AND so at last we gained the top, and looked forth the edge of the forest, where the ground was very stony and like the crest of a quarry; and no more trees between us and the brink of the cliff below, three hundred yards below

---

This Selection and the two following exemplify different phases of Description; and presuppose a knowledge of the Rhetoric as far as page 353. Involving the same general principles, the selections are chosen largely with the view of illustrating kinds of description not fully exemplified in the Rhetoric.

The known care that Mr. Blackmore bestows on his descriptions of natural scenery is ample warrant for studying the present selection as a skilful work of literary art. A critical journal says: "Mr. Blackmore's descriptive passages in his novels are justly esteemed one of their great attractions. He does not trust to his imagination for these delightful landscapes, but spends months at a time in the places where he lays the scenes of his stories; and his studies of moor, forest, and garden are pursued with the keen eye of a painter and a naturalist, and the ardor of a lover."

The glen here described was the stronghold of the Doones, a band of marauders and murderers who in the seventeenth century were the terror of the countryside, in Somersetshire and Devonshire. It is here described twice, from different points of view: first, as visited by way of reconnoissance, by John Ridd and his uncle Reuben Huckaback; and secondly, as visited by John's mother, soon after the Doones had

it might be, all strong slope and gliddery. And now for the first time I was amazed at the appearance of the Doones' stronghold, and understood its nature. For when I had been even in the valley, and climbed the cliffs to escape from it, about seven years agone, I was no more than a stripling boy, noting little, as boys do, except for their present purpose, and even that soon done with. But now, what with the fame of the Doones, and my own recollections, and Uncle Ben's insistence, all my attention was called forth, and the end was simple astonishment.

The chine of highland, whereon we stood, curved to the right and left of us, keeping about the same elevation, and crowned with trees and brushwood. At about half a mile in front of us, but looking as if we could throw a stone to strike any man upon it, another crest just like our own

---

murdered her husband. In both cases John Ridd is the assumed describer.

The two descriptions afford a good opportunity to study how the point of view influences the details of a description; see Rhet. p. 329. What do you learn as to the position and distance of the point of view in the first description? see ll. **1–5, 17.** What in the second? see ll. **34–36, 46.** In which do you find the details more particularized, and why? In the first description only general shapes and masses of color are given; but trace, in the second, the degrees of minuteness according to the distance from the point of view. Lines **50–58.**

Report in each case the comprehensive outline; see Rhet. p. 330. How does the first description answer to Rhet. p. 331, bottom? What feature of outline common to both? What ideas are given as to the size of the valley?

Trace in each case the sequence of details from point to point; see Rhet. p. 332. How does the sequence differ in the two? Of what advantage is the " little river " in the second description for determining the sequence of details?

Point out the words that answer to Rhet. p. 341, 1. What words contain a metaphorical suggestiveness or personification? see Rhet.

20 bowed around to meet it; but failed by reason of two narrow clefts, of which we could only see the brink. One of these clefts was the Doone-gate, with a portcullis of rock above it, and the other was the chasm by which I had once made entrance. Betwixt them, where the hills fell back, 25 as in a perfect oval, traversed by the winding water, lay a bright green valley, rimmed with sheer black rock, and seeming to have sunken bodily from the bleak rough heights above. It looked as if no frost could enter, neither winds go ruffling: only spring and hope and comfort 30 breathe to one another. Even now the rays of sunshine dwelt and fell back on one another, whenever the clouds lifted; and the pale blue glimpse of the growing day seemed to find young encouragement.

II. From the Doone-Gate.

In the early afternoon she came to the hollow and bar-
35 ren entrance, where in truth there was no gate, only darkness to go through. If I get on with this story, I shall have

---

p. 339, 2. What touches in the description answer to Rhet. p. 345, 1? What effect has this upon the description? How is simile, at least implied simile, employed in outlining, ll. **18, 27**? What simile describes the positions of the houses, l. **60**? What type of prose diction do you discern in ll. **28-33, 50-55, 65-69**? Does it correspond fittingly with its occasion? see Rhet. p. 338, bottom.

How is contrast or antithesis (see Rhet. p. 340, 3) employed to vivify the description, in ll. **65-69**? How intimated in ll. **28-30**? What contrast is used to set off the beauty of the valley in ll. **24-28**?

In what state of mind is the scene represented as viewed, in both cases (ll. **6, 14, 44**)? What contrast in scenery probably leads in each case to that state of mind (ll. **1-3, 34-36, 41-43**)? How is this mood made to heighten the effect (cf. Rhet. p. 342), — by infusing itself into the scene, or by accentuating the contrast? Blackmore seems to be fond of suffusing a scene, as it were, with the emotion of the spectator;

to tell of it by-and-by, as I saw it afterwards; and will
not dwell there now. Enough that no gun was fired at
her, only her eyes were covered over, and somebody led
her by the hand, without any wish to hurt her.

A very rough and headstrong road was all that she remembered, for she could not think as she wished to do,
with the cold iron pushed against her. At the end of this
road they delivered her eyes, and she could scarce believe
them.

For she stood at the head of a deep green valley, carved
from out the mountains in a perfect oval, with a fence of
sheer rock standing round it, eighty feet or a hundred high;
from whose brink black wooded hills swept up to the sky-
line. By her side a little river glided out from under
ground with a soft dark babble, unawares of daylight; then
growing brighter, lapsed away, and fell into the valley.
There, as it ran down the meadow, alders stood on either
marge, and grass was blading out upon it, and yellow tufts
of rushes gathered, looking at the hurry. But farther
down, on either bank, were covered houses, built of stone,

---

thus, in describing the Wizard's Slough, in Chapter XXXI. of this same
romance, he chooses as the spectator John Fry, a rather cowardly fellow, with a superstitious belief in uncanny stories, and represents him
as quaking with fear and amazement. The reader is thus prepared with
keener interest to read: "For there was the Wizard's Slough itself, as
black as death, and bubbling, with a few scant yellow reeds in a ring
around it. Outside these bright water-grass of the liveliest green was
creeping, tempting any unwary foot to step and plunge and founder.
And on the marge were blue campanula, sundew, and forget-me-not,
such as no child could resist. On either side the hill fell back, and the
ground was broken with tufts of rush and flag and mares-tail, and a few
rough alder-trees overclogged with water. And not a bird was seen or
heard — neither rail nor water-hen, wagtail nor reed-warbler." — Is this
"subjective description," as defined, Rhet. p. 343, bottom?

square and roughly cornered, set as if the brook were meant to be the street between them. Only one room high they were, and not placed opposite each other, but in and out, as skittles are; only that the first of all, which proved to be the captain's, was a sort of double house, or rather, two houses joined together by a plank-bridge over the river.

Fourteen cots my mother counted, all very much of a pattern, and nothing to choose between them, unless it were the captain's. Deep in the quiet valley there, away from noise, and violence, and brawl, save that of the rivulet, any man would have deemed them homes of simple mind and innocence. Yet not a single house stood there but was the home of murder.

From LORNA DOONE.

A word may be said finally regarding the language of the above descriptions, which seems almost affectedly quaint. Note for instance "looked forth the edge," l. 1; "strong slope and gliddery," l. 5; "seven years agone," l. 9; "rough and headstrong road," l. 41; "soft dark babble," l. 51. This is due partly to Mr. Blackmore's natural manner, which is strongly individual, and partly to his endeavor to imitate what was supposably the language of the time and place of which he was writing.

XVII.

ARTHUR PENRHYN STANLEY.

TRIUMPHAL ENTRY OF CHRIST TO JERUSALEM.

LET us briefly go through the points which occur in the Sacred History, of the last days of Christ, during which alone He appears for any continuous period in Jerusalem and its neighborhood. From Bethany we must begin. A wild mountain-hamlet, screened by an intervening ridge 5 from the view of the top of Olivet, perched on its broken

---

The writer's object in recounting this scene, — which may be gathered from his characterization of it as the scene "which, with the one exception of the conversation at the well of Jacob, stands alone in the Gospel history for the vividness and precision of its localization," — will suggest quite naturally the kind of description we are here to expect. He evidently wishes, on the one hand, to put together the successive features of the event as accurately as possible, and on the other, to increase their realism by connecting them at their various stages with the natural features of the country, as observed by a traveller of to-day.

We look therefore partly for a description of an event, and partly for successive descriptions of natural scenery from the "traveller's point of view." How does this illustrate Rhet. p. 345, 2, and why is it not narration? How does it illustrate Rhet. p. 346, 3; and how are the successive points of view determined from ll. **4-18**; **49-54**; **65-67**; **89-92**?

How does the description of Bethany, ll. **4-11**, illustrate Rhet. p. 331, bottom? — What part does epithet play (cf. Rhet. p. 341, 1) as an accessory, in these lines? — Is **intervening**, l. **5**, an epithet? — How do the words **perched**, l. **6**, and **clustering**, l. **10**, illustrate Rhet.

plateau of rock, the last collection of human habitations before the desert-hills which reach to Jericho — this is the modern village of El-Lazarieh, which derives its name from its clustering round the traditional site of the one house and grave which give it an undying interest. High in the distance are the Peræan mountains; the foreground is the deep descent to the Jordan valley. On the further side of that dark abyss Martha and Mary knew that Christ was abiding when they sent their messenger; up that long ascent they had often watched His approach — up that long ascent He came when, outside the village, Martha and Mary met Him, and the Jews stood round weeping.

Up that same ascent He came, also, at the beginning of the week of His Passion. One night He halted in the village, as of old; the village and the desert were then all alive, — as they still are once every year at the Greek Easter, — with the crowd of Paschal pilgrims moving to and fro between Bethany and Jerusalem. In the morning, He set forth on His journey. Three pathways lead, and probably always led, from Bethany to Jerusalem; one, a steep footpath over the summit of Mount Olivet; another, by a long circuit over its northern shoulder, down the valley which parts it from Scopus; the third, the natural continuation of the road by which mounted travellers always

---

p. 345, 1? — 9. **El-Lazarieh**, this Arabic name, derived from the name *Lazarus*, connects the village in what manner with John xi. 1–44? — What descriptive touches in ll. **11–18**, and by what means obtained? — Is the realistic effect heightened by the repetition of the localizing phrases, ll. **11, 13, 15, 16, 19**, always at the beginning of the clause or sentence, and sometimes in identical terms? Cf. Rhet. p. 161, 74. — **12. The Peræan mountains** are beyond the Jordan, eastward from Bethany.

What illustration in l. **22** of Rhet. p. 337? How does this also

approach the city from Jericho, over the southern shoulder, between the summit which contains the Tombs of the Prophets and that called the "Mount of Offence." There can be no doubt that this last is the road of the Entry of Christ, not only because, as just stated, it is and must ₃₅ always have been the usual approach for horsemen and for large caravans, such as then were concerned, but also because this is the only one of the three approaches which meets the requirements of the narrative which follows.

Two vast streams of people met on that day. The one ₄₀ poured out from the city, and as they came through the gardens whose clusters of palm rose on the south-eastern corner of Olivet, they cut down the long branches, as was their wont at the Feast of Tabernacles, and moved upwards towards Bethany, with loud shouts of welcome. ₄₅ From Bethany streamed forth the crowds who had assembled there on the previous night, and who came testifying to the great event at the sepulchre of Lazarus.

---

illustrate Rhet. p. 156, 67? — **39. Which,** — there are three reasons why *that* would be the preferable relative here; can you give them? See Rhet. pp. 127-131. — In ll. 37-39 we see an indication of the writer's object in making the succeeding description: he wishes to trace the road that "meets the requirements of the narrative," as found in Matthew xxi. 1-11; Mark xi. 1-11; Luke xix. 29-44; John xii. 12-19. This is one of the few events that are given, with greater or less fulness, by all four of the Gospel writers.

All the details of the procession here given are carefully made out from the several narratives, often from minute study of various readings, the implications of the Greek tenses, and the like, the object being to reproduce with the greatest exactness the actual scene.

What heightened or descriptive words can you point out in the paragraph, ll. **40-48**? — Reconstruct the sentence, ll. **46-48**, so that it will balance better with the two sentences preceding. The beginning of the sentence, l. **40**, leads us to expect what beginning here?

The road soon loses sight of Bethany. It is now a rough, but still broad and well-defined mountain track, winding over rock and loose stones ; a steep declivity below on the left ; the sloping shoulder of Olivet above it on the right ; fig-trees below and above, here and there growing out of the rocky soil. Along the road the multitudes threw down the branches which they had cut as they went along, or spread out a rude matting formed of the palm-branches they had already cut as they came out. The larger portion — those, perhaps, who escorted Him from Bethany — unwrapped their loose cloaks from their shoulders, and stretched them along the rough path, to form a momentary carpet as He approached.

The two streams met midway. Half of the vast mass, turning round, preceded, the other half followed. Gradually the long procession swept up and over the ridge, where first begins "the descent of the Mount of Olives " towards Jerusalem. At this point the first view is caught

---

Point out how complete is the outline description, ll. 49-54, as to the various features of the road ; the surroundings ; the vegetation ; the character of the soil. Much is condensed in very little space. Point out what is given by implication, according to Rhet. p. 158, 2. — This outline description of the road furnishes the background, so to say, on which the writer portrays the general scene of the multitudes before and behind making up the jubilant procession. Why do we call this scene description rather than narration?

64. By what trope (see Newman (p. 83), ll. 134, 135, note) is the description of the procession vivified? — By what position of the adverb? — **65.** The carefulness with which this exact point of view is determined is indicated in the following note, appended to the account : "Luke xix. 37, 'as He drew near, even now ($\check{\eta}\delta\eta$), at the descent of the Mount of Olives ($\pi\rho\grave{o}s$ $\tau\hat{\eta}$ $\kappa\alpha\tau\alpha\beta\acute{\alpha}\sigma\epsilon\iota$ $\tau o\hat{v}$ $\check{o}\rho o v s$ $\tau\hat{\omega}\nu$ $\grave{\epsilon}\lambda\alpha\iota\hat{\omega}\nu$)', *i.e.*, at the point where the road over the Mount begins to descend. This exactly applies to such a shoulder of the hill as I have described, and

of the south-eastern corner of the city. The Temple and the more northern portions are hid by the slope of Olivet on the right; what is seen is only Mount Zion, now for the most part a rough field, crowned with the Mosque of David and the angle of the western walls, but then covered with houses to its base, surmounted by the Castle of Herod, on the supposed site of the palace of David, from which that portion of Jerusalem, emphatically the "City of David," derived its name. It was at this precise point, "as He drew near, at the descent of the Mount of Olives,"—(may it not have been from the sight thus opening upon them?) —that the shout of triumph burst forth from the multitude, "Hosanna to the Son of David! Blessed is He that cometh in the name of the Lord. Blessed is the kingdom that cometh of our father *David.* Hosanna . . . peace . . . glory in the highest." There was a pause as the shout rang through the long defile; and, as the Pharisees who stood by in the crowd complained, He pointed to the stones which, strewn beneath their feet, would immediately "cry out" if "these were to hold their peace."

Again the procession advanced. The road descends a

---

is entirely inapplicable to the first view, the first 'nearing' of the city, on crossing the direct summit. The expression would then have been 'at the top of the mount.'"— The glimpse of part of the city, here described, ll. **67-75**, serves as the background on which to portray the second stage of the scene, the Hosanna-shout of the multitude. Is there any attempt at picturesqueness in this description of the south-eastern corner of the city?— What serves as the suggestion, ll. **73-75**, to connect the view with the multitude's triumphal shout, ll. **79-82**? It is not so much the picturesqueness as the historical associations of the view, that connects it with the shout; hence perhaps the absence of heightened detail.— What realistic touch in l. **83** to aid in the conception of the scene at this moment?

slight declivity, and the glimpse of the city is again withdrawn behind the intervening ridge of Olivet. A few
90 moments, and the path mounts again, it climbs a rugged ascent, it reaches a ledge of smooth rock, and in an instant the whole city bursts into view. As now the dome of the Mosque El-Aksa rises like a ghost from the earth before the traveller stands on the ledge, so then must have
95 risen the Temple tower; as now the vast enclosure of the Mussulman sanctuary, so then must have spread the Temple courts; as now the gray town on its broken hills, so then the magnificent city, with its background — long since vanished away — of gardens and suburbs on the western
100 plateau behind. Immediately below was the Valley of the Kedron, here seen in its greatest depth as it joins the Valley of Hinnom, and thus giving full effect to the great peculiarity of Jerusalem seen only on its eastern side — its situation as of a city rising out of a deep abyss. It is
105 hardly possible to doubt that this rise and turn of the road,

---

The impressiveness of the next view, ll. **91-104**, is evidently due largely to the suddenness with which it is obtained. How is this fact prepared for in ll. **89-91**? See Rhet. p. 364, 1. — **91**. What illustration of Rhet. p. 181, 4? — **92**. What illustration of Rhet. p. 345, 1? — What two accessories heighten the description in l. **93**? — **96. Mussulman sanctuary,** — of what, previously mentioned, is this term a repetition? — **Must have spread,** — note that this verb belongs equally to the previous clause, but is expressed only here. Does this cause any lack of clearness? — **97, 100.** Trace the climax, as produced by different terms, epithet, and amplitude. — **104. A city rising out of a deep abyss,** — how does this influence our conception of the view already described? — The foregoing view of the city, which emphasizes its peculiar beauty, suddenly bursting into view, is the background on which we are to imagine the scene of Christ's weeping over Jerusalem. This scene is left undescribed here; but the Scripture account, Luke xix. 41-44, indicates that Christ's tears were called forth by the sudden thought of

— this rocky ledge, — was the exact point where the multitude paused again, and " He, when He beheld the city, wept over it."

Nowhere else on the Mount of Olives is there a view like this. By the two other approaches, above mentioned, over the summit, and over the northern shoulder, of the hill, the city reveals itself gradually; there is no partial glimpse like that which has just been described as agreeing so well with the first outbreak of popular acclamation, still less is there any point where, as here, the city and Temple would suddenly burst into view, producing the sudden and affecting impression described in the Gospel narrative. And this precise coincidence is the more remarkable because the traditional route of the Triumphal Entry is over the summit of Olivet; and the traditional spot of the lamentation is at a place half-way down the mountain, to which the description is wholly inapplicable, whilst no tradition attaches to this, the only road by which a large procession could have come; and this, almost the only spot of the Mount of Olives which the Gospel narrative fixes with exact certainty, is almost the only unmarked

---

the contrast between this, " the most impressive view which the neighborhood of Jerusalem furnishes," and the desolation so soon to come upon the fated city: "And when He was come near, He beheld the city, and wept over it, saying, ' If thou hadst known, even thou, at least in this thy day, the things which belong unto thy peace!—but now they are hid from thine eyes. For the days shall come upon thee, that thine enemies shall cast a trench about thee, and compass thee round, and keep thee in on every side, and shall lay thee even with the ground, and thy children within thee; and they shall not leave in thee one stone upon another; because thou knewest not the time of thy visitation.'" These words seem to show indications of the same emotion which so naturally fills the traveller of the present day, at the sight of this impressive view.

spot, — undefiled or unhallowed by mosque or church, chapel or tower — left to speak for itself, that here the Lord's feet stood, and here His eyes beheld what is still the most impressive view which the neighborhood of Jerusalem furnishes, — and the tears rushed forth at the sight.

From SINAI AND PALESTINE.

How does the harmony between the scene and the actions, as traced in the foregoing notes, furnish illustration of Rhet. p. 342? — Evidently this very "indication of effects" was one great object of the writer; for it serves, better than any other feature of the description, a kind of argumentative purpose, by increasing the probability that this road was the actual scene of the Triumphal Entry, — a fact which he desires to establish in the face of the hitherto accepted tradition.

XVIII.

JOHN RICHARD GREEN.

THE CHARACTER OF QUEEN ELIZABETH.

ENGLAND's one hope lay in the character of her queen. Elizabeth was now in her twenty-fifth year. Personally she had more than her mother's beauty; her figure was commanding, her face long but queenly and intelligent, her eyes quick and fine. She had grown up amidst the

---

The present Selection, which Mr. Green himself regarded as the best passage in his Short History, may be studied as a notable example of what may be called analytical description: description, that is, in which the writer must make his plan rather than discover it. Explain this character of the material by Rhet. p. 262, 2, and p. 348, 2; and show how, in the broad sense, the laws of association on which it is founded, according to Rhet. pp. 273-275, make it differ from ordinary local or temporal description.

Observe that this is not the same passage that is quoted from and analyzed, Rhet. pp. 331, 333; that being from Green's longer history of the English people.

In a description of character like this, obviously the main problem is, how to group a large number of complex details and traits so as to produce unity of effect; nor can the quality of picturesqueness be sought, so much as strikingness and unity. In the attainment of these results, two means here used seem to predominate over others: grouping by antithesis, and illustration by the concrete. What may antithesis effect toward unity? See Rhet. p. 340. How may the concrete work to strength and definiteness? See Rhet. p. 155, 66.

The description, occurring as it does at a determinate point in the history of a people (the time when Elizabeth succeeded to the throne), begins with what lies nearest, her personal appearance and accomplish-

liberal culture of Henry's court a bold horsewoman, a good shot, a graceful dancer, a skilled musician, and an accomplished scholar. She studied every morning the Greek Testament, and followed this by the tragedies of Sophocles or orations of Demosthenes, and could "rub up her rusty Greek" at need to bandy pedantry with a Vice-Chancellor. But she was far from being a mere pedant. The new literature which was springing up around her found constant welcome in her court. She spoke Italian and French as fluently as her mother-tongue. She was familiar with Ariosto and Tasso. Even amidst the affectation and love of anagrams and puerilities which sullied her later years, she listened with delight to the "Faery Queen," and found a smile for "Master Spenser" when he appeared in her presence. Her moral temper recalled in its strange contrasts the mixed blood within her veins. She was at once

---

ments at that time. Is there something here that may be regarded as the point of view, according to Rhet. p. 329? Observe, the moment of Elizabeth's accession can be taken as the point of view only in the sense of a starting-point, or defining-point, for the character here portrayed has traits revealed or developed throughout her reign.

Lines 1-8. — Report on the traits here recounted as determined by (1) the time when the description begins, (2) the ease of observing them, (3) their relation to Elizabeth's position. — What trait is selected, ll. **8-20**, for amplification, and what means of amplification is employed? See Rhet. p. 290. — How does l. **12** suggest an antithetic grouping in the details describing her scholarliness? Show how the points of the antithesis are brought together in adjacent sentences. — What significance in the word **bandy**, l. **11**, as suggested by its derivation? — What is an **anagram** (l. **17**)? — Is the word **sullied**, l. **17**, happily chosen? — **20.** Is there any close connection between the section of the description here beginning and the preceding? What reasons for and what reasons against putting this section in a paragraph by itself? Compare Rhet. p. 193. — On what principle of grouping, as revealed in ll. **20-22**, is the description of "her moral temper" determined? — Of the traits derived

the daughter of Henry and of Anne Boleyn. From her
father she inherited her frank and hearty address, her love
of popularity and of free intercourse with the people, her
dauntless courage and her amazing self-confidence. Her
harsh, manlike voice, her impetuous will, her pride, her furious outbursts of anger, came to her with her Tudor blood.
She rated great nobles as if they were schoolboys; she met
the insolence of Essex with a box on the ear; she would break
now and then into the gravest deliberations to swear at her
ministers like a fishwife. But strangely in contrast with
the violent outlines of her Tudor temper stood the sensuous, self-indulgent nature she derived from Anne Boleyn.
Splendor and pleasure were with Elizabeth the very air she
breathed. Her delight was to move in perpetual progresses
from castle to castle through a series of gorgeous pageants,
fanciful and extravagant as a caliph's dream. She loved
gaiety and laughter and wit. A happy retort or a finished
compliment never failed to win her favor. She hoarded
jewels. Her dresses were innumerable. Her vanity remained, even to old age, the vanity of a coquette in her
teens. No adulation was too fulsome for her, no flattery
of her beauty too gross. "To see her was heaven," Hatton
told her, "the lack of her was hell." She would play with
her rings that her courtiers might note the delicacy of her
hands; or dance a coranto that the French ambassador,

---

from her father (ll. **22-31**), report what are described in general terms,
and what in the concrete. — Note how the expression is varied between
sentences ll. **22-25** and **25-27** in giving lists of traits. — In the detail-
sentence, ll. **28-31**, typical incidents are used to portray general traits.
Note how the elements of comparison and contrast are made to heighten
the effect. — **31-43**. Many details are here grouped together to illustrate one side of her character; what law of association (Rhet. pp.
273-275) gives them the right to be together? The strikingness of

hidden dexterously behind a curtain, might report her sprightliness to his master. Her levity, her frivolous laughter, her unwomanly jests, gave color to a thousand scandals. Her character, in fact, like her portraits, was utterly without shade. Of womanly reserve or self-restraint she knew nothing. No instinct of delicacy veiled the voluptuous temper which had broken out in the romps of her girlhood and showed itself almost ostentatiously throughout her later life. Personal beauty in a man was a sure passport to her liking. She patted handsome young squires on the neck when they knelt to kiss her hand, and fondled her " sweet Robin," Lord Leicester, in the face of the court.

It was no wonder that the statesmen whom she outwitted held Elizabeth almost to the last to be little more than a frivolous woman, or that Philip of Spain wondered how "a wanton" could hold in check the policy of the Escurial. But the Elizabeth whom they saw was far from being all of Elizabeth. The wilfulness of Henry, the triviality of Anne Boleyn, played over the surface of a nature hard as steel, a temper purely intellectual, the very type of reason

---

these details corresponds with the picturesqueness of natural descriptions; they are, so to speak, mentally picturesque. — How do the actions of Elizabeth, recorded ll. **44-50**, illustrate Rhet. p. 348, 3? — Lines **50-58** may be regarded as a summary of her personal traits in one, the most comprehensive and most apparent. How does this summary prepare for the subject of the next paragraph, as expressed ll. 63-67? — What adjustment of sentences to each other, l. **51**, and what stress is thereby effected?

59-62. As related to their paragraph, what office have these lines, and how do they serve to heighten the subject? — **64.** What words in this line serve to summarize very briefly what has been said in previous paragraph? — Line **64**, by intimating what kind of elements of Elizabeth's character have been already given, implies transition to what contrasted kind in this paragraph? — Read now this paragraph carefully, and report its subject, as related to preceding. — Point out how, in

untouched by imagination or passion. Luxurious and
pleasure-loving as she seemed, Elizabeth lived simply and
frugally, and she worked hard. Her vanity and caprice
had no weight whatever with her in state affairs. The
coquette of the presence-chamber became the coolest and
hardest of politicians at the council-board. Fresh from
the flattery of her courtiers, she would tolerate no flattery
in the closet; she was herself plain and downright of speech
with her counsellors, and she looked for a corresponding
plainness of speech in return. If any trace of her sex
lingered in her actual statesmanship, it was seen in the
simplicity and tenacity of purpose that often underlies a
woman's fluctuations of feeling. It was this in part which
gave her her marked superiority over the statesmen of her
time. No nobler group of ministers ever gathered round
a council-board than those who gathered round the council-
board of Elizabeth. But she was the instrument of none.
She listened, she weighed, she used or put by the counsels
of each in turn, but her policy as a whole was her own. It
was a policy, not of genius, but of good sense. Her aims
were simple and obvious: to preserve her throne, to keep
England out of war, to restore civil and religious order.
Something of womanly caution and timidity perhaps backed
the passionless indifference with which she set aside the
larger schemes of ambition which were ever opening before
her eyes. She was resolute in her refusal of the Low
Countries. She rejected with a laugh the offers of the

---

ll. **67–79**, every sentence is introduced by an antithetic reminder of the preceding paragraph. These sentences serve to amplify the paragraph-subject; report now how this subject is *applied*, ll. **77–86**, and to what summary it is steered, l. **85**. — Report further how this summary is amplified, ll. **86–96**, and how at the end a definition is given to what has been expounded at length (cf. Rhet. p. 294, 3, top), which in turn has

Protestants to make her "head of the religion" and "mis-
95 tress of the seas." But her amazing success in the end
sprang mainly from this wise limitation of her aims. She
had a finer sense than any of her counsellors of her real
resources; she knew instinctively how far she could go,
and what she could do. Her cold, critical intellect was
100 never swayed by enthusiasm or by panic either to exagger-
ate or to underestimate her risks or her power.

Of political wisdom indeed, in its larger and more generous sense, Elizabeth had little or none; but her political
tact was unerring. She seldom saw her course at a glance,
105 but she played with a hundred courses, fitfully and discur-
sively, as a musician runs his fingers over the key-board,
till she hit suddenly upon the right one. Her nature was

---

a sentence of amplification. — How is the last sentence, ll. **99-101**, connected with the general subject of the paragraph?

Keeping in mind still the author's great problem, of grouping so as
to bring large numbers of discordant details into unity, and recalling
how the two paragraphs just studied have dealt respectively with the
surface-elements and with the deeper elements of Elizabeth's character,
and how traits illustrating these, and therefore grouped by the law of
similarity, have been adduced, we go on now to find what law of grouping is chosen in the succeeding. Read this paragraph (ll. **102-168**) and
the next (ll. **169-280**) carefully through, and report with what general
aspects of the subject they deal. The sentence ll. **102-104**, compared
with the sentences ll. **169-174**, suggests what antithesis as the basis of
these two paragraphs? Report how the subordinate traits detailed
ll. **104-124**; ll. **124-141**; ll. **142-151**; ll. **151-168**, are related to and
illustrate the first member of the antithesis. — What assertion in the
previous paragraph, especially in ll. **96-99**, which serves as suggestion
for this paragraph, and indeed is so vividly recalled that its influence
attracts by antithesis the beginning of the sentence ll. 102-104 to inverted
order? — Is **political tact** (l. 103) a great mental quality or a small
one? — By what figure is it illustrated? — **105. A hundred**, — compare
a thousand, ll. 49, 125, and consider how much more vivid it is to use

essentially practical and of the present. She distrusted a plan in fact just in proportion to its speculative range or its outlook into the future. Her notion of statesmanship lay in watching how things turned out around her, and in seizing the moment for making the best of them. A policy of this limited, practical, tentative order was not only best suited to the England of her day, to its small resources and the transitional character of its religious and political belief, but it was one eminently suited to Elizabeth's peculiar powers. It was a policy of detail, and in details her wonderful readiness and ingenuity found scope for their exercise. "No War, my Lords," the Queen used to cry imperiously at the council-board, "No War!" but her hatred of war sprang less from her aversion to blood or to expense, real as was her aversion to both, than from the fact that peace left the field open to the diplomatic manœuvres and intrigues in which she excelled. Her delight in the consciousness of her ingenuity broke out in a thousand puckish freaks, — freaks in which one can hardly see any purpose beyond the purpose of sheer mystification. She revelled in "bye-ways" and "crooked ways." She played with grave cabinets as a cat plays with a mouse, and with much of the same feline delight in the mere embarrassment of her victims. When she was weary of mystifying foreign statesmen she turned to find fresh sport in mystifying her

---

a definite number than an indefinite. This is one favorite means of making style concrete. — Report how each of the subordinate traits brought to light in this paragraph is applied (ll. **112–117**; ll. **137–141**; ll. **164–168**) directly, as soon as it is detailed, to the England of Elizabeth's day. — **126. Puckish**, — what is the origin of this word, and what makes it a happily chosen word here? — What figure illustrates this trait of her character? — **130. Feline**, — what value has this Latin derivative here, as related to the repetition of ideas? Try the effect of

own ministers. Had Elizabeth written the story of her reign she would have prided herself, not on the triumph of England or the ruin of Spain, but on the skill with which she had hoodwinked and outwitted every statesman in Europe during fifty years. Nor was her trickery without political value. Ignoble, inexpressibly wearisome as the Queen's diplomacy seems to us now, tracing it as we do through a thousand despatches, it succeeded in its main end. It gained time, and every year that was gained doubled Elizabeth's strength. Nothing is more revolting in the Queen, but nothing is more characteristic, than her shameless mendacity. It was an age of political lying, but in the profusion and recklessness of her lies Elizabeth stood without a peer in Christendom. A falsehood was to her simply an intellectual means of meeting a difficulty; and the ease with which she asserted or denied whatever suited her purpose was only equalled by the cynical indifference with which she met the exposure of her lies as soon as their purpose was answered. The same purely intellectual view of things showed itself in the dexterous use she made of her very faults. Her levity carried her gaily over moments of detection and embarrassment where better women would have died of shame. She screened her tentative and hesitating statesmanship under the natural timidity and vacillation of

---

using still the common term. — **136. Hoodwinked,** — report on the derivation and meaning of this word. How does it differ from **outwitted?** — **138.** How does this line recall the writer's grouping of traits in this paragraph? — Report the different words used for *lying*, ll. **143–146**, and the source from which each is derived. — What summarizing characteristic, mentioned twice in ll. **146–153**, serves to connect and unify the subject of this paragraph with the subject of the preceding? (cf. l. 66). — Derivation of the word **cynical,** l. **149?** of the word **dexterous,** l. **152?** — L. **157** indicates a climax; trace it. — Show how

her sex. She turned her very luxury and sports to good account. There were moments of grave danger in her reign when the country remained indifferent to its perils, as it saw the Queen give her days to hawking and hunting, and her nights to dancing and plays. Her vanity and affectation, her womanly fickleness and caprice, all had their part in the diplomatic comedies she played with the successive candidates for her hand. If political necessities made her life a lonely one, she had at any rate the satisfaction of averting war and conspiracies by love sonnets and romantic interviews, or of gaining a year of tranquillity by the dexterous spinning out of a flirtation.

As we track Elizabeth through her tortuous mazes of lying and intrigue, the sense of her greatness is almost lost in a sense of contempt. But wrapped as they were in a cloud of mystery, the aims of her policy were throughout temperate and simple, and they were pursued with a singular tenacity. The sudden acts of energy which from time to time broke her habitual hesitation proved that it was no hesitation of weakness. Elizabeth could wait and finesse; but when the hour was come she

---

closely, in this paragraph, the ideas are felted together (to use Dr. Whately's expression) in the transitions between traits, ll. **124, 142, 151**. In each case what suggestion of the preceding is taken up and carried on, as if all were moving in the same line?

In the next paragraph, ll. **169-280**, report how its subject is brought out by antithesis, ll. **206-208**; how it is stated casually, l. **219**; and how it is recognized in one aspect, ll. **248, 249**. — Report now on the subdivisions of this paragraph, as indicated ll. **171-195**; ll. **195-205**; ll. **206-219**; ll. **219-280**. — What touch, ll. **273-275**, serves to bring this paragraph into unity with traits mentioned before ? — **177. Finesse**, — a noun used as a verb, though not so used for the first time by Green. See Webster's Dict. — Point out how, as in previous paragraphs, the subjects preceding are referred to by antithesis. Cf. note on ll. **67-79**.

could strike, and strike hard. Her natural temper indeed
tended to a rash self-confidence rather than to self-distrust.
180 She had, as strong natures always have, an unbounded confidence in her luck. "Her Majesty counts much on Fortune," Walsingham wrote bitterly; "I wish she would trust
more in Almighty God." The diplomatists who censured
at one moment her irresolution, her delay, her changes of
185 front, censure at the next her "obstinacy," her iron will,
her defiance of what seemed to them inevitable ruin.
"This woman," Philip's envoy wrote after a wasted re-
monstrance, "this woman is possessed by a hundred
thousand devils." To her own subjects, indeed, who
190 knew nothing of her manœuvres and retreats, of her "bye-
ways" and "crooked ways," she seemed the embodiment
of dauntless resolution. Brave as they were, the men who
swept the Spanish Main or glided between the icebergs of
Baffin's Bay never doubted that the palm of bravery lay
195 with their Queen. Her steadiness and courage in the pur-
suit of her aims was equalled by the wisdom with which
she chose the men to accomplish them. She had a quick
eye for merit of any sort, and a wonderful power of enlist-
ing its whole energy in her service. The sagacity which
200 chose Cecil and Walsingham was just as unerring in its
choice of the meanest of her agents. Her success indeed
in securing from the beginning of her reign to its end,
with the single exception of Leicester, precisely the right
men for the work she set them to do, sprang in great

— What antithesis is implied in the inversion for adjustment, l. **189**? —
What sentence-adjustment, l. **192**? — Trace how the transition is made,
ll. **195–199**, from bravery to sagacity. — **201**. **Meanest**; also **225**.
From what provincial use of the word *mean* is this to be distinguished,
and how? — **201–208**. What trait common to the two is used to make

measure from the noblest characteristic of her intellect. If in loftiness of aim her temper fell below many of the tempers of her time, in the breadth of its range, in the universality of its sympathy it stood far above them all. Elizabeth could talk poetry with Spenser and philosophy with Bruno; she could discuss Euphuism with Lyly, and enjoy the chivalry of Essex; she could turn from talk of the last fashions to pore with Cecil over despatches and treasury books; she could pass from tracking traitors with Walsingham to settle points of doctrine with Parker, or to calculate with Frobisher the chances of a north-west passage to the Indies. The versatility and many-sidedness of her mind enabled her to understand every phase of the intellectual movement of her day, and to fix by a sort of instinct on its higher representatives. But the greatness of the Queen rests above all on her power over her people. We have had grander and nobler rulers, but none so popular as Elizabeth. The passion of love, of loyalty, of admiration which finds its most perfect expression in the "Faery Queen," throbbed as intensely through the veins of her meanest subjects. To England, during her reign of half a century, she was a virgin and a Protestant Queen; and her immorality, her absolute want of religious enthusiasm, failed utterly to blur the brightness of the national ideal.

---

the transition from sagacity to versatility? — **206.** Point out suspense, and the use of it, the more noticeable here because it puts off what is expected at this point. — **210. Euphuism,** — see explanation of this, Rhet. p. 192, note. — Of what character is the assertion, ll. **216-219**, as related to preceding? — The last trait of character treated in this paragraph, is introduced, l. **219**, more abruptly than usual. Between what ideas is the adversative relation expressed by **but**? — This trait, or fact, which takes up the rest of the paragraph, shows clear indications of subdivision; see if you can set down its three related aspects from a

Her worst acts broke fruitlessly against the general devo‑
230 tion. A Puritan, whose hand she cut off in a freak of
tyrannous resentment, waved his hat with the hand that
was left, and shouted, "God save Queen Elizabeth!" Of
her faults, indeed, England beyond the circle of her court
knew little or nothing. The shiftings of her diplomacy
235 were never seen outside the royal closet. The nation at
large could only judge her foreign policy by its main out‑
lines, by its temperance and good sense, and above all
by its success. But every Englishman was able to judge
Elizabeth in her rule at home, in her love of peace, her
240 instinct of order, the firmness and moderation of her gov‑
ernment, the judicious spirit of conciliation and com‑
promise among warring factions which gave the country an
unexampled tranquillity at a time when almost every other
country in Europe was torn with civil war. Every sign of
245 the growing prosperity, the sight of London as it became
the mart of the world, of stately mansions as they rose on
every manor, told, and justly told, in Elizabeth's favor.
In one act of her civil administration she showed the bold‑
ness and originality of a great ruler; for the opening of
250 her reign saw her face the social difficulty which had so
long impeded English progress, by the issue of a commis‑
sion of inquiry which ended in the solution of the problem
by the system of poor-laws. She lent a ready patronage
to the new commerce; she considered its extension and
255 protection as a part of public policy, and her statue in the

---

study of (1) ll. **219-244**; (2) **244-271** (for the articulation of this, see Rhet. p. 275, 3); (3) **271-280**. — **236**. Is only rightly placed? — Point out, in ll. **230-232, 254-258,** and **276-279** how Rhet. p. 291, 2 (top of page) is exemplified. — What influence causes the sentence in‑version, l. **232**? — How are the two sentences, ll. **235-244**, balanced

centre of the London Exchange was a tribute on the part of the merchant class to the interest with which she watched and shared personally in its enterprises. Her thrift won a general gratitude. The memories of the Terror and of the Martyrs threw into bright relief the aversion from bloodshed which was conspicuous in her earlier reign, and never wholly wanting through its fiercer close. Above all there was a general confidence in her instinctive knowledge of the national temper. Her finger was always on the public pulse. She knew exactly when she could resist the feeling of her people, and when she must give way before the new sentiment of freedom which her policy unconsciously fostered. But when she retreated, her defeat had all the grace of victory; and the frankness and unreserve of her surrender won back at once the love that her resistance had lost. Her attitude at home in fact was that of a woman whose pride in the well-being of her subjects, and whose longing for their favor, was the one warm touch in the coldness of her natural temper. If Elizabeth could be said to love anything, she loved England. "Nothing," she said to her first Parliament, in words of unwonted fire, "nothing, no worldly thing under the sun, is so dear to me as the love and good-will of my subjects." And the love and good-will which were so dear to her she fully won.

---

together? — **261. Aversion from,** — this preposition is quite in accord with the derivation of the word *aversion* ; but usage nowadays is more is favor of *aversion to.* Compare ll. 121, 122. — **265.** What striking figure expresses strongly her relation to public affairs? Cf. Rhet. p. 156, 67. — What means, ll. **265-268,** of preserving unity of idea with what has been said previously? Cf. ll. **97-101.**

The last paragraph, ll. **281-333,** begins not with the main trait that is the subject of the paragraph, but with a subordinate and derived fact,

She clung perhaps to her popularity the more passionately that it hid in some measure from her the terrible loneliness of her life. She was the last of the Tudors, the last of Henry's children; and her nearest relatives were Mary Stuart and the House of Suffolk, one the avowed, the other the secret claimant of her throne. Among her mother's kindred she found but a single cousin. Whatever womanly tenderness she had, wrapt itself around Leicester; but a marriage with Leicester was impossible, and every other union, could she even have bent to one, was denied to her by the political difficulties of her position. The one cry of bitterness which burst from Elizabeth revealed her terrible sense of the solitude of her life. "The Queen of Scots," she cried at the birth of James, "has a fair son, and I am but a barren stock." But the loneliness of her position only reflected the loneliness of her nature. She stood utterly apart from the world around her, sometimes above it, sometimes below it, but never of it. It was only on its intellectual side that Elizabeth touched the England of her day. All its moral aspects were simply dead to her. It was a time when men were being lifted into nobleness by the new moral energy which seemed suddenly to pulse through the whole people, when honor and enthusiasm took colors of poetic beauty, and religion became a chivalry.

---

which leads up to the subject. How is this opening consideration connected with the previous paragraph? How is it led onward to the main subject, ll. **296-300**? — What is the subject of this paragraph, as brought to light in the last-mentioned lines? How is it related with the traits that have been recounted previously? — What aspects does this trait take, as seen in ll. **301-315**; **315-320**; **322-328**; **328-333**? Into what two antithetic groups do they fall? — **281. Perhaps**, — find a better place for this word in the sentence. — It is to be noted that Green occasionally uses very strong and striking adjectives; point out

But the finer sentiments of the men around her touched Elizabeth simply as the fair tints of a picture would have touched her. She made her market with equal indifference out of the heroism of William of Orange or the bigotry of Philip. The noblest aims and lives were only counters on her board. She was the one soul in her realm whom the news of St. Bartholomew stirred to no thirst for vengeance; and while England was thrilling with its triumph over the Armada, its Queen was coolly grumbling over the cost, and making her profit out of the spoiled provisions she had ordered for the fleet that saved her. To the voice of gratitude, indeed, she was for the most part deaf. She accepted services such as were never rendered to any other English sovereign without a thought of return. Walsingham spent his fortune in saving her life and her throne, and she left him to die a beggar. But, as if by a strange irony, it was to this very want of sympathy that she owed some of the grander features of her character. If she was without love, she was without hate. She cherished no petty resentments; she never stooped to envy or suspicion of the men who served her. She was indifferent to abuse. Her good humor was never ruffled by the charges of wantonness and cruelty with which the Jesuits filled every court in Europe. She was insensible to fear. Her life became at last the mark for assassin after assassin, but the thought of peril was the one hardest to bring home to her. Even

---

such in ll. **282, 293**, also ll. **25, 40, 95, 143, 180**, preceding. — A thing that has constantly been noticed, too, and might be traced in much minuter detail, is the ceaseless play of antithesis, direct and hidden, so constant as to be well-nigh a mannerism. But it certainly has worked, along with skilful grouping of ideas, to produce a very unified and self-consistent portrayal of an exceeding complex character.

when the Catholic plots broke out in her very household she would listen to no proposals for the removal of Catholics from her court.

From A SHORT HISTORY OF THE ENGLISH PEOPLE.

From the indications that have been furnished in the notes, tabulate the points treated in the paragraphs, showing how they are related to one another, and how their subdivisions are related to them. Endeavor also, from the foregoing description and analysis, to express the character of Elizabeth, as to its most cardinal features, in one sentence.

NOTES ON DESCRIPTION IN PREVIOUS SELECTIONS.

SOME of the Selections already studied for their style are works of description, whose authors are celebrated for their masterly work in portrayal. Let us examine the workmanship of two or three of them.

Ruskin: Pages 36–47. — Ruskin's description of St. Mark's, Venice, is widely celebrated as a masterpiece in its kind. Much of this celebrity is due, no doubt, to the gorgeousness of its language, which has already been examined; but it will be profitable to investigate also whether underneath this splendor of diction there is rigor and definiteness enough of outline to give solidity and practical value to the treatment.

Let us look first at the description of the exterior, ll. **138–180**. Notice first by what narrative touches, ll. **127–130**, and ll. **138–141**, the first sight of the church is made impressive; explain by Rhet. p. 345, 1. — What point of view do these lines determine? What contrast, detailed previously (ll. 63–126) heightens the effect of the scene from this point of view, and how are the spectator's emotions thus enlisted? Cf. Rhet. pp. 342, 343. — For the comprehensive outline of this description, it is obvious that we are to investigate in two lines, — seeking the outline as to form, which is here the subordinate feature, and the outline as to color, material, decoration, which are the predominating features in the writer's mind. — As to form, what general shape is outlined, l. **142**? — Into what feature, beginning with the ground, is this general outline first broken, l. **144**? This feature is traced in detail to l. **170**. — **167. The broad archivolts** are the inner contour, or vaulted ceiling, of the arches, here described as seen from below. — The façade of the church of St. Mark's appears to be divided by a long balcony into two divisions, the lower one of which has been outlined. No mention is here made of the balcony, or indeed of any feature not distinguished by rich artistic decoration; but from ll. **170, 171**, what is the general make-up of the upper division? How are the arches surmounted, l. **175**? — We thus see that bits of outline are interspersed, merely enough to be a bare framework for the gorgeous wealth of color and sculpture and design in which the writer revels. These latter have been largely studied in the examination of Ruskin's style; observe, however, what a surpassingly rich effect is produced by the narrative touches, ll. **175–178.**

Let us now note a few features of the description of the interior, ll. **217–259.** What general outline is given, ll. **221–223?** What conditions, as to light, are given for observation? — What appropriateness in calling the church **a vast cave,** l. **221?** — The description, from l. **218** to l. **235,** centres in what feature? From l. **235** to l. **259** in what main feature? See Rhet. p. 257, examples. What characteristic, ll. **242–245,** gives unity to the bewildering mass of artistic detail in this last section? — This whole description, both exterior and interior, is not a matter-of-fact description but idealized by imagination, — as the note, p. 47, preceding, says: "It is the idealized St. Mark's, as seen through the mist of time in the clear light of its first creation — and indeed farther back still, in the artist's mind that conceived it — that the writer has placed before us."

Carlyle: Pages 56–63. — We know from Carlyle's own testimony that he valued very highly the power of graphic description, and students of his writings have found his own describing power especially manifest in the portrayal of persons. See Rhet. p. 338, examples. Let us see how he describes Coleridge's personal appearance, in ll. **13–38** of this Selection.

What may be taken as the point of view, l. **13?** See Rhet. p. 329. Some of the details, as in ll. **25, 30,** are such as would necessarily presuppose a somewhat elderly man; while all are fully in harmony with this initial note of his age. — What *most general* feature of his appearance (ll. **15–17**) corresponding to the comprehensive outline is given, and how made picturesque and impressive? How summarized, l. **29 ?** — Between this outline and its summary, trace now the regular order and sequence in which the details of his appearance are given. What *two* characteristics emerge from the examination, as the unifying traits of his character? — After the summary, l. **29,** in what characteristic is the description centred, and with what appropriateness is this feature singled out for special treatment? — To what further summary, at the end of the paragraph, is this description conducted? — What means and what accessories of description are predominantly used here?

XIX.

THOMAS HUGHES.

ST. AMBROSE CREW WIN THEIR FIRST RACE.

HARK!—the first gun. The report sent Tom's heart into his mouth again. Several of the boats pushed off at once into the stream; and the crowds of men on the bank began to be agitated, as it were, by the shadow of the coming excitement. The St. Ambrose fingered their oars, put a last dash of grease on their rollocks, and settled their feet against the stretchers.

"Shall we push her off?" asked bow.

This Selection and the two that follow will be studied for the manner in which they exemplify principles of Narration; and presuppose a knowledge of the Rhetoric as far as page 382. It is to be observed that this Handbook can exhibit only such aspects of narration as can be exemplified on a small scale, and must omit such larger features of movement, perspective, combined narratives, and the like, as can ordinarily be shown only in stories of too great length to be given here.

The present Selection exemplifies the kind of narration that is nearest like description; explain what this is, and its principle, by Rhet. p. 370. Accordingly, we look to find the interest of each part not subordinated to a coming *dénouement*, but concentrated in the individual details as they occur; and what modification of the style will this naturally produce?

As this account is taken from the middle of a chapter, we miss the descriptive introduction that is usually appended to stories standing independently. Nor is the account brought to a formal ending. How is its place in its larger story explained, Rhet. p. 370, bottom?

"No; I can give you another minute," said Miller, who
was sitting, watch in hand, in the stern; "only be smart
when I give the word."

The captain turned on his seat, and looked up the boat.
His face was quiet, but full of confidence, which seemed to
pass from him into the crew. Tom felt calmer and stronger,
as he met his eye. "Now mind, boys, don't quicken," he
said, cheerily; "four short strokes to get way on her, and
then steady. Here, pass up the lemon."

The style suitable to this account may be gathered from two considerations: 1. It deals, in a descriptive spirit, with a scene of intense energy in action; 2. The author is recounting from actual reminiscence what deeply interests him. Later in the chapter he thus addresses his readers: "You, I know, will pardon the enthusiasm which stirs our pulses, now in sober middle age, as we call up again the memories of this the most exciting sport of our boyhood (for we were but boys, then, after all)." From these considerations we expect and demand that it be spirited, that is, enter congenially into the vigor and action it is employed to portray.

Lines 1–8. What emotional indication, at the outset, of the intense feeling connected with the scene? — By what condensing metaphor indicated in the case of the hero, Tom Brown? — How is the coming excitement suggested in the case of the other boats? — **6. Rollocks,** — the same as *row-locks*, which word is in this country colloquially pronounced rŭl-uks. — As to the boating-terms and tropes used throughout this account the author says later, appealing to his "readers of the gentler sex": "You will pardon, though I fear hopelessly unable to understand the above sketch; your sons and brothers will tell you it could not have been made less technical."

10. Be smart, — from what American provincialism is this to be distinguished, — and how?

12–15. What contrast to the prevailing excitement here suggested, and of what use is the suggestion toward the coming victory? — **15–17.** How do these words illustrate Rhet. p. 77, 3, and by contrast, p. 80, 2? Change into written style, supplying all ellipses. — The captain's quiet confidence and his cheery words correspond with the

And he took a sliced lemon out of his pocket, put a small piece in his own mouth, and then handed it to Blake, who followed his example, and passed it on. Each man took a 20 piece; and just as bow had secured the end, Miller called out, —

" Now, jackets off, and get her head out steadily."

The jackets were thrown on shore, and gathered up by the boatman in attendance. The crew poised their oars, No. 25 2 pushing out her head, and the captain doing the same for the stern. Miller took the starting-rope in his hand.

" How the wind catches her stern," he said; " here, pay out the rope one of you. No, not you — some fellow with a strong hand. Yes, you'll do," he went on, as Hardy 30 stepped down the bank and took hold of the rope; "let me

---

description of him given earlier in the book: " Altogether a noble specimen of a very noble type of our countrymen. Tall and strong of body; courageous and even-tempered; tolerant of all men; sparing of speech, but ready in action; a thoroughly well-balanced, modest, quiet Englishman." He is the Jervis, mentioned ll. 181, 199.

21. Miller, the coxswain, with his abrupt and peremptory manner (cf. l. 164), has also been described before: " A slight, resolute, fiery little man, with curly black hair. He was peculiarly qualified by nature for the task which he had set himself; and it takes no mean qualities to keep a boat's crew well together and in order. Perhaps he erred a little on the side of over-strictness and severity; and he certainly would have been more popular had his manner been a thought more courteous: but the men who rebelled most against his tyranny grumblingly confessed that he was a firstrate coxswain."

30. Hardy, a man little known to the other college men, being a servitor, but a friend of Tom Brown's, and, as it transpires afterwards, one of the best rowers in the college.

What influence have these details of getting the boat ready before starting, as given ll. **24–48**, upon our confidence and sympathy, as regards the success of the race? That is, how do they prepare for the account yet to come?

have it foot by foot as I want it. Not too quick; make the most of it — that'll do. Two and three, just dip your oars in to give her way."

The rope paid out steadily, and the boat settled to her place. But now the wind rose again, and the stern drifted in toward the bank.

"You *must* back her a bit, Miller, and keep her a little further out or our oars on stroke side will catch the bank."

"So I see; curse the wind. Back her, one stroke all. Back her, I say!" shouted Miller.

It is no easy matter to get a crew to back her an inch just now, particularly as there are in her two men who have never rowed a race before, except in the torpids, and one who has never rowed a race in his life.

However, back she comes; the starting-rope slackens in Miller's left hand, and the stroke, unshipping his oar, pushes the stern gently out again.

There goes the second gun! one short minute more, and we are off. Short minute, indeed! you wouldn't say so if you were in the boat, with your heart in your mouth and trembling all over like a man with the palsy. Those sixty seconds before the starting-gun in your first race — why, they are a little lifetime.

"By Jove, we are drifting in again," said Miller, in horror. The captain looked grim but said nothing; it was too late now for him to be unshipping again. "Here, catch hold of the long boat-hook, and fend her off."

49–54. What irregularities of expression, — condensation, exclamation, pleonasm, — indicating a heightened style, and due to what? The excitement, so easily roused by the successive guns, is described again in l. **74**, where the pent-up life and energy is represented as "held in leash, as it were."

Hardy, to whom this was addressed, seized the **boat-hook**, and, standing with one foot in the **water**, pressed the end 60 of the boat-hook against the gunwale, at the full stretch of his arm, and so, by main force, kept the stern out. There was just room for **stroke** oars to dip, and that was all. The starting-rope **was as taut as** a harp-string; will Miller's left hand hold out? 65

It is an awful moment. But the coxswain, though almost dragged backwards off his seat, is equal to the occasion. He holds his watch in his right hand with the tiller rope.

"Eight seconds more only. Look out for the flash. 70 Remember, all eyes in the boat."

There it comes, at last — the flash of the starting-gun. Long before the sound of the report can roll up the river, the whole pent-up life and energy which has been held in leash, as it were, for the last six minutes, is loose, and 75 breaks away with a bound and a dash which he who has felt it will remember for his life, but the like of which, will he ever feel again? The starting-ropes drop from the

---

64. What indication of the writer's throwing himself into the scene?

66. Is the word **awful** correctly used? Does the kind of diction in which the whole is written permit liberties? See Rhet. p. 77, 4.

72-81. As the most intense part of the account, note in these lines the irregularities of expression due to the emotional and descriptive feeling. What influence causes the pleonasm, l. **72**? What influence attracts the time-clause, l. **73**, to the beginning of its sentence? — **74. Pent-up,** — how does this epithet illustrate Rhet. p. 158, examples, 2? — **Has been held,** — is this in concord with its subject? See Rhet. p. 110, 2. — **75. Is loose,** — the verb and its construction as brief as may be, for the sake of rapid condensation. — **76.** Point out how Rhet. p. 169, 87 is illustrated in this line. How does the rhythm aid in the description? — **77.** What influence causes the inversion in this and the next line? — **78-81.** Point out the words that especially

coxswain's hands, the oars flash into the water, and gleam
on the feather, the spray flies from them, and the boats
leap forward.

The crowds on the bank scatter, and rush along, each
keeping as near as may be to its own boat. Some of the
men on the towing-path, some on the very edge of, often
in, the water; some slightly in advance, as if they could
help to drag their boat forward; some behind, where they
can see the pulling better; but all at full speed, in wild
excitement, and shouting at the top of their voices to those
on whom the honor of the college is laid.

"Well pulled, all!" "Pick her up there, five!" "You're
gaining every stroke!" "Time in the bows!" "Bravo,
St. Ambrose!"

On they rush by the side of the boats, jostling one
another, stumbling, struggling, and panting along.

For a quarter of a mile along the bank the glorious,
maddening hurly-burly extends, and rolls up the side of the
stream.

For the first ten strokes, Tom was in too great fear of
making a mistake to feel or hear or see. His whole soul

---

contain the life and spirit of the passage. — Of this whole paragraph,
ll. **72–81**, what is the fitting movement? See Rhet. p. 365, 2. Which
is the predominating means of gaining rapidity here, the omission of
details or the manner in which they are given?

82–97. The first two lines of this passage cover about all that is actually narrative in it; the rest being descriptive. How is this descriptive feeling indicated in the structure of the sentence, ll. **83–89**? — **84. On the very edge of, often in,** — explain the construction by Rhet. p. 159, examples, 2. — What is left to be understood in ll. **90–92**? — In ll. **93–97**, point out the descriptive words, and the words in which sound corresponds to sense. — What distinction in position of the adverb, l. **93**? — What is the origin of the word **hurly-burly**, l. **96**?

98–133. The style of this paragraph is distinctly less rapid than the

was glued to the back of the man before him, his one 100
thought to keep time and get his strength into the stroke.
But as the crew settled down into the well-known long sweep,
what we may call consciousness returned; and, while every
muscle in his body was straining, and his chest heaved,
and his heart leapt, every nerve seemed to be gathering 105
new life, and his senses to wake into unwonted acuteness.
He caught the scent of wild thyme in the air, and found
room in his brain to wonder how it could have got there,
as he had never seen the plant near the river, or smelt it
before. Though his eye never wandered from the back of 110
Diogenes, he seemed to see all things at once. The boat
behind, which seemed to be gaining;—it was all he could
do to prevent himself from quickening on the stroke as he
fancied that;—the eager face of Miller, with his compressed lips, and eyes fixed so earnestly ahead that Tom 115
could almost feel the glance passing over his right shoulder;

---

style of the paragraphs preceding it, being a kind of interlude of quieter description by way of taking breath. This is manifest in the diction by the fewer irregularities, the fuller constructions, and the less intense suggestiveness of individual words.— **100.** What striking trope in this line, and what is the use of it?— **103. What we may call consciousness,**— why the amplitude, instead of merely the last quoted word?— What implied antithesis in ll. **103–106**?— How does this description of a mental state, ll. **107–125**, exemplify Rhet. p. 348, 3, and what accessories does it employ? What name would you give to the mental state described?— **111. Diogenes,**— thus described earlier in the book: "He was a heavy, burly man, naturally awkward in his movements, but gifted with a sort of steady, dogged enthusiasm, and by dint of hard and constant training had made himself into a most useful oar, fit for any place in the middle of the boat. . . . He was the most good-natured man in the world, very badly dressed, very short-sighted, and called everybody 'old fellow.' His name was simple Smith, generally known as Diogenes Smith, from an eccentric habit which he had of

coxswain's hands, the oars flash into the water, and gleam
on the feather, the spray flies from them, and the boats
leap forward.

The crowds on the bank scatter, and rush along, each
keeping as near as may be to its own boat. Some of the
men on the towing-path, some on the very edge of, often
in, the water; some slightly in advance, as if they could
help to drag their boat forward; some behind, where they
can see the pulling better; but all at full speed, in wild
excitement, and shouting at the top of their voices to those
on whom the honor of the college is laid.

"Well pulled, all!" "Pick her up there, five!" "You're
gaining every stroke!" "Time in the bows!" "Bravo,
St. Ambrose!"

On they rush by the side of the boats, jostling one
another, stumbling, struggling, and panting along.

For a quarter of a mile along the bank the glorious,
maddening hurly-burly extends, and rolls up the side of the
stream.

For the first ten strokes, Tom was in too great fear of
making a mistake to feel or hear or see. His whole soul

---

contain the life and spirit of the passage. — Of this whole paragraph,
ll. **72-81**, what is the fitting movement? See Rhet. p. 365, 2. Which
is the predominating means of gaining rapidity here, the omission of
details or the manner in which they are given?

82-97. The first two lines of this passage cover about all that is actually narrative in it; the rest being descriptive. How is this descriptive feeling indicated in the structure of the sentence, ll. **83-89**? — **84. On the very edge of, often in,** — explain the construction by Rhet. p. 159, examples, 2. — What is left to be understood in ll. **90-92**? — In ll. **93-97**, point out the descriptive words, and the words in which sound corresponds to sense. — What distinction in position of the adverb, l. **93**? — What is the origin of the word **hurly-burly,** l. **96**?

98-133. The style of this paragraph is distinctly less rapid than the

was glued to the back of the man before him, his one 100
thought to keep time and get his strength into the stroke.
But as the crew settled down into the well-known long sweep,
what we may call consciousness returned ; and, while every
muscle in his body was straining, and his chest heaved,
and his heart leapt, every nerve seemed to be gathering 105
new life, and his senses to wake into unwonted acuteness.
He caught the scent of wild thyme in the air, and found
room in his brain to wonder how it could have got there,
as he had never seen the plant near the river, or smelt it
before. Though his eye never wandered from the back of 110
Diogenes, he seemed to see all things at once. The boat
behind, which seemed to be gaining ;—it was all he could
do to prevent himself from quickening on the stroke as he
fancied that ;— the eager face of Miller, with his compressed lips, and eyes fixed so earnestly ahead that Tom 115
could almost feel the glance passing over his right shoulder ;

---

style of the paragraphs preceding it, being a kind of interlude of quieter description by way of taking breath. This is manifest in the diction by the fewer irregularities, the fuller constructions, and the less intense suggestiveness of individual words.— **100**. What striking trope in this line, and what is the use of it?— **103. What we may call consciousness**,— why the amplitude, instead of merely the last quoted word?— What implied antithesis in ll. **103–106**?— How does this description of a mental state, ll. **107–125**, exemplify Rhet. p. 348, 3, and what accessories does it employ? What name would you give to the mental state described?— **111. Diogenes**,— thus described earlier in the book: "He was a heavy, burly man, naturally awkward in his movements, but gifted with a sort of steady, dogged enthusiasm, and by dint of hard and constant training had made himself into a most useful oar, fit for any place in the middle of the boat. . . . He was the most good-natured man in the world, very badly dressed, very short-sighted, and called everybody 'old fellow.' His name was simple Smith, generally known as Diogenes Smith, from an eccentric habit which he had of

the flying banks and the shouting crowd; see them with his bodily eyes he could not, but he knew, nevertheless, that Grey had been upset and nearly rolled down the bank into the water in the first hundred yards, that Jack was bounding and scrambling and barking along by the very edge of the stream; above all, he was just as well aware as if he had been looking at it, of a stalwart form in cap and gown, bounding along, brandishing the long boat-hook, and always keeping just opposite the boat; and amid all the Babel of voices, and the dash and pulse of the stroke, and the laboring of his own breathing, he heard Hardy's voice coming to him again and again, and clear as if there had been no other sound in the air, "Steady, two! steady! well pulled! steady, steady." The voice seemed to give him strength and keep him to his work. And what work it was! he had had many a hard pull in the last six weeks, but never aught like this.

But it can't last forever; men's muscles are not steel, or their lungs bulls' hide, and hearts can't go on pumping a

---

making an easy chair of his hip-bath." — **119. Grey**, — thus described earlier, in a conversation between Tom and Hardy: "'You must have seen him here sometimes in the evenings.' 'Yes, I remember; the fellow with a stiff neck, who won't look you in the face.' 'Ay; but he is a sterling man at the bottom, I can tell you.'" — **120. Jack**, — "a white bull-dog, . . . a gem in his way; for his brow was broad and massive, and wrinkled about the eyes; his skin was as fine as a lady's, and his tail taper and nearly as thin as a clay pipe; but he had a way of going snuzzling about the calves of strangers which was not pleasant for nervous people." — **123. A stalwart form**, — the name is delayed by suspense till l. **127**; see Rhet. p. 147, examples, 2. — **133. Aught**, — is this condensed form to be explained by Rhet. p. 71, cf. 50?

134. Can't, — how is the effectiveness of the description aided by the colloquial diction? — **Or**, see also l. 109. A slight inaccuracy in this writer's diction, *or* where *nor* is the correct particle. An inaccu-

hundred miles an hour long, without bursting. The St. Ambrose boat is well away from the boat behind, there is a great gap between the accompanying crowds; and now, as they near the Gut, she hangs for a moment or two in hand, though the roar from the bank grows louder 140 and louder, and Tom is already aware that the St. Ambrose crowd is melting into the one ahead of them.

"We must be close to Exeter!" The thought flashes into him, and, it would seem, into the rest of the crew at the same moment; for, all at once, the strain seems taken 145 off their arms again; there is no more drag; she springs to the stroke as she did at the start; and Miller's face, which had darkened for a few seconds, lightens up again.

Miller's face and attitude are a study. Coiled up into the smallest possible space, his chin almost resting on his 150 knees, his hands close to his sides, firmly but lightly feeling the rudder, as a good horseman handles the mouth of a free-going hunter; if a coxswain could make a bump by his own exertions, surely he will do it. No sudden jerks of the St. Ambrose rudder will you see, watch as you will from 155 the bank; the boat never hangs through fault of his, but easily and gracefully rounds every point. "You're gain-

---

racy that is often carelessly indulged in nowadays.— **135.** What striking trope gives vigor to the description? Would it be so effective if poetic?— **136. sq.** It will be noted that the progress of the boat since the start has not been narrated, but presupposed while the attention of the reader has been directed to something else; and now it is resumed and *described* at a single point. This illustrates how the descriptive element predominates here over the narrative.

143-148. What descriptive words import vividness and vigor into the passage, according to the spirited points of the action?— **145. All at once, etc.,**— observe that a moment of accomplished act is described, not the act narrated in progress.

149-157. What effectiveness and significance are gained by inserting

ing! you're gaining!" he now and then mutters to the captain, who responds with a wink, keeping his breath for other matters. Isn't he grand, the captain, as he comes forward like lightning, stroke after stroke, his back flat, his teeth set, his whole frame working from the hips with the regularity of a machine? As the space still narrows, the eyes of the fiery little coxswain flash with excitement, but he is far too good a judge to hurry the final effort before the victory is safe in his grasp.

The two crowds are mingled now, and no mistake; and the shouts come all in a heap over the water: "Now, St. Ambrose, six strokes more." "Now, Exeter, you're gaining; pick her up." "Mind the Gut, Exeter." "Bravo, St. Ambrose!" The water rushes by, still eddying from the strokes of the boat ahead. Tom fancies now he can hear their oars and the workings of their rudder, and the voice of their coxswain. In another moment both boats are in the Gut, and a perfect storm of shouts reaches them from the crowd, as it rushes madly off to the left to the foot-bridge, amidst which "Oh, well steered, well steered, St. Ambrose!" is the prevailing cry. Then Miller, motionless as a statue till now, lifts his right hand and whirls the tassel round his head. "Give it her now, boys,

---

the description of Miller just at this place? — **159.** The captain's silence is of course necessary here; but in general, also, the description of him is, "The stroke was in general a man of marvellous few words, having many better uses than talking to put his breath to." — **160–163.** How does the enthusiastic description of the captain, so entirely from a student's point of view, aid in the action and its result? — **161. Like lightning,** — how does this heighten the descriptive feeling, in accordance with Rhet. p. 99?

167. See note on l. **136 sq.** — What aids to condensed and strong expression in ll. **168** and **175**? See Rhet. p. 156, 67. — **179. Motionless as a statue, etc.,** — how does this particular aid what succeeds?

six strokes and we're into them." Old Jervis lays down that great broad back, and lashes his oar through the water with the might of a giant, the crew catch him up in another stroke, the tight new boat answers to the spurt, and Tom feels a little shock behind him, and then a grating sound, as Miller shouts, "Unship oars, bow and three!" and the nose of the St. Ambrose boat glides quietly up the side of the Exeter, till it touches their stroke oar.

"Take care where you're coming to." It is the coxswain of the bumped boat who speaks.

Tom finds himself within a foot or two of him when he looks round; and, being utterly unable to contain his joy, and yet unwilling to exhibit it before the eyes of a gallant rival, turns away towards the shore, and begins telegraphing to Hardy.

"Now, then, what are you at there in the bows? Cast her off, quick. Come, look alive! Push across at once out of the way of the other boats."

"I congratulate you, Jervis," says the Exeter stroke, as the St. Ambrose boat shoots past him. "Do it again next race and I shan't care."

From TOM BROWN AT OXFORD.

— 182. Point out the epithets and the trope that are here employed to heighten the description. — 181-188. What call for accelerated movement here? See Rhet. p. 366. Observe that the movement is accelerated here at the end by the omission of intermediate details; in l. 184, for instance, the bumping of the other boat comes immediately after the beginning of the spurt.

Why is it better, here at the end, to relapse into a quiet and undescriptive style, in spite of the excitement of the action? See Rhet. p. 368, 4.

XX.

JOSEPH HENRY SHORTHOUSE.

A MYSTERIOUS INCIDENT.

It was two nights after the execution of Lord Strafford. The guard was set at Whitehall and the "all night" served up. The word for the night was given, and the whole palace was considered as under the sole command of Inglesant, as the esquire in waiting. He had been round to the several gates and seen that the courts and ante-

---

As the narrative given in the foregoing Selection was discursive, that is, centred mostly in description, with the moving and spirited portrayal of its details, so that of the present Selection centres in an action, in which we look for the balanced and skilful arrangement of its successive stages. As therefore the action itself—what in larger stories would be called the *plot*—supplies the interest, what characteristic does Rhet. p. 370 lead us to look for in the style?

Though occurring within a chapter of a larger work, this account, with all its approaches, is complete in itself. The writer's reason for giving it, as also the general nervous unquiet manifest throughout the incident, may be gathered from the following words in the paragraph preceding: "That such a man, by the simple clamor of popular opinion, should have been arrested, tried, and executed in a few days, with no effort but the most degrading and puny one made on his behalf by his royal master and friend, certainly must have produced a terror and excitement, one would think, unequalled in history. That the King never recovered from it is not surprising; one would have thought he would never have held up his head again. That the royal party was amazed and confounded is not wonderful; one would have thought it would have been impossible ever to have formed a royal party afterwards."

rooms were quiet and clear of idlers, and then came up
into the anteroom outside the privy chamber, and sat down
alone before the fire. In the room beyond him were two
gentlemen of the privy chamber, who slept in small beds
drawn across the door opening into the royal bedchamber
beyond. The King was in his room, in bed, but not asleep;
Lord Abergavenny, the gentleman of the bedchamber in
waiting, was reading Shakespeare to him before he slept.
Inglesant took out a little volume of the classics, of the
series printed in Holland, which it was the custom of the
gentlemen of the Court, and those attached to great nobles,
to carry with them to read in antechambers while in waiting. The night was perfectly still, and the whole palace
wrapped in a profound quiet that was almost oppressive to
one who happened to be awake. Inglesant could not read;
the event that had just occurred, the popular tumults, the
shock of feeling which the royal party had sustained, the
fear and uncertainty of the future, filled his thoughts.
The responsibility of his post sat on him to-night like a
nightmare, and with very unusual force: a sense of approaching terror in the midst of the intense silence fascinated him and became almost insupportable. His fancy
filled his mind with images of some possible oversight and
of some unseen danger which might be lurking even then
in the precincts of the vast rambling palace.

Lines 1-31. Explain the office of this first paragraph by Rhet. p. 369, 1. Does this introductory description admit any details not necessary, or at least helpful, to the proper understanding of the story? How does it answer to the proper style of an introduction, as prescribed Rhet. p. 272? — How does the detail, ll. **5-7**, help the story? — What influence has the detail, ll. **19-21**, as preparing for the mysterious event? — How do ll. **21-31** illustrate Rhet. p. 367, 2? — **31. Of the vast rambling palace,** — give the full force of this phrase of implication; see Rhet. p. 158, examples, 2.

Gradually, however, all these images became confused and the sense of terror dulled, and he was on the point of falling asleep, when he was startled by the ringing sound of arms and the challenge of the yeoman of the guard, on the landing outside the door. The next instant, a voice, calm and haughty, which sent a tremor through every nerve, gave back the word, "Christ." Inglesant started up and grasped the back of his chair in terror.

Gracious Heaven! who was this that knew the word? In another moment the hangings across the door were drawn sharply back, and with a quick step, as one who went straight to where he was expected and had a right to be, the intruder entered the antechamber. It wore the form and appearance of Strafford — it was Strafford — in dress, and mien, and step. Taking no heed of Inglesant, crouched back in terror against the carved chimney-piece, the apparition crossed the room with a quick step, drew the hangings that screened the door of the privy chamber,

---

How do ll. **32, 33** illustrate Rhet. p. 367, 3? — The lines, **40–50**, comprising as they do the central feature of the incident, need to be carefully written. How do they illustrate Rhet. p. 364, 1? — Does l. **40** fully explain Inglesant's terror? — **37.** What other cause of his terror may we infer from **which sent a tremor through every nerve?**

42. As one who, etc. This particular, with its contrast to the terror and impotence of the esquire, whose duty it was to guard the house, adds greatly to the impressiveness of the account. One is reminded of a note to Coleridge's "Ancient Mariner": "The journeying moon, and the stars that still sojourn, yet still move onward; and everywhere the blue sky belongs to them, and is their appointed rest, and their native country, and their own natural homes, *which they enter unannounced, as lords that are certainly expected.*" — **44, 45.** What is the use of the amplitude in telling who it was? — How do the descriptive details, ll. **47, 55,** illustrate Rhet. p. 349? Explain also by Rhet. p. 342. — **48. With a quick step,** — compare the position and stress of this phrase with its

and disappeared. Inglesant recovered in a moment, sprang
across the room, and followed the figure through the door.
He saw nothing; but the two gentlemen raised themselves
from their couches, startled by his sudden appearance and
white, scared look, and said, "What is it, Mr. Esquire?"

Before Inglesant, who stood with eyes and mouth open,
the picture of terror, could recover himself, the curtain of
the bedchamber was drawn hastily back, and the Lord
Abergavenny suddenly appeared, saying in a hurried,
startled voice:—

---

first occurrence, l. **42.**—**50. And disappeared,**—observe that this is the last that is given in direct narration of the movements of the apparition; the rest is brought out by the words of those present, as they recount their connection with the scene.

A problem of unity arises; for the event in its successive stages occurred in four different places: the landing outside the door, the anteroom, the privy chamber, and the royal bedchamber. To have followed the apparition from point to point in direct narration would have shifted and dissipated the scene quite inconsistently with unity of effect; yet what occurred in each of these places must in some way be brought to light. The unity that cannot be preserved by place may, however, be preserved by the actors and by the manner of recounting. Which one of the actors was present in every stage of the event that is directly narrated? In all these he was the determining agent, or at least the principal one. In the only parts where he was not, ll. **73-76, 80-88**, what is there in the manner of recounting to subordinate its effect? What liberties have accordingly to be taken with the order of time? See ll. **68-76,** and **78**; and compare Rhet. p. 361, 2.

Another thing also may be noted: the way in which the various actors are subordinated to the event, and to the two principal observers. How many actually saw the apparition? How was Lord Abergavenny related to the occurrence? See ll. **80 sq.** How the two gentlemen? ll. **52-54.** How the guard? ll. **71-76.** This subordination makes two persons stand out with special prominence: Inglesant, as the one through whom the various incidents came to be known, and the King, as the one whom the event most concerned.

⁶⁰ "Send for Mayern; send for Dr. Mayern, the King is taken very ill!"

Inglesant, who by this time was recovered sufficiently to act, seized the opportunity to escape, and, hurrying through the antechamber and down the staircase to the guard-room, ⁶⁵ he found one of the pages, and despatched him for the Court physician. He then returned to the guard at the top of the staircase.

"Has anyone passed?" he asked.

"No," the man said; "he had seen no one."

⁷⁰ "Did you challenge no one a moment ago?"

The man looked scared, but finally acknowledged what he feared at first to confess, lest it should be thought he had been sleeping at his post, — that he had become suddenly conscious of, as it seemed to him, some presence in ⁷⁵ the room, and found himself the next moment, to his confusion, challenging the empty space.

Failing to make anything of the man, Inglesant returned to the privy chamber, where Lord Abergavenny was relating what had occurred.

⁸⁰ "I was reading to the King," he repeated, "and His Majesty was very still, and I began to think he was falling asleep, when he suddenly started upright in bed, grasped the book on my knee with one hand, and with the other pointed across the chamber to some object upon which his

---

69. "*He had seen no one,*" — what modification in the report of conversation (see Rhet. p. 127, 24), — corresponding to the *oratio obliqua* of the Latin literature? — **73–76.** Comparing these lines with ll. 34–36, what do you gather that the man saw and heard, as compared with Inglesant? — **Had become suddenly conscious,** — is the word *conscious* accurate here? Compare De Quincey (p. 14), l. 98 and note.

77. To make anything of the man, — how explained by Rhet. p. 46, 14? — Observe that in the scene of Lord Abergavenny's relation,

gaze was fixed with a wild and horror-stricken look, while
he faintly tried to cry out. In a second the terror of the
sight, whatever it was, overcame him, and he fell back on
the bed with a sharp cry."

"Mr. Inglesant saw something," said both the gentlemen at once; "he came in here as you gave the alarm."

"I saw nothing," said Inglesant; "whatever frightened me I must tell the King."

Dr. Mayern, who lodged in the palace, soon arrived; and as the King was sensible when he came, he merely prescribed some soothing drink, and soon left. The moment he was gone, the King called Abergavenny into the room alone to him, and questioned him as to what had occurred. Abergavenny told him all he knew, adding that the esquire in waiting, Mr. Inglesant, was believed to have seen something by the gentlemen of the privy chamber, whom he had aroused. Inglesant was sent for, and found the King and Abergavenny alone. He declined to speak before the latter, until the King positively commanded him to do so. Deadly pale, with his eyes on the ground, and speaking with the greatest difficulty, he then told his story; of the

---

Inglesant is present, being, so to say, the unifying element in every part of the story.

On the description of the King, ll. **82-88**, compare note to ll. 47, 55.

— **87. Whatever it was,** — from this it is evident that Abergavenny saw nothing; see also l. 122.

92. The postponing of Inglesant's revelation until he could make it directly to the King gives opportunity to relate the *dénouement*, the most intense and exciting part of the event, in the King's presence. At the same time it confines the event to the three who alone are directly concerned with it.

93-95. How does the doctor's visit, despatched in so few words, illustrate Rhet. p. 365, 2? Compare also the brief repetition, ll. **105-107,**

deep silence, his restlessness, the sentry's challenge, and the apparition that appeared. Here he stopped.

"And this figure," said Abergavenny in a startled whisper, "did you know who it was?"

"Yes, I knew him," said the young man; "would to God I had not."

"Who was it?"

Paler, if possible, than before, and with a violent effort, Inglesant forced himself to look at the King.

A contortion of pain, short but terrible to see, passed over the King's face, but he rose from the chair in which he sat (for he had risen from the bed and even dressed himself), and, with that commanding dignity which none ever assumed better than he, he said, —

"Who was it, Mr. Esquire?"

"My Lord Strafford."

Abergavenny stepped back several paces, and covered his face with his hands. No one spoke. Inglesant dared not stir, but remained opposite to the King, trembling in every limb, and his eyes upon the ground like a culprit. The King continued to stand with his commanding air, but stiff and rigid as a statue; it seemed as though he had strength to command his outward demeanor, but no power besides.

---

which illustrates the skill of modern narration, as compared with ancient; compare, for instance, the narrative repetitions, given in identical words, in Job i. 6–8, ii. 1–3; also i. 13–19.

What preparation is made, according to Rhet. p. 367, 2, in ll. **102–120**, for the *dénouement?* How is it shown in the agitation of all three? How is it rendered more impressive by Abergavenny's questioning? What influence has Inglesant's refusal to answer, ll. 91, 102, 114, upon the impressiveness of the end, and acccording to what principle? — **121**. Observe that the answer is given in the fewest words possible,

The silence grew terrible. At last the King was able to make a slight motion with his hand. Inglesant seized the opportunity, and, bowing to the ground, retired backward to the door. As he closed the door the King turned towards Abergavenny, but the room was empty. The King was left alone.

From JOHN INGLESANT.

---

the reader being already in possession of the story, and this one detail being all that is necessary to supply the key, so to say, of the whole.

Does the scene that follows this revelation, ll. **122–135**, need for its recounting any descriptive or heightened language? Why not?

XXI.

SIR WALTER SCOTT.

AN HISTORICAL INCIDENT RETOLD.

The following, from Fuller's "Worthies of England," is the source from which we get the well-known incident of Walter Raleigh and the cloak: —

"This Captain Raleigh coming out of Ireland to the English court in good habit (his clothes being then a considerable part of his estate) found the Queen walking, till, meeting with a plashy place, she seemed to scruple going thereon. Presently Raleigh cast and spread his new plush cloak on the ground; whereon the Queen trod gently, rewarding him afterwards with many suits, for his so free and seasonable tender of so fair a foot cloth. Thus an advantageous admission into the first notice of a prince is more than half a degree to preferment."

[Raleigh, Blount, and Tracy, who are in the service of the Earl of Sussex, are sent to propitiate Queen Elizabeth, whose displeasure the Earl has through Raleigh's agency incurred.]

"COME with me, Tracy, and come you too, Master Walter Wittypate, that art the cause of our having all this ado. Let us see if thy neat brain, that frames so many flashy fireworks, can help out a plain fellow at need with some of
5 thy shrewd devices."

The present Selection, besides being a well-constructed story in itself, exemplifies two important elements in the art of narration.

First, in exhibiting the use made, by an acknowledged master in his art, of a pre-existing material already known to us, it exhibits also what additions, accessories, and colorings are regarded as necessary to give artistic life to an original narrative-germ, whatever it is.

Secondly, it illustrates the important office that conversation holds in the structure of a narrative. It was a rule of a recent leading story-

"Never fear, never fear," exclaimed the youth, "it is I will help you through — let me but fetch my cloak."

"Why, thou hast it on thy shoulders," said Blount — "the lad is mazed."

"No, this is Tracy's old mantle," answered Walter; "I go not with thee to court unless as a gentleman should."

"Why," said Blount, "thy braveries are like to dazzle the eyes of none but some poor groom or porter."

---

writer that "no single word of conversation should ever be introduced which did not plainly either (1) develop the character speaking, or (2) forward the plot." These are at least the two main ends of conversation; and the present Selection will help us to see how they are subserved.

In the appended extract from Fuller, Raleigh is represented as "coming out of Ireland to the English court"; but in order to introduce him more naturally to Queen Elizabeth, and at the same time make him fill an important part in his story, Scott has represented him as temporarily in the service of the Earl of Sussex, one of the leading characters in the novel of Kenilworth.

A little before the beginning of this Selection Blount and Raleigh are thus described: "There was a remarkable contrast in their dress, appearance, and manners. The attire of the elderly gentleman, a person as it seemed of quality, and in the prime of life, was very plain and soldier-like, his stature low, his limbs stout, his bearing ungraceful, and his features of that kind which express sound common sense, without a grain of vivacity or imagination. The younger, who seemed about twenty, or upwards, was clad in the gayest habit used by persons of quality at the period, wearing a crimson velvet cloak richly ornamented with lace and embroidery, with a bonnet of the same, encircled with a gold chain turned three times round it, and secured by a medal. His hair was adjusted very nearly like that of some fine gentlemen of our own time, that is, it was combed upwards and made to stand as it were on end; and in his ears he wore a pair of silver ear-rings, having each a pearl of considerable size. The countenance of this youth, besides being regularly handsome and accompanied by a fine person, was animated and striking in a degree that seemed to speak at once the firmness

"I know that," said the youth; "but I am resolved I will have my own cloak, ay, and brush my doublet to boot, ere I stir forth with you."

"Well, well," said Blount, "here is a coil about a doublet and a cloak — get thyself ready, a God's name!"

They were soon launched on the princely bosom of the broad Thames, upon which the sun now shone forth in all its splendor.

"There are two things scarce matched in the universe," said Walter to Blount — "the sun in heaven, and the Thames on the earth."

"The one will light us to Greenwich well enough," said Blount, "and the other would take us there a little faster, if it were ebb tide."

"And this is all thou think'st — all thou carest — all thou deem'st the use of the King of Elements, and the King of Rivers, to guide three such poor caitiffs, as thyself, and me, and Tracy, upon an idle journey of courtly ceremony!"

"It is no errand of my seeking, faith," replied Blount,

---

of a decided and the fire of an enterprising character, the power of reflection, and the promptitude of determination."

Lines 1–82. In this preliminary conversation, which, with interspersed description serves to introduce the principal scene, we look to see suggested all the elements necessary to the understanding of the story. What is naturally the first topic of conversation, ll. **1–18**, and what the good of introducing it? How does it illustrate Rhet. p. 357? In the discussion of it how do Raleigh's and Blount's contrasted characters reveal themselves? — By the short narrative lines, **19–21**, a new topic of conversation is introduced; how is it steered to the introduction of the principal scene, ll. **35–39**? What further traits of Raleigh and Blount are revealed in the discussion of this topic? Note especially the contrast, ll. **22–31**. — How does the descriptive paragraph, ll. **40–50**, exemplify Rhet. p. 369, 2? — This picture of the Queen's barge (see also ll. 169–171) is conformed, so far as it goes, to what trait of

"and I could excuse both the sun and the Thames the trouble of carrying me where I have no great mind to go, and where I expect but dog's wages for my trouble — and by my honor," he added, looking out from the head of the boat, "it seems to me as if our message were a sort of labor in vain; for see, the Queen's barge lies at the stairs, as if her Majesty were about to take water."

It was even so. The royal barge, manned with the queen's watermen, richly attired in the regal liveries, and having the banner of England displayed, did indeed lie at the great stairs which ascended from the river, and along with it two or three other boats for transporting such part of her retinue as were not in immediate attendance on the royal person. The yeomen of the guard, the tallest and most handsome men whom England could produce, guarded with their halberds the passage from the palace gate to the river side, and all seemed in readiness for the Queen's coming forth, although the day was yet so early.

"By my faith, this bodes us no good," said Blount; "it must be some perilous cause puts her Grace in motion thus untimeously. By my counsel, we were best put back again, and tell the Earl what we have seen."

Elizabeth's character, as revealed in Green (see *ante*, No. XVIII.), ll. 34-37? How do ll. **46-50** conform to Green's description, ll. 55-58?

51-54. It will be noticed that in the conversations Scott conforms his diction with care throughout to the characteristics, real or supposed, of Elizabethan idiom; cf. Rhet. p. 82. This is done partly by catchwords, as in ll. 18, 32, 36, 51, 76, where Elizabethan oaths and expletives are used, and partly by old words and idioms. Point out and explain the archaisms in this paragraph. What supposable old idiom in l. **53**? — Notice that the expletives are all attributed to Blount, probably as an old soldier, while Raleigh's speech is not only free from them but of a higher and more refined order than Blount's.

55 "Tell the Earl what we have seen!" said Walter; "why, what have we seen but a boat, and men with scarlet jerkins, and halberds in their hands? Let us do his errand, and tell him what the Queen says in reply."

So saying, he caused the boat to be pulled towards a 60 landing-place at some distance from the principal one, which it would not, at that moment, have been thought respectful to approach, and jumped on shore, followed, though with reluctance, by his cautious and timid companions. As they approached the gate of the palace, one 65 of the sergeant porters told them they could not at present enter, as her Majesty was in the act of coming forth. The gentlemen used the name of the Earl of Sussex; but it proved no charm to subdue the officer, who alleged in reply, that it was as much as his post was worth, to dis-70 obey in the least tittle the commands which he had received.

"Nay, I told you as much before," said Blount; "do, I pray you, my dear Walter, let us take boat and return."

"Not till I see the Queen come forth," returned the 75 youth, composedly.

"Thou art mad, stark mad, by the mass!" answered Blount.

51–82. In the conversation and narration covered by these lines a new contrast between Blount and Raleigh comes to light, — what is it? How is it suggested and set off by antithesis, ll. **78–82**? Blount has already, in the paragraph preceding this Selection, expressed in characteristic words the cause of his fears: "'A plague on it,' said Blount, as he descended the stairs, ' had he sent me with a cartel to Leicester, I think I should have done his errand indifferently well. But to go to our gracious Sovereign, before whom all words must be lackered over either with gilding or with sugar, is such a confectionery matter as clean baffles my poor old English brain.'" But here is a juncture where Blount's weakness is Raleigh's strength; what contrasted mood is

"And thou," said Walter, "art turned coward of the sudden. I have seen thee face half a score of shag-headed Irish kernes to thy own share of them, and now thou wouldst blink and go back to shun the frown of a fair lady!"

At this moment the gates opened, and ushers began to issue forth in array, preceded and flanked by the band of Gentlemen Pensioners. After this, amid a crowd of lords and ladies, yet so disposed around her that she could see and be seen on all sides, came Elizabeth herself, then in the prime of womanhood, and in the full glow of what in a Sovereign was called beauty, and who would in the lowest rank of life have been truly judged a noble figure, joined to a striking and commanding physiognomy. She leant on the arm of Lord Hunsdon, whose relation to her by her mother's side often procured him such distinguished marks of Elizabeth's intimacy.

The young cavalier we have so often mentioned had probably never yet approached so near the person of his Sovereign, and he pressed forward as far as the line of warders permitted, in order to avail himself of the present opportunity. His companion, on the contrary, cursing his imprudence, kept pulling him backwards, till Walter shook him off impatiently, and letting his rich cloak drop care-

---

revealed in ll. **72–75**? Observe that Blount for once forgets his swagger, and fairly entreats.

In all the story thus far, Blount is obviously introduced only as a subordinate character, having significance merely as a foil to Raleigh. How do the traits of his character, as shown in the foregoing, serve to set off Raleigh's? Recount now the traits of Raleigh's character that have appeared, and show how they bear upon the success ascribed to him alike by Fuller and by this incident. Thus we are in all points ready to enter upon the incident and its results.

lessly from one shoulder; a natural action, which served, however, to display to the best advantage his well-proportioned person. Unbonneting at the same time, he fixed his eager gaze on the Queen's approach, with a mixture of respectful curiosity, and modest yet ardent admiration, which suited so well with his fine features, that the warders, struck with his rich attire and noble countenance, suffered him to approach the ground over which the Queen was to pass, somewhat closer than was permitted to ordinary spectators. Thus the adventurous youth stood full in Elizabeth's eye, — an eye never indifferent to the admiration which she deservedly excited among her subjects, or to the fair proportions of external form which chanced to distinguish any of her courtiers. Accordingly, she fixed her keen glance on the youth, as she approached the place where he stood, with a look in which surprise at his boldness seemed to be unmingled with resentment, while a trifling accident happened which attracted her attention towards him yet more strongly. The night had been rainy, and just where the young gentleman stood, a small quantity of mud interrupted the Queen's passage. As she hesitated to pass on, the gallant, throwing his cloak from his shoulders, laid it on the miry spot, so as to ensure her stepping over it dryshod. Elizabeth looked at the young man, who accompanied this act of devoted courtesy with a profound reverence, and a blush that overspread

---

The paragraph ll. 83-94 may be taken as occasion for noting, what has perhaps already been observed, that Sir Walter Scott's eminence as a writer lies in his wonderful invention rather than in his style. In the latter, indeed, he is so hasty and careless, sometimes so lumbering, as to be, grammatically at least, far from a model. Note, for instance, 86. **yet so disposed,**—what is the actual subject of this participle, and what its apparent grammatical subject? Cf. Rhet. p. 115, 10. How

his whole countenance. The Queen was confused, and blushed in her turn, nodded her head, hastily passed on, and embarked in her barge without saying a word.

"Come along, Sir Coxcomb," said Blount; "your gay cloak will need the brush to-day, I wot. Nay, if you had meant to make a foot-cloth of your mantle, better have kept Tracy's old drap-de-bure, which despises all colors."

"This cloak," said the youth, taking it up and folding it, "shall never be brushed while in my possession."

"And that will not be long, if you learn not a little more economy — we shall have you in *cuerpo* soon, as the Spaniard says."

Their discourse was here interrupted by one of the Band of Pensioners.

"I was sent," said he, after looking at them attentively, "to a gentleman who hath no cloak, or a muddy one. — You, sir, I think," addressing the younger cavalier, "are the man; you will please to follow me."

"He is in attendance on me," said Blount, "on me, the noble Earl of Sussex's master of horse."

"I have nothing to say to that," answered the messenger; "my orders are directly from her Majesty, and concern this gentleman only."

---

can the sentence be corrected? — **89. And who**, etc., — see preceding, p. 73, note on Huxley, l. 109; also note p. 87 on Thackeray, l. 104. How correct this sentence? — This whole sentence, ll. 85-91, is careless; observe, for instance, the crude inaccuracy of "*who* would have been truly judged *a noble figure, joined to a* striking and commanding *physiognomy*." — **95. The young cavalier we have so often mentioned**, — does this repetition for *Raleigh* comport with the acquaintance we may be supposed by this time to have with him? Observe that in l. **78** he is called **Walter**.

In the next paragraph, ll. **95-130**, which contains the significant

So saying, he walked away, followed by Walter, leaving the others behind, Blount's eyes almost starting from his head with the excess of his astonishment. At length he gave vent to it in an exclamation — "Who the good jere would have thought this!" And shaking his head with a mysterious air, he walked to his own boat, embarked, and returned to Deptford.

The young cavalier was, in the meanwhile, guided to the water-side by the Pensioner, who showed him considerable respect; a circumstance which, to persons in his situation, may be considered as an augury of no small consequence. He ushered **him** into one of the wherries which lay ready to attend the Queen's barge, which was already proceeding up the river, with the advantage of that flood-tide, of which, in the course of their descent, Blount had complained to his associates.

The two rowers used **their** oars with such expedition at **the** signal **of** the Gentleman Pensioner, that they very soon **brought their** little skiff under the stern of the Queen's boat, where she sate beneath an awning, attended by two or three ladies, and the nobles of her household. She looked more than once at the wherry in which the young adventurer was seated, spoke to those around her, and

---

stage of the whole account, observe first how approach is made to the central incident. What incident is introduced to insure the Queen's attention, ll. **100-104**? — Compare also ll. 111-115. How is this conformed to Elizabeth's character? — see Green, l. 55. How is even this trifling incident accounted for and made natural? — But introducing it incurred a slight improbability, or at least may not have seemed sufficient in itself to insure the Queen's attention; how is the probability increased, ll. **107-111**? — How is the way to the main incident further smoothed, l. **120**? — The detail ll. 104-106 is introduced to comport with Raleigh's known character; compare also ll. 354-360. In an appended

seemed to laugh. At length one of the attendants, by the
Queen's order apparently, made a sign for the wherry to
come alongside, and the young man was desired to step
from his own skiff into the Queen's barge, which he performed with graceful agility at the fore part of the boat,
and was brought aft to the Queen's presence, the wherry
at the same time dropping into the rear. The youth under-
went the **gaze of Majesty, not the less** gracefully, that his
self-possession was mingled with embarrassment. The
muddied cloak still hung upon his arm, and formed the
natural topic with which the Queen introduced the conversation.

"You have this day spoiled a gay mantle in our service,
young man. We thank you for your service, though the
manner of offering it was unusual, and something **bold.**"

"In a sovereign's need," answered the youth, "it is each
liege man's duty to be bold."

"God's pity! that was well said, my lord," said the
Queen, turning to a grave person who sate by her, and
answered with a grave inclination of the head, and something of a mumbled assent.

"Well, young man, your gallantry shall **not** go unre-
warded. **Go** to the wardrobe **keeper,** and he shall have

---

note Scott says: "None of Elizabeth's courtiers knew better than he how
to make his court to her personal vanity, or could more justly estimate
the quantity of flattery which she could condescend to swallow. Being
confined in the Tower for some offence, and understanding the Queen
was about to pass to Greenwich in her barge, he insisted on approaching the window, that he might see, at whatever distance, the Queen of
his Affections, the most beautiful object which the earth bore on its surface. The Lieutenant of the Tower (his own particular friend) threw
himself between his prisoner and the window; while Sir Walter, apparently influenced by a fit of unrestrainable passion, swore he would not

orders to supply the suit which you have cast away in our service. Thou shalt have a suit, and that of the newest cut, I promise thee, on the word of a princess."

200 "May it please your grace," said Walter, hesitating, "it is not for so humble a servant of your Majesty to measure out your bounties; but if it became me to choose—"

"Thou wouldst have gold, I warrant me," said the Queen, interrupting him; "fie, young man! I take shame to say, 205 that, in our capital, such and so various are the means of thriftless folly, that to give gold to youth is giving fuel to fire, and furnishing them with the means of self-destruction. If I live and reign, these means of unchristian excess shall be abridged. Yet thou mayst be poor," she 210 added, "or thy parents may be—It shall be gold, if thou wilt, but thou shalt answer to me for the use on't."

Walter waited patiently until the Queen had done, and then modestly assured her, that gold was still less in his wish than the raiment her Majesty had before offered.

215 "How, boy!" said the Queen, "neither gold nor garment? What is it thou wouldst have of me then?"

"Only permission, madam—if it is not asking too high an honor—permission to wear the cloak which did you this trifling service."

---

be debarred from seeing his light, his life, his goddess! A scuffle ensued, *got up* for effect's sake, in which the Lieutenant and his captive grappled and struggled with fury,—tore each other's hair,—and at length drew daggers, and were only separated by force. The Queen being informed of this scene exhibited by her frantic adorer, it wrought, as was to be expected, much in favor of the captive Paladin. There is little doubt that his quarrel with the Lieutenant was entirely contrived for the purpose which it produced."— How does the amplitude of this whole paragraph illustrate Rhet. p. 364, 1?—**119. While a trifling accident, etc.**,—is it felicitous to subordinate the introduction of the

"Permission to wear thine own cloak, thou silly boy!" said the Queen.

"It is no longer mine," said Walter; "when your Majesty's foot touched it, it became a fit mantle for a prince, but far too rich a one for its former owner."

The Queen again blushed; and endeavored to cover, by laughing, a slight degree of not unpleasing surprise and confusion.

"Heard you ever the like, my lords? The youth's head is turned with reading romances — I must know something of him, that I may send him safe to his friends. — What art thou?"

"A gentleman of the household of the Earl of Sussex, so please your Grace, sent hither with his Master of Horse, upon a message to your Majesty."

In a moment the gracious expression which Elizabeth's face had hitherto maintained, gave way to an expression of haughtiness and severity.

"My Lord of Sussex," she said, "has taught us how to regard his messages, by the value he places upon ours. We sent but this morning the physician in ordinary of our chamber, and that at no usual time, understanding his lordship's illness to be more dangerous than we had be-

---

main incident, which has been so prepared for, by putting it in a while-clause? How amend the expression so as to bring it out better? — Compare the actual telling of the incident, for amplitude, with the extract from Fuller quoted at the beginning. — Observe the number and variety of the designations of Raleigh, and estimate how they correspond with the circumstances of their introduction; see ll. **95**, **100**, **111**, **116**, **121**, **123**, **126**. Are they always felicitously chosen, and is it elegant to vary so constantly?

Scott's great skill as a story-teller is nowhere more felicitously shown than in the manner in which he makes one part of the story prepare,

fore apprehended. There is at no court in Europe a man more skilled in this holy and most useful science than Dr.
245 Masters, and he came from Us to our subject. Nevertheless, he found the gate of Say's Court defended by men with culverins, as if it had been on the Borders of Scotland, not in the vicinity of our court; and when he demanded admittance in our name, it was stubbornly refused.
250 For this slight of a kindness, which had but too much of condescension in it, we will receive, at present at least, no excuse; and some such we suppose to have been the purport of my Lord of Sussex's message."

This was uttered in a tone, and with a gesture, which
255 made Lord Sussex's friends who were within hearing tremble. He to whom the speech was addressed, however, trembled not; but with great deference and humility, as soon as the Queen's passion gave him an opportunity,

---

whether by direct suggestion or by antithesis, for the other. The intercalary conversation, ll. **131–139**, is steered to what suggestion, and how does it prepare for the messenger from the Queen? See Rhet. p. 366, 1. How does it also illustrate Rhet. p. 367, 3?—The words exchanged between the messenger and Blount, together with Blount's astonishment, ll. **142–157**, have what suggestiveness as regards the importance of what is yet to come? See Rhet. p. 367, 2. How is this suggestiveness further increased, and the nature and result of the coming interview foreshadowed, in the paragraph, ll. **158–166**?

167–185. This paragraph, which seems merely to fill up an interstice in the account, really makes also the last notes of preparation for the interview. How does it indicate the Queen's mood? How does it indicate, in Raleigh's actions, a predetermination toward the Queen's favor, as corresponding with her character?—**183.** Observe how the mention of the cloak—what the Germans would perhaps call the *cloak-motif*—serves at each prominent point as the suggestive unifier and connecting-link of the story; see ll. 7, 101, 123, 183, 346.

In the conversation that ensues, which extends to the end of the

he replied: — "So please your most gracious Majesty, I was charged with no apology from the Earl of Sussex." 260

"With what were you then charged, sir?" said the Queen, with the impetuosity which, amid nobler qualities, strongly marked her character; "was it with a justification? — or, God's death, with a defiance?"

"Madam," said the young man, "my Lord of Sussex 265 knew the offence approached towards treason, and could think of nothing save of securing the offender, and placing him in your Majesty's hands, and at your mercy. The noble Earl was fast asleep when your most gracious message reached him, a potion having been administered to 270 that purpose by his physician; and his Lordship knew not of the ungracious repulse your Majesty's royal and most comfortable message had received, until after he awoke this morning."

Selection, we look for three main features: 1. That on Elizabeth's side it comport with the dignity of a queen, and with the historical character of *this* queen in particular; 2. That on Raleigh's side it comport with the position of a subject, and with the known character of this subject in particular; 3. That it be conducted, without superfluities, to the goal, also historically known, of Elizabeth's complacency and favor. Of course that it should be worded in the Elizabethan diction goes without saying; also that the words of each interlocutor take their cue always from what the previous speaker has said.

The introductory topic, as mentioned in l. **184**, suggests itself: the cloak which has served the queen's need. How is the naturalness of its mention still further increased?

191. How does the Queen's remark on Raleigh's answer illustrate Green, l. 38, and what aid is thus given toward the object of the conversation?

200-202. The extreme delicacy of Raleigh's answer recognizes that it is an indecorum in a subject to demur to the sovereign's will; just as l. **212** recognizes the indecorum of interrupting her, though she inter-

"And which of his domestics, then, in the name of Heaven, presumed to reject my message, without even admitting my own physician to the presence of him whom I sent him to attend?" said the Queen, much surprised.

"The offender, madam, is before you," replied Walter, bowing very low; "the full and sole blame is mine; and my lord has most justly sent me to abye the consequences of a fault, of which he is as innocent as a sleeping man's dreams can be of a waking man's actions."

"What! was it thou? — thou thyself, that repelled my messenger and my physician from Say's Court?" said the Queen. "What could occasion such boldness in one who seems devoted — that is, whose exterior bearing shows devotion — to his Sovereign?"

"Madam," said the youth, — who, notwithstanding an assumed appearance of severity, thought that he saw

---

rupts him and others freely (ll. 203, 322). It will be noted also how Raleigh conforms to what De Quincey mentions afterward in the account of his own interview with royalty: "I was well aware, before I saw him [George III.], that in the royal presence, . . . I must have no voice except for *answers*; I was to originate nothing myself." The questions are all asked by the Queen. How are these touches in Raleigh's demeanor explained in ll. **350–352**?

The Queen's freedom and impetuosity, as illustrated ll. **203, 215, 228, 261, 284**, and often, compares how with Green's portrayal of her character, Green, ll. 23–26, 50–52? — Line **220** may be compared with Green, l. 28. — **222–224**. This remark again finds the Queen at a peculiarly susceptible point of her character; compare Green, ll. 40–43; and thus far, by a limited display of his own character he has evidently reached a high position in her esteem. Raleigh has already been represented, in what precedes our Selection, as desiring court favor: in this skilfully managed conversation, and in his refusal of all substantial reward, does Scott regard him as *playing a part*, and shrewdly adapting himself to what he knows of the Queen's peculiarities, or is he also

something in the Queen's face that resembled not implacability, — "we say in our country, that the physician is for the time the liege sovereign of his patient. Now, my noble master was then under dominion of a leach, by whose advice he hath greatly profited, who had issued his commands that his patient should not that night be disturbed, on the very peril of his life."

"Thy master hath trusted some false varlet of an empiric," said the Queen.

"I know not, madam, but by the fact, that he is now — this very morning — awakened much refreshed and strengthened, from the only sleep he hath had for many hours."

The nobles looked at each other, but more with the purpose to see what each thought of this news, than to exchange any remarks on what had happened. The Queen

---

sincere? Compare the poetic trait in his character, as revealed in ll. **22-31**, and the following, from the preceding chapter: "The look of the younger gallant had in it something imaginative; he was sunk in reverie, and it seemed as if the empty space of air betwixt him and the wall were the stage of a theatre on which his fancy was mustering his own *dramatis personæ*, and treated him with sights far different from those which his awakened and earthly vision could have offered."

But there remains an important part of the story unsatisfied (compare note at beginning); nor has Raleigh yet displayed the more manly and brave side of his character. How is this effected in the section of conversation, ll. **230-288**? On what suggestion is the current of conversation turned into the new channel? — The Queen's words and demeanor, ll. **250-256**, seem suddenly to cut off all conciliation; furnishing therefore what test for Raleigh's character and what task for his tact to meet? — Illustrate ll. **254-256** by Green, ll. **25-31**. — What antithesis is thus prepared, to set off the succeeding? — What traits of character are revealed in Raleigh's words, ll. **259-260**; **265-274**; **279-283**? What evidence, in ll. **289-292** that this conduct was not without

answered hastily, and without affecting to disguise her satisfaction, "By my word, I am glad he is better. But thou wert over bold to deny the access of my Doctor Masters. Know'st thou not that Holy Writ saith, 'in the multitude of counsel there is safety'?"

"Ay, madam," said Walter, "but I have heard learned men say, that the safety spoken of is for the physicians, not for the patient."

"By my faith, child, thou hast pushed me home," said the Queen, laughing; "for my Hebrew learning does not come quite at a call.— How say you, my Lord of Lincoln? Hath the lad given a just interpretation of the text?"

"The word *safety*, my most gracious madam," said the Bishop of Lincoln, "for so hath been translated, it may be somewhat hastily, the Hebrew word, being—"

"My Lord," said the Queen, interrupting him, "we said we had forgotten our Hebrew.— But for thee, young man, what is thy name and birth?"

"Raleigh is my name, most gracious Queen, the youngest son of a large but honorable family of Devonshire."

"Raleigh?" said Elizabeth, after a moment's recollection, "have we not heard of your service in Ireland?"

---

a calculated wisdom, frankly appealing to the stronger and nobler side of the Queen's character? With this latter, compare Green, ll. 74-76, 195-199.

The section of conversation, ll. **289-323**, reveals Raleigh's readiness in resource and his wit in retort;— how are these qualities illustrated, for instance, in ll. **300-303** and **312-314**? Both of these would appeal strongly to Elizabeth.— How are his own lightness and wit set off by contrast in the answer of the Bishop of Lincoln, ll. **319-321**? What assumed character comes to light in these last few words?— The whole passage about Hebrew illustrates, by allusion, what accomplishment of Elizabeth? See Green, ll. 7-12.

"I have been so fortunate as to do some service there, madam," replied Raleigh, "scarce, however, of consequence sufficient to reach your Grace's ears."

"They hear farther than you think of," said the Queen, graciously, "and have heard of a youth who defended a ford in Shannon against a whole band of wild Irish rebels, until the stream ran purple with their blood and his own."

"Some blood I may have lost," said the youth looking down, "but it was where my best is due; and that is in your Majesty's service."

The Queen paused and then said hastily, "You are very young to have fought so well, and to speak so well. But you must not escape your penance for turning back Masters — the poor man hath caught cold on the river; for our order reached him when he was just returned from certain visits in London, and he held it matter of loyalty and conscience instantly to set forth again. So hark ye, Master Raleigh, see thou fail not to wear thy muddy cloak, in token of penitence, till our pleasure be farther known. And here," she added, giving him a jewel of gold, in the form of a chess-man, "I give thee this to wear at the collar."

Raleigh, to whom nature had taught intuitively, as it were, those courtly arts which many scarce acquire from long experience, knelt, and, as he took from her hand the

---

In the concluding section of the conversation, ll. **323–349**, the story is conducted to its termination and result. How is this section connected with the preceding? What does it reveal of Raleigh's character and what of Elizabeth's? — **326. Large but honorable,** — is this a natural adversative relation? See Rhet. p. 142, 45. — **340.** What indication in this line of what Scott evidently intended in the character of Raleigh's conversation? — Does the penance inflicted by the Queen (l. 346) indicate to some degree that she was sensible to his delicate gallantry? Compare l. 220.

jewel, kissed the fingers which gave it. He knew, perhaps, better than almost any of the courtiers who sur-
355 rounded her, how to mix the devotion claimed by the Queen, with the gallantry due to her personal beauty — and in this, his first attempt to unite them, he succeeded so well, as at once to gratify Elizabeth's personal vanity, and her love of power.

From KENILWORTH.

What indication, in ll. **354-360**, of Scott's design in retelling this incident of Raleigh and the cloak? How does the story illustrate each of the two elements here represented as successfully united? What evidence of skilful design displayed in the beginning, — skilful as adapted to illustrate the character of both Raleigh and the Queen, — in making him one of the household of the Earl of Sussex at this juncture?

XXII.

JOHN STUART MILL.

THE MEANING OF THE TERM NATURE.

NATURE, natural, and the group of words derived from them, or allied to them in etymology, have at all times filled a great place in the thoughts and taken a strong hold on the feelings of mankind. That they should have done so is not surprising, when we consider what the words, in 5 their primitive and most obvious signification, represent; but it is unfortunate that a set of terms which play so great a part in moral and metaphysical speculation, should have acquired many meanings different from the primary one, yet sufficiently allied to it to admit of confusion. 10 The words have thus become entangled in so many foreign

---

This Selection and the one following are studied as exemplifying the principles of Exposition; and presuppose a knowledge of the Rhetoric as far as page 406.

The present Selection illustrates Exposition as applied to the exact definition of an idea; a definition that is to be constructed with special care, on account of the importance of the idea, the commonness of the term used to express it, and the ambiguities inhering in its popular and ordinary use. We may accordingly call this Philosophical Exposition.

The warrant that the exposition will be conducted carefully, and the spirit of caution and calm judgment which should guide every one's work in exposition, are alike found in the habitual method of Mr. Mill. "At the same time that he was peculiarly deliberate and slow in forming opinions," says his editor, "he had a special dislike

associations, mostly of a very powerful and tenacious character, that they have come to excite, and to be the symbols of, feelings which their original meaning will by no means justify; and which have made them one of the most copious sources of false taste, false philosophy, false morality, and even bad law.

The most important application of the Socratic Elenchus, as exhibited and improved by Plato, consists in dissecting large abstractions of this description; fixing down to a precise definition the meaning which as popularly used they merely shadow forth, and questioning and testing the common maxims and opinions in which they bear a part. It is to be regretted that among the instructive specimens of this kind of investigation which Plato has left, and to which subsequent times have been so much indebted for whatever intellectual clearness they have attained, he has not enriched posterity with a dialogue περὶ φύσεως. If the idea denoted by the word had been subjected to his searching analysis, and the popular commonplaces in which it figures had been submitted to the

---

to the utterance of half-formed opinions. He declined altogether to be hurried into premature decision on any point to which he did not think he had given sufficient time and labor to have exhausted it to the utmost limit of his own thinking powers. And, in the same way, even after he had arrived at definite conclusions, he refused to allow the curiosity of others to force him to the expression of them before he had bestowed all the elaboration in his power upon their adequate expression, and before, therefore, he had subjected to the test of time, not only the conclusions themselves, but also the form in which he had thrown them."

The last sentence of this Selection, ll. **146–148**, indicates what object and what limitation, in making this exposition? What reason is apparent in the first paragraph, ll. **1–17**, for making it, and how are its importance and its difficulty indicated? Being the starting-point and basis of a long essay, comprising 65 pages in the book from which it is

ordeal of his powerful dialectics, his successors probably would not have rushed, as they speedily did, into modes of thinking and reasoning of which the fallacious use of that word formed the corner stone; a kind of fallacy from which he was himself singularly free.

According to the Platonic method which is still the best type of such investigations, the first thing to be done with so vague a term is to ascertain precisely what it means. It is also a rule of the same method, that the meaning of an abstraction is best sought for in the concrete — of an universal in the particular. Adopting this course with the word Nature, the first question must be, what is meant by the "nature" of a particular object? as of fire, of water, or of some individual plant or animal? Evidently the *ensemble* or aggregate of its powers or properties: the modes in which it acts on other things (counting among those things the senses of the observer) and the modes in which other things act upon it; to which, in the case of a sentient being, must be added, its own capacities of feeling, or being conscious. The Nature of the thing means

---

taken, this exposition evidently ought to be the subject of much discrimination and care.

18-36. This paragraph is merely preliminary to the exposition, but contains some things important to be noted. — **18. The Socratic Elenchus,** — a kind of argument conducted mainly by searching exposition, and applied most generally to refutation of some prevailing notion. Its principal office is very well defined here. — **20. Large abstractions of this description,** — what does this sentence imply as regards their inaccuracy, and what as regards the importance of exactly defining them? — **28. A dialogue** περὶ φύσεως, — *i.e.*, concerning Nature. Plato's philosophical works are in the form of dialogue. — **32. Dialectics,** — derivation and definition? — Lines **33-35** indicate how important exposition is, as related to argumentation; compare also ll. 15-17 for its importance as related to action.

all this; means its entire capacity of exhibiting phenomena.
And since the phenomena which a thing exhibits, however
much they vary in different circumstances, are always the
same in the same circumstances, they admit of being
described in general forms of words, which are called the
laws of the thing's nature. Thus it is a law of the nature
of water that under the mean pressure of the atmosphere
at the level of the sea, it boils at 212° Fahrenheit.

As the nature of any given thing is the aggregate of its
powers and properties, so Nature in the abstract is the
aggregate of the powers and properties of all things.
Nature means the sum of all phenomena, together with
the causes which produce them; including not only all
that happens, but all that is capable of happening; the
unused capabilities of causes being as much a part of the
idea of Nature as those which take effect. Since all phenomena which have been sufficiently examined are found
to take place with regularity, each having certain fixed
conditions, positive and negative, on the occurrence of
which it invariably happens; mankind have been able to

The order pursued in this exposition is the order of investigation, or inductive; according to Rhet. p. 276, 2, 1, what kind of beginning do we expect? How is this inductive order inculcated in the Platonic method? — Point out now, from ll. **42-52**, how the word is first particularized or made concrete. What is the first definition constructed of it? Can you trace in it the genus and differentia of a logical definition? See Rhet. pp. 387, 388. — How do ll. **46-51** amplify the definition? See Rhet. p. 390, 2. — How is this amplification then summarized into a new and perhaps exacter, though less easy definition? — **52. Phenomena**, — what is the derivation and definition of this word? How does this derivation accord with the verb **exhibits**? — Evidently this second and harder definition is introduced as the basis for defining the related term *laws* of a thing's nature; construct a definition of this related term from the data given here. — How do ll. **57-59** exemplify Rhet. p. 394?

ascertain, either by direct observation or by reasoning processes grounded on it, the conditions of the occurrence of many phenomena; and the progress of science mainly consists in ascertaining those conditions. When discovered they can be expressed in general propositions, which are called laws of the particular phenomenon, and also, more generally, Laws of Nature. Thus, the truth that all material objects tend towards one another with a force directly as their masses and inversely as the square of their distance, is a law of Nature. The proposition that air and food are necessary to animal life, if it be as we have good reason to believe, true without exception, is also a law of nature, though the phenomenon of which it is the law is special, and not, like gravitation, universal.

Nature, then, in this its simplest acceptation, is a collective name for all facts, actual and possible; or (to speak more accurately) a name for the mode, partly known to us and partly unknown, in which all things take place. For the word suggests, not so much the multitudinous detail of the phenomena, as the conception which might be formed

---

From the paragraph, ll. 60–85, point out how the foregoing first definition is repeated and broadened. — How is the second, more difficult, definition repeated and broadened? — The nature of a particular thing is defined as "its entire capacity of exhibiting phenomena"; beginning the definition of Nature, in general, with "the sum of all phenomena," how much more must we add to make it as comprehensive as the other definition suggests? — Lines 67–78 repeats in more general terms what definition of the preceding paragraph? — How is exposition by exemplification employed in this paragraph? — Thus it will be seen that this paragraph corresponds very closely, as to its ideas and their grouping, with the previous one; but it represents what further stage in the inductive order which is chosen as the plan of investigation?

86–95. In this paragraph the two definitions already constructed are how simplified? — 89. **For the word suggests,** — the word *for* indi-

of their manner of existence as a mental whole, by a mind
possessing a complete knowledge of them: to which conception it is the aim of science to raise itself, by successive
steps of generalization from experience.

Such, then, is a correct definition of the word Nature.
But this definition corresponds only to one of the senses
of that ambiguous term. It is evidently inapplicable to
some of the modes in which the word is familiarly employed. For example, it entirely conflicts with the common form of speech by which Nature is opposed to Art,
and natural to artificial. For in the sense of the word
Nature which has just been defined, and which is the true
scientific sense, Art is as much Nature as anything else;
and everything which is artificial is natural — Art has no
independent powers of its own: Art is but the employment of the powers of Nature for an end. Phenomena
produced by human agency, no less than those which as
far as we are concerned are spontaneous, depend on the
properties of the elementary forces, or of the elementary
substances and their compounds. The united powers of

---

cates that a reason is given for a statement preceding; what do the lines
succeeding, **89-95**, thus explain? — What is here represented as the
object of science?

98. That ambiguous term, — what is the derivation of the word
ambiguous, and why is the term *Nature* so called? — The definition
already given leaves no room for exposition by antithesis (see Rhet.
p. 392); and yet in one of its senses the word Nature has an antithetic
term, — Art. How, in this first and scientific definition, is Art related
to Nature (ll. **102-107**)? How is this distinction amplified, ll. **107-113**?
— How do ll. **115-128** expound the idea? In each example, trace the
two sides, man's and nature's. How do laws of nature emerge from
this distinction in each case? — **128-131**. To what simple summary
and explanation is all human and artistic agency reduced here? **131**. A
good example of how the most learned exposition tends to plainness

the whole human race could not create a new property of
matter in general, or of any one of its species. We can
only take advantage for our purposes of the properties
which we find. A ship floats by the same laws of specific
gravity and equilibrium, as a tree uprooted by the wind
and blown into the water. The corn which men raise for
food, grows and produces its grain by the same laws of
vegetation by which the wild rose and the mountain straw-
berry bring forth their flowers and fruit. A house stands
and holds together by the natural properties, the weight
and cohesion of the materials which compose it: a steam
engine works by the natural expansive force of steam,
exerting a pressure upon one part of a system of arrange-
ments, which pressure, by the mechanical properties of
the lever, is transferred from that to another part where
it raises the weight or removes the obstacle brought into
connexion with it. In these and all other artificial operations the office of man is, as has often been remarked, a
very limited one; it consists in moving things into certain
places. We move objects, and by doing this, bring some
things into contact which were separate, or separate others
which were in contact : and by this simple change of place,
natural forces previously dormant are called into action,

---

and simplicity. How is this idea amplified, and how does the amplification exemplify Rhet. p. 391, 3?— The definition of Nature given
already is thus made to absorb and include all that opposes it, namely,
the idea Art, which is antithetic to some aspects of Nature.

139–148. It remains now merely to make the discrimination between
meanings, for the sake of which this exposition largely exists. What
part of the larger idea does the smaller idea of Nature, here given, include? Notice that for the definition of this smaller idea, ll. **143–146**,
the previous paragraph has been accumulating material. — From this
definition of Nature, what definition would you give to its antithesis Art?

and produce the desired effect. Even the volition which designs, the intelligence which contrives, and the muscular force which executes these movements, are themselves powers of Nature.

It thus appears that we must recognize at least two principal meanings in the word Nature. In one sense, it means all the powers existing in either the outer or the inner world and everything which takes place by means of those powers. In another sense, it means, not everything which happens, but only what takes place without the agency, or without the voluntary and intentional agency, of man. This distinction is far from exhausting the ambiguities of the word; but it is the key to most of those on which important consequences depend.

From THREE ESSAYS ON RELIGION: *Essay on* NATURE.

The language of the foregoing exposition, while simple in construction, sometimes very plain, and never ornamental, uses learned and philosophical terms freely, and evidently seeks exactness. The main definition becomes clear largely by repetition (see Rhet. p. 393); trace, for instance, the different forms that it takes.

XXIII.

JOHN RUSKIN.

OF THE PATHETIC FALLACY.

[Mr. Ruskin begins with a discussion, somewhat remote from the subject and therefore omitted here, of the philosophical terms *objective* and *subjective*, the use of which he does not like.]

Now, therefore, putting these tiresome and absurd words quite out of our way, we may go on at our ease to examine the point in question, — namely, the difference between the ordinary, proper, and true appearances of things to us; and the extraordinary, or false appearances, when we are 5 under the influence of emotion, or contemplative fancy; false appearances, I say, as being entirely unconnected

---

The foregoing Selection has given an example of Exposition put to its more strict and severe work of defining and discriminating general ideas, a work which, though nourishing and satisfying to deep thinkers, is to rapid and indolent readers dry, and indeed does not make much appeal to the literary sense, apart from the sense for definiteness and accuracy. The present Selection exemplifies the use of Exposition in literary criticism, addressed to the reader of general culture, and put in a style adapted to give pleasure as well as instruction to all.

Lines 1-9. What is the exact subject of exposition laid down in this paragraph? By what antithetical adjectives are the two sides of the subject set over against each other? Does the word proper need any antithesis? What is probably its exact meaning in the author's mind, as connected with its derivation? Why does the word false need special exegesis, in ll. 7-9? — How is this subject explained, Rhet. p. 343, bottom? — **6. Emotion . . . contemplative fancy,** — how does the Rhetoric (pp. 71, 73) connect these influences with prose style?

with any real power or character in the object, and only imputed to it by us.

For instance—

> "The spendthrift crocus, bursting through the mould
> Naked and shivering, with his cup of gold."

This is very beautiful, and yet very untrue. The crocus is not a spendthrift, but a hardy plant; its yellow is not gold, but saffron. How is it that we enjoy so much the having it put into our heads that it is anything else than a plain crocus?

It is an important question. For, throughout our past reasonings about art, we have always found that nothing could be good or useful, or ultimately pleasurable, which was untrue. But here is something pleasurable in written poetry which is nevertheless *un*true. And what is more,

---

10-17. To begin with a concrete instance, which is evidently to be explained, thus leading the subject gradually up to the general idea expounded, is to adopt what order of procedure? See Rhet. pp. 276–279. How does this comport with the character of the subject?—
11. The couplet here quoted is from Oliver Wendell Holmes, given, according to a footnote, at second hand, as "quoted by Miss Mitford, in her Recollections of a Literary Life."— The several quotations given, as far as l. 104, serve to introduce and illustrate, in a concrete way, the various aspects of the subject.

And first of all, what question, l. **15**, opens the discussion? Note how much more hearty and homely interest is given to the subject by putting the question in plain language instead of philosophical,—"the having it put into our heads that," etc., instead of, e.g. *the fallacious subjective impression that*, etc. It is very largely this employment of everyday language that makes the present exposition so interesting.

18-25. How is the foregoing question related to the general principle of truth?— 20. **Which was untrue,**—if instead of this expression we should say "unless it was true," how would the relation of the suc-

if we think over our favorite poetry, we shall find it full of this kind of fallacy, and that we like it all the more for being so.

It will appear also, on consideration of the matter, that this fallacy is of two principal kinds. Either, as in this case of the crocus, it is the fallacy of wilful fancy, which involves no real expectation that it will be believed; or else it is a fallacy caused by an excited state of the feelings, making us, for the time, more or less irrational. Of the cheating of the fancy we shall have to speak presently; but, in this chapter, I want to examine the nature of the other error, that which the mind admits, when affected strongly by emotion. Thus, for instance, in Alton Locke: —

> "They rowed her in across the rolling foam —
> The cruel, crawling foam."

The foam is not cruel, neither does it crawl. The state of mind which attributes to it these characters of a living creature is one in which the reason is unhinged by grief. All violent feelings have the same effect. They produce in us a falseness in all our impressions of external things, which I would generally characterize as the "Pathetic Fallacy."

---

ceeding antithesis, l. 22, be put in clearer light? — **24. This kind of fallacy,** — here is suggested the main term of the subject expounded; define a fallacy.

27–45. This fallacy, once introduced, is after all too broad a term for the present discussion. Explain how it is narrowed, by Rhet. p. 396, III. On what principle is the division made? See Rhet. p. 397. — Of the two members, one is chosen for present treatment: what is done with the other? — Of the exposition of the member chosen, explain the first step by Rhet. p. 394. How does the example fulfil the requisite

Now we are in the habit of considering this fallacy as eminently a character of poetical description, and the temper of mind in which we allow it, as one eminently poetical, because passionate. But, I believe, if we look well into the matter, that we shall find the greatest poets do not often admit this kind of falseness, — that it is only the second order of poets who much delight in it.

Thus, when Dante describes the spirits falling from the bank of Acheron "as dead leaves flutter from a bough," he gives the most perfect image possible of their utter lightness, feebleness, passiveness, and scattering agony of despair, without, however, for an instant losing his own clear perception that *these* are souls, and *those* are leaves: he makes no confusion of one with the other. But when Coleridge speaks of

"The one red leaf, the last of its clan,
That dances as often as dance it can,"

he has a morbid, that is to say, a so far false, idea about the leaf: he fancies a life in it, and will, which there are

---

at the bottom of the page? — What general proposition is deduced from this step of exposition, and what general term? Explain the word **pathetic**, l. **44**, comparing its meaning here with its derivation.

46–52. Having thus deduced and defined the object expounded, the author proceeds to give it what place and application in poetical literature? This leads, in ll. **49–52**, to what classification of poets? In a footnote to this paragraph, Ruskin says: "I admit two orders of poets, but no third; and by these two orders I mean the Creative (Shakspere, Homer, Dante), and Reflective or Perceptive (Wordsworth, Keats, Tennyson). But both of these must be *first*-rate in their range, though their range is different; and with poetry second-rate in *quality* no one ought to be allowed to trouble mankind."

53–89. In this paragraph three examples are adduced, as basis for a succeeding step in the exposition. — What does the quotation from

not; confuses its powerlessness with choice, its fading
death with merriment, and the wind that shakes it with
music. Here, however, there is some beauty, even in the
morbid passage; but take an instance in Homer and Pope.
Without the knowledge of Ulysses, Elpenor, his youngest
follower, has fallen from an upper chamber in the Circean
palace, and has been left dead, unmissed by his leader, or
companions, in the haste of their departure. They cross
the sea to the Cimmerian land; and Ulysses summons the
shades from Tartarus. The first which appears is that of
the lost Elpenor. Ulysses, amazed, and in exactly the
spirit of bitter and terrified lightness which is seen in
Hamlet, addresses the spirit with the simple, startled
words: —

"Elpenor! How camest thou under the Shadowy darkness? Hast thou come faster on foot than I in my black ship?"

Which Pope renders thus: —

"O, say, what angry power Elpenor led
To glide in shades, and wander with the dead?
How could thy soul, by realms and seas disjoined,
Outfly the nimble sail, and leave the lagging wind?"

I sincerely hope the reader finds no pleasure here, either in the nimbleness of the sail, or the laziness of the wind!

Dante exemplify? Observe how, in his vivid imagination of the spirits in Acheron, the descriptive impulse seizes Ruskin, in ll. **55, 56,** and culminates in the striking phrase **scattering agony of despair**; what force in the epithet? — What does the quotation from Coleridge exemplify? — **63. Morbid,** — what is the derivation of this word, and in what sense is it used here? — The quotation from Pope leads to what contrast with Coleridge? (Cf. ll. 86, 87 with l. 67.) — **76. Which is seen in Hamlet,** — the reference is to the line, Hamlet, Act I,

And yet how is it that these conceits are so painful now, when they have been pleasant to us in the other instances? For a very simple reason. They are not a *pathetic* fallacy at all, for they are put into the mouth of the wrong passion — a passion which never could possibly have spoken them — agonized curiosity. Ulysses wants to know the facts of the matter; and the very last thing his mind could do at the moment would be to pause, or suggest in any wise what was *not* a fact. The delay in the first three lines, and conceit in the last, jar upon us instantly, like the most frightful discord in music. No poet of true imaginative power could possibly have written the passage.

Therefore, we see that the spirit of truth must guide us in some sort, even in our enjoyment of fallacy. Coleridge's fallacy has no discord in it, but Pope's has set our teeth on edge. Without farther questioning, I will endeavor to state the main bearings of this matter.

The temperament which admits the pathetic fallacy, is, as I said above, that of a mind and body in some sort too

---

sc. v., where Hamlet addresses the ghost of his father, "Well said, old mole! canst work i' the ground so fast?" — **88.** Compare the question here deduced with the question already asked, l. **15.** It denotes, as we see, an antithetic phase of the subject.

90-99. Compare the answer to the question, as contained in this paragraph, with the case of the quotation from Coleridge. Why is the latter more natural and true? — **96. The delay in the first three lines,** — explain how this delay is effected. — **Conceit,** — compare l. **88.** What is meant by a *conceit*, as the word is here used?

100-104. The answer to the foregoing question, like the former (ll. 18-22) is related to the principle of truth. — **101. In some sort,** — in what sort, then, as here revealed, must "the spirit of truth guide us even in our enjoyment of fallacy"? — At this point (l. 104), the concrete instances are all in, to serve as a basis for explaining "the main bearings" of the matter; so here begins the more abstract portion.

weak to deal fully with what is before them or upon them;
borne away, or over-clouded, or over-dazzled by emotion;
and it is a more or less noble state, according to the force
of the emotion which has induced it. For it is no credit
to a man that he is not morbid or inaccurate in his percep-
tions, when he has no strength of feeling to **warp** them;
and it is in general a sign of higher capacity and stand in
the ranks of **being,** that the emotions should be strong
enough to vanquish, partly, the intellect, and make it
believe what they choose. But it is still a grander condition when the intellect also rises, till it is strong enough
to assert its rule against, or together with, the utmost
efforts of the passions; and the whole man stands in an
iron glow, white hot, perhaps, but still strong, and in no-
wise evaporating; **even if he melts, losing none of** his
weight.

So, then, **we** have the three **ranks:** the man who per-

Lines 105–188 constitute a new section of the exposition, in which the human mind is estimated according to its relation to the pathetic fallacy, **and men** are classified on that basis.

105–122. This paragraph works out, in a general way, a **basis, or** furnishes material, in a brief psychological study, for the classification. In the first sentence, ll. **105–110,** to what one cause, or principle, is the pathetic fallacy reduced? — **108.** What figure of speech do you notice here, and what does it effect? Do you see in it a casual exposition by division? — **110. For it is no credit,** — the word *for* indicates that this sentence gives a reason for something; what is that something here accounted for, and is it expressed or implied? — How do the sentences, ll. **110–122,** exemplify Rhet. p. **105?** — Point out, in this paragraph, **how** metaphor and trope are **used to make the** abstract ideas vivid; also personification. — **119–122.** In these lines the man is associated with what material, and is the metaphor consistent throughout? — An iron glow, — what is the force of this epithet?

123–137. These lines contain the first, or preliminary classification,

ceives rightly, because he does not feel, and to whom the primrose is very accurately the primrose, because he does not love it. Then, secondly, the man who perceives wrongly, because he feels, and to whom the primrose is anything else than a primrose: a star, or a sun, or a fairy's shield, or a forsaken maiden. And then, lastly, there is the man who perceives rightly in spite of his feelings, and to whom the primrose is forever nothing else than itself — a little flower, apprehended in the very plain and leafy fact of it, whatever and how many soever the associations and passions may be, that crowd around it. And, in general, these three classes may be rated in comparative order, as the men who are not poets at all, and the poets of the second order, and the poets of the first; only, however great a man may be, there are always some subjects which *ought* to throw him off his balance; some, by which his poor human capacity of thought should be conquered, and brought into the inaccurate and vague state of perception, so that the language of the highest inspiration becomes broken, obscure, and wild in metaphor, resembling that of the weaker man, overborne by weaker things.

And thus, in full, there are four classes: the men who feel nothing, and therefore see truly; the men who feel

---

sufficient to include the data given in the previous paragraph, but confessedly incomplete. On what principle of division are men classified? See Rhet. p. 397. — How is each member of the division made concrete and plain? — Finally, how does he *name* the three classes? — **137–144.** What consideration, expressed in these lines, makes it evident that this preliminary division is not complete? How does this therefore, by transgression, illustrate Rhet. p. 398, 1? What is the use in adopting an incomplete division thus deliberately, and completing it before the reader's eyes?

145–153. Draw out the division here given, and put it in tabular

strongly, think weakly, and see untruly (second order of
poets); the men who feel strongly, think strongly, and see
truly (first order of poets); and the men who, strong as
human creatures can be, are yet submitted to influences 150
stronger than they, and see in a sort untruly, because what
they see is inconceivably above them. This last is the
usual condition of prophetic inspiration.

I separate these classes, in order that their character
may be clearly understood; but of course they are united 155
each to the other by imperceptible transitions, and the
same mind, according to the influences to which it is subjected, passes at different times into the various states.
Still, the difference between the great and less man is, on
the whole, chiefly in this point of *alterability*. That is to 160
say, the one knows too much, and perceives and feels too
much of the past and future, and of all things beside and
around that which immediately affects him, to be in any
wise shaken by it. His mind is made up; his thoughts
have an accustomed current; his ways are stedfast; it is 165
not this or that new sight which will at once unbalance
him. He is tender to impression at the surface, like a
rock with deep moss upon it; but there is too much mass
of him to be moved. The smaller man, with the same

---

form. What is there, in the range over which it extends, to guarantee
that it is complete, that is, that it is fully commensurate with the divided whole? See Rhet. p. 398, 1. Does the division also agree with
Rhet. p. 399, 2? — How does the division stand the test of the three
Rules of Division, given Rhet. pp. 400 and 401?

154-158. What is there in these lines to indicate that Ruskin regards the object expounded as a *concept* of the mind (cf. Rhet. pp. 384,
385), rather than as an object of sense? — **160. Alterability,** — how
is this quality expounded in what succeeds? — **167. He is tender to
impression, etc.,** — what is the utility of the simile that follows, and

170 degree of sensibility, is at once carried off his feet; he
wants to do something he did not want to do before; he
views all the universe in a new light through his tears;
he is gay or enthusiastic, melancholy or passionate, as
things come and go to him. Therefore the high creative
175 poet might even be thought, to a great extent, impassive
(as shallow people think Dante stern), receiving indeed all
feelings to the full, but having a great centre of reflection
and knowledge in which he stands serene, and watches the
feeling, as it were, from far off.
180 Dante, in his most intense moods, has entire command
of himself, and can look around calmly, at all moments,
for the image or the word that will best tell what he sees
to the upper or lower world. But Keats and Tennyson,
and the poets of the second order, are generally themselves
185 subdued by the feelings under which they write, or, at
least, write as choosing to be so, and therefore admit certain expressions and modes of thought which are in some
sort diseased or false.

Now so long as we see that the *feeling* is true, we par-

---

is it to be regarded as an ornament? — **169-174**. Point out the homely
and everyday language here used for expository purposes, — a good
illustration, but no better than many another in this same Selection, of
the kind of expression that should be sought for such difficult work. —
174. Therefore, — this sentence is illative to what preceding idea?

180-188. How does this paragraph exemplify Rhet. p. 394? — **185.**
Note the saving clause here, indicative of carefulness of statement.
Such carefulness is evidence in itself of broad thinking; how?

At this point the exposition proper, in its definitions and divisions,
is complete; and from l. 189 to the end, the treatment consists of a
series of examples and explanations, designed to bring out more clearly
various aspects of the subject. How is this object indicated, and comprising what features, in ll. **422-426**?

189-208. With what aspect of the case does this paragraph deal?

don, or are even pleased by, the confessed fallacy of sight which it induces: we are pleased, for instance, with those lines of Kingsley's, above quoted, not because they fallaciously describe foam, but because they faithfully describe sorrow. But the moment the mind of the speaker becomes cold, that moment every such expression becomes untrue, as being forever untrue in the external facts. And there is no greater baseness in literature than the habit of using these metaphorical expressions in cool blood. An inspired writer, in full impetuosity of passion, may speak wisely and truly of "raging waves of the sea, foaming out their own shame"; but it is only the basest writer who cannot speak of the sea without talking of "raging waves," "remorseless floods," "ravenous billows," and so forth; and it is one of the signs of the highest power in a writer to check all such habits of thought, and to keep his eyes fixed firmly on the *pure fact*, out of which if any feeling comes to him or his reader, he knows it must be a true one.

To keep to the waves, I forget who it is who represents a man in despair, desiring that his body may be cast into the sea,

"*Whose changing mound, and foam that passed away*,
Might mock the eye that questioned where I lay."

Show how exposition by antithesis and exposition by exemplification are combined. — **192-194.** How does the antithetic statement here made illustrate Rhet. p. 349? — How do ll. **196-208** corroborate Rhet. p. 47, rule 15?

209. To keep to the waves, — a reminiscence, probably, of the example last recalled to mind, l. 191, with perhaps an indirect allusion to the one last quoted, ll. 79-85, which, however, is only remotely associated with waves. What advantage (see other examples, ll. 53-62, ll. 375-410) in thus preserving parallelism of suggestion in the exam-

Observe, there is not a single false or even overcharged expression. "Mound" of the sea-wave is perfectly simple and true; "changing" is as familiar as may be; "foam that passed away," strictly literal; and the whole line descriptive of the reality with a degree of accuracy which I know not any other verse, in the range of poetry, that altogether equals. For most people have not a distinct idea of the clumsiness and massiveness of a large wave. The word "wave" is used too generally of ripples and breakers, and bendings in light drapery or grass: it does not by itself convey a perfect image. But the word "mound" is heavy, large, dark, definite; there is no mistaking the kind of wave meant, nor missing the sight of it. Then the term "changing" has a peculiar force also. Most people think of waves as rising and falling. But if they look at the sea carefully, they will perceive that the waves do not rise and fall. They change. Change both place and form, but they do not fall; one wave goes on, and on, and still on; now lower, now higher, now tossing its mane like a horse, now building itself together like a wall, now shaking, now steady, but still the same wave, till at last it seems struck by something, and changes, one knows not how, — becomes another wave.

The close of the line insists on this image, and paints it still more perfectly, — "foam that passed away." Not

---

ples? — How does the section ll. **214-227**, in the kind of exposition employed, exemplify Rhet. p. 390, 2? — How do ll. **227-236** answer to Rhet. p. 391, 3? What striking metaphor, almost like a personification, betrays the writer's descriptive delight in portraying the object? How does the same figure exemplify Rhet. p. 92, 3?

240. The absolute ocean fact, — how does this substantiate ll. 203-208? Observe, in order to express himself with exactness and vigor, both of which qualities are here needed, the author turns a noun

merely melting, disappearing, but passing on, out of sight, on the career of the wave. Then, having put the absolute ocean fact as far as he may before our eyes, the poet leaves us to feel about it as we may, and to trace for ourselves the opposite fact,—the image of the green mounds that do not change, and the white and written stones that do not pass away; and thence to follow out also the associated images of the calm life with the quiet grave, and the despairing life with the fading foam: —

"Let no man move his bones."
"As for Samaria, her king is cut off like the foam upon the water."

But nothing of this is actually told or pointed out, and the expressions, as they stand, are perfectly severe and accurate, utterly uninfluenced by the firmly governed emotion of the writer. Even the word "mock" is hardly an exception, as it may stand merely for "deceive" or "defeat," without implying any impersonation of the waves.

It may be well, perhaps, to give one or two more instances to show the peculiar dignity possessed by all pas-

---

into an adjective. It is an epithet employed not for picturesqueness, but for condensed energy. — **242. And trace for ourselves the opposite fact**, — what kind of exposition is here employed? — **248, 249.** The two citations here given quite break off the grammatical continuity; why are they introduced, and what do they exemplify?

251. Perfectly severe, — what is the exact force of this word, as here used? How distinguished from **accurate**, l. 252? — **253-255.** What evidence of care in the study and estimation of words? There is no procedure so particular as exposition in measuring and maintaining the exact suggestion of words, and Ruskin's exposition is fully worthy of the requirement.

256-259. What is the object in giving the coming instances, and by what one word best represented? How does this object differ from the one last in mind (ll. 189-191)? — **256. One or two more instances,**

sages which thus limit their expression to the pure fact, and leave the hearer to gather what he can from it. Here is a notable one from the Iliad. Helen, looking from the Scæan gate of Troy over the Grecian host, and telling Priam the names of its captains, says at last : —

"I see all the other dark-eyed Greeks; but two I cannot see, — Castor and Pollux, — whom one mother bore with me. Have they not followed from fair Lacedæmon, or have they indeed come in their sea-wandering ships, but now will not enter into the battle of men, fearing the shame and the scorn that is in me?"

Then Homer : —

"So she spoke. But them, already, the life-giving earth possessed, there in Lacedæmon, in the dear fatherland."

Note, here, the high poetical truth carried to the extreme. The poet has to speak of the earth in sadness, but he will not let that sadness affect or change his thoughts of it. No; though Castor and Pollux be dead, yet the earth is our mother still, fruitful, life-giving. These are the facts of the thing. I see nothing else than these. Make what you will of them. . . .

— only one of the instances is quoted here, though the author gives two ; the second, though a fine instance, depends for its effect on the reader's understanding of a French poem, of which it quotes thirty-six lines.

271-277. On what antithesis does the effectiveness of this instance depend? — **275, 277.** Note the effect of the short sentences, and compare Rhet. p. 186, 1. The same manner of expression is employed, at greater length, in the comment on the French poem mentioned above : " Yes, that is the fact of it. Right or wrong, the poet does not say. What you may think about it, he does not know. He has nothing to do with that. There lie the ashes of the dead girl in her chamber. There they danced, till the morning, at the Ambassador's of France. Make what you will of it." Curious examples these, of the effect of instances of a peculiar kind on the writer's manner of expression.

Now in this there is the exact type of the consummate poetical temperament. For, be it clearly and constantly remembered, that the greatness of a poet depends upon the two faculties, acuteness of feeling, and command of it. A poet is great, first in proportion to the strength of his passion, and then, that strength being granted, in proportion to his government of it; there being, however, always a point beyond which it would be inhuman and monstrous if he pushed this government, and, therefore, a point at which all feverish and wild fancy becomes just and true. Thus the destruction of the kingdom of Assyria cannot be contemplated firmly by a prophet of Israel. The fact is too great, too wonderful. It overthrows him, dashes him into a confused element of dreams. All the world is, to his stunned thought, full of strange voices. "Yea, the fir-trees rejoice at thee, and the cedars of Lebanon, saying, Since thou art gone down to the grave, no feller is come up against us." So, still more, the thought of the presence of Deity cannot be borne without this great astonishment. "The mountains and the hills shall break forth before you into singing, and all the trees of the field shall clap their hands."

---

277. The instance here omitted, with the comment thereon, takes up about a page and a half of the original.

278–282. The explanation here given virtually repeats what has already been asserted, ll. 49–52; how does it add to and complete it? — **284–298.** The explanation here added is quite necessary, or at least very serviceable, to open further an idea that has been merely suggested before (ll. 137–144; 149–153), but not exemplified. — The Scripture citations, ll. 292 and 297, which may be found in Isaiah xiv. 8 and lv. 12, evidence Ruskin's intimate familiarity not only with the words but with the very tissue and spirit of the Bible, a familiarity which, more than any other one thing perhaps, has operated to form both his literary style and his general view of things.

300 But by how much this feeling is noble when it is justified by the strength of its cause, by so much it is ignoble when there is not cause enough for it; and beyond all other ignobleness is the mere affectation of it, in hardness of heart. Simply bad writing may almost always, as above 305 noticed, be known by its adoption of these fanciful metaphorical expressions, as a sort of current coin; yet there is even a worse, at least a more harmful, condition of writing than this, in which such expressions are not ignorantly and feelinglessly caught up, but, by some master, skilful in 310 handling, yet insincere, deliberately wrought out with chill and studied fancy; as if we should try to make an old lava stream look red-hot again, by covering it with dead leaves, or white-hot, with hoar frost.

When Young is lost in veneration, as he dwells on the 315 character of a truly good and holy man, he permits himself for a moment to be overborne by the feeling so far as to exclaim —

> "Where shall I find him? angels, tell me where.
> You know him; he is near you; point him out.
> 320 Shall I see glories beaming from his brow,
> Or trace his footsteps by the rising flowers?"

Do lines 90–104, preceding, require the further elucidation given to the idea with which they deal, in ll. **300–361**? — **304. As above noticed,** — see ll. 194–203. — **307. A worse, at least a more harmful,** — what is the advantage of the second of these words over the first? Cf. Rhet. p. 31, note. Why use the first at all, if it is to be so immediately corrected?

308. Are not, etc., but, etc., — note the different orders of the verbs in these two clauses; what stress is thus effected? — **310. Chill and studied fancy,** — note how much more effective is this epithet *chill* than the word *cold* would be. Why? — **311–313.** Analyze the figure here by Rhet. p. 395.

314 sq. The quotation from Young may be "true and right" as regards emotion, but it is not very remarkable poetry. How does it *flat*

This emotion has a worthy cause, and is thus true and right. But now hear the cold-hearted Pope say to a shepherd girl:—

> "Where'er you walk, cool gales shall fan the glade! 325
> Trees, where you sit, shall crowd into a shade;
> Your praise the birds shall chant in every grove,
> And winds shall waft it to the powers above.
> But would you sing, and rival Orpheus' strain,
> The wondering forests soon should dance again; 330
> The moving mountains hear the powerful call,
> And headlong streams hang, listening, in their fall."

This is not, nor could it for a moment be mistaken for, the language of passion. It is simple falsehood, uttered by hypocrisy; definite absurdity, rooted in affectation, and 335 coldly asserted in the teeth of nature and fact. Passion will indeed go far in deceiving itself; but it must be a strong passion, not the simple wish of a lover to tempt his mistress to sing. Compare a very closely parallel passage in Wordsworth, in which the lover has lost his mistress:— 340

> "Three years had Barbara in her grave been laid,
> When thus his moan he made:—
>
> 'Oh, move, thou cottage, from behind yon oak,
> Or let the ancient tree uprooted lie,
> That in some other way yon smoke 345
> May mount into the sky.

---

a note, as described and exemplified Rhet. p. 83?— From the foregoing it appears that this citation from Young is introduced merely to prepare for and set off by antithesis the succeeding from Pope. — Exactly what does the citation from Pope exemplify?— How do the lines, and especially ll. **331, 332**, exemplify what is said of hyperbole, Rhet. p. 99?— What consideration, according to Ruskin, saves the citation from Wordsworth, ll. **341–350**, from being overstrained and ludicrous? Point out exactly what it illustrates.

'If still behind yon pine-tree's ragged bough,
   Headlong, the waterfall must come,
   Oh, let it, then, be dumb —
350   Be anything, sweet stream, but that which thou art now.'"

Here is a cottage to be moved, if not a mountain, and a waterfall to be silent, if it is not to hang listening; but with what different relation to the mind that contemplates them! Here, in the extremity of its agony, the soul cries out wildly
355 for relief, which at the same moment it partly knows to be impossible, but partly believes possible, in a vague impression that a miracle *might* be wrought to give relief even to a less sore distress, — that nature is kind, and God is kind, and that grief is strong; it knows not well what *is* possible
360 to such grief. To silence a stream, to move a cottage wall, — one might think it could do as much as that!

I believe these instances are enough to illustrate the main point I insist upon respecting the pathetic fallacy, — that so far as it *is* a fallacy, it is always the sign of a mor-
365 bid state of mind, and comparatively of a weak one. Even in the most inspired prophet it is a sign of the incapacity of his human sight or thought to bear what has been revealed to it. In ordinary poetry, if it is found in the thoughts of the poet himself, it is at once a sign of his
370 belonging to the inferior school; if in the thoughts of the characters imagined by him, it is right or wrong according to the genuineness of the emotion from which it springs; always, however, implying necessarily *some* degree of weakness in the character.

362-374. In this paragraph the author begins to summarize his thought. — **364. A morbid state of mind,** — in what sense are we to take the term *morbid* here? It is evidently to be regarded as not inconsistent with the possibility of being right as well as wrong (l. 371). — **373. Some degree of weakness,** — how is this implication related

Take two most exquisite instances from master hands. 375
The Jessy of Shenstone, and the Ellen of Wordsworth,
have both been betrayed and deserted. Jessy, in the
course of her most touching complaint, says : —

> " If through the garden's flowery tribes I stray,
>   Where bloom the jasmines that could once allure, 380
> ' Hope not to find delight in us,' they say,
>   ' For we are spotless, Jessy, we are pure.' "

Compare with this some of the words of Ellen : —

> " ' Ah, why,' said Ellen, sighing to herself,
> ' Why do not words, and kiss, and solemn pledge, 385
> And nature, that is kind in woman's breast,
> And reason, that in man is wise and good,
> And fear of Him who is a righteous Judge, —
> Why do not these prevail for human life,
> To keep two hearts together, that began 390
> Their springtime with one love, and that have need
> Of mutual pity and forgiveness, sweet
> To grant, or be received ; while that poor bird —
> O, come and hear him ! Thou who hast to me
> Been faithless, hear him ; — though a lowly creature, 395
> One of God's simple children, that yet know not
> The Universal Parent, *how* he sings !
> As if he wished the firmament of heaven
> Should listen, and give back to him the voice
> Of his triumphant constancy and love. 400
> The proclamation that he makes, how far
> His darkness doth transcend our fickle light.' "

---

to the examples further adduced? — see the explanation of them, ll.
405-421. — **377. Have both, etc.**, — compare note on l. 209. — **405.
Insuperable**, — a rather unusual sense in which to employ the word.
Can you suggest an equivalent? — **405-421**. Exactly what phase of the
subject do these examples round out and illustrate?

The perfection of both these passages, as far as regards truth and tenderness of imagination in the two poets, is quite insuperable. But, of the two characters imagined, Jessy is weaker than Ellen, exactly in so far as something appears to her to be in nature which is not. The flowers do not really reproach her. God meant them to comfort her, not to taunt her; they would do so if she saw them rightly.

Ellen, on the other hand, is quite above the slightest erring emotion. There is not the barest film of fallacy in all her thoughts. She reasons as calmly as if she did not feel. And, although the singing of the bird suggests to her the idea of its desiring to be heard in heaven, she does not for an instant admit any veracity in the thought. "As if," she says, — "I know he means nothing of the kind; but it does verily seem as if." The reader will find, by examining the rest of the poem, that Ellen's character is throughout consistent in this clear though passionate strength.

It then being, I hope, now made clear to the reader in all respects that the pathetic fallacy is powerful only so far as it is pathetic, feeble so far as it is fallacious, and, therefore, that the dominion of Truth is entire, over this, as over every other natural and just state of the human mind, we may go on to the subject for the dealing with which this prefatory inquiry became necessary; and why necessary, we shall see forthwith.

From MODERN PAINTERS, Vol. III.

422-426. Another summary, introduced subordinately, but adding an important element of definition to the previous one, ll. 362-374. What does it add to that? — **424. Feeble,** — this word stands here, by way of antithesis to *powerful*, in l. 423, as the equivalent of *morbid* and *weak*, ll. 364, 365. — **And therefore,** etc., — how does this summarize and complete what is said previously, ll. **100, 101**?

NOTES ON EXPOSITION IN PREVIOUS SELECTIONS.

SEVERAL of the Selections already given, being expository, may be profitably studied both for the individual qualities they display, as to choice and treatment of subject, and for the models of exposition that they afford, to guide and influence other writers. Let us look at a few of the more prominent features of them.

De Quincey : Pages 8–16. — Quite in accordance with the refined and refining quality of his mind, De Quincey has chosen a peculiarly subtle idea to expound. What is it, as gathered from the first paragraph, ll. **1–9**?

The exposition groups itself around two questions: 1. What object is to be accomplished (defined in ll. 37–84); and 2. How the knocking at the gate works in accomplishing it (set forth in ll. 84–132).

1. In defining the object to be accomplished, what change is to be wrought in our ordinary view of murder? What gives importance to the close exposition of the idea of sympathy? Explain ll. **51–53**, together with the note thereon, by Rhet. p. 389, 1. How is this object necessitated by the claims of poetry? — In the case before us, in order to satisfy the claims of poetical treatment, what antithesis (notice that De Quincey views this as an instrument of exposition, l. 74) must be presented, and how does the character of Duncan affect the requirement of it, as to energy? Exactly what office does De Quincey attribute to the knocking at the gate (l. **82**) in promoting the object?

2. In setting forth this office of the knocking at the gate, what means of exposition is first used, ll. **84–113**? See Rhet. p. 395. Do the two cases illustrate exactly the same point? Cf. ll. 86 and 99. — What call is there to labor, as De Quincey evidently does, to make the description of the city streets, ll. **89–95**, particularly vivid, and what kind of exposition does this involve? How does he explain his object, l. **103**? — In *applying* his analogies to the case in hand, on what means of exposition does he bestow especial labor, in ll. **115–124**, also ll. **124–132**? See Rhet. p. 393. Does the importance of these passages in the treatment require such pains?

Professor Minto says of De Quincey, "The great obstacle to his success in exposition was the want of simplicity. He was . . . too persistently scholastic for the ordinary reader, making an almost ostentatious use of logical forms and scientific technicalities." Can you point out instances of this over-learnedness, as measured by the requirements of the subject (which in this case is especially subtle), and as related to the capacity of the readers to whom such a subject would appeal?

Burke: Pages 18–23. — The idea of National Chivalry, here expounded, is an idea of very different kind from that treated by De Quincey, and potent in a very different region, so to say, of the human mind. It is an oratorical idea, and we may call this, although occurring in a discourse published in epistolary form, a good example of oratorical exposition. We look therefore for the expedients of spoken discourse, and for the more large and striking expository elements.

The idea being introduced, l. **18**, what step of exposition is first taken, ll. **18–20**? By what means of exposition is this followed, ll. **20–31**? For both of these questions, see Rhet. p. 393; and compare Rhet. pp. 293, 3, and 292, 1. What expository force have the lines **1–18**, which precede the introduction of the idea?

It is only indirectly that the exposition of the idea of National Chivalry enters into the treatment of Burke's present subject; but the succeeding paragraphs, by defining its effect in civilization, and the baneful effect of its opposite on national temper and the commonwealth, deepens and broadens our idea of what it is, and what is its importance.

Huxley: Pages 67–75. — What idea has the author to expound? What means of exposition is used, ll. **9–55**? Trace it. — How is exposition by definition employed, ll. **122–136**? Explain by Rhet. p. 391, 3.

Newman: Pages 76–80. — Trace the analogy, ll. **1–45**, and evolve from it a definition of the author's idea. — How is the paragraph, ll. **46–68**, related to the exposition of the idea? Does it set it forth directly? — How is the analogy modified in the paragraph, ll. **69–83**, and what different phase of the idea does it elucidate, as compared with the first paragraph?

Addison: Pages 141–146. — How does the exposition of the obverse enter into the presentation of Addison's idea? — What is the most useful and striking means of exposition that he employs, in the first paragraph? By what expository means is the subject finished and applied?

XXIV.

JOHN TYNDALL.

THE METEORIC THEORY OF THE SUN'S HEAT.

IF we know the velocity and weight of any projectile, we can calculate with ease the amount of heat developed by the destruction of its moving force. For example, knowing as we do the weight of the earth and the velocity with which it moves through space, a simple calculation enables 5 us to state the exact amount of heat which would be developed, supposing the earth to strike against a target

---

The principles of Argumentation are so numerous and complex that it would take much more space than this Handbook has at command to exemplify them all. Some of the more usual and important aspects of the subject, however, will be studied in this Selection and the one following; which presuppose a knowledge of the Rhetoric as far as page 446.

The present Selection exemplifies some of the main procedures of an Inductive Argument (Rhet. pp. 416–423), as applied to scientific investigation. The argument invites our study as literature, its aim being not only scholarly but popular; or, as the author defines the aim of the book from which it is taken, "to combine soundness of matter with a style which should arouse interest and sympathy in persons uncultured in science." It may thus be regarded as a fair specimen of the kind of writing which has done so much in this century to popularize scientific culture and modes of thought.

For what basis do we look, according to Rhet. p. 416, as the beginning of our induction? How is this requisite supplied, in ll. **24–28**? Is the argument to be *a priori* or *a posteriori?* See Rhet. p. 417.

A hypothesis is not "made up out of whole cloth"; there are always

strong enough to stop its motion. We could tell, for example, the number of degrees which this amount of heat would impart to a globe of water equal to the earth in size. Mayer and Helmholtz have made this calculation, and found that the quantity of heat which would be generated by this colossal shock would be quite sufficient, not only to fuse the entire earth, but to reduce it, in great part, to vapor. Thus, by the simple stoppage of the earth in its orbit, "the elements" might be caused "to melt with fervent heat." The amount of heat thus developed would be equal to that derived from the combustion of fourteen globes of coal, each equal to the earth in magnitude. And if, after the stoppage of its motion, the earth should fall into the sun, as it assuredly would, the amount of heat generated by the blow would be equal to that developed by the combustion of 5,600 worlds of solid carbon.

Knowledge such as that which you now possess has caused philosophers, in speculating on the mode in which the sun's power is maintained, to suppose the solar heat and light to be caused by the showering down of meteoric matter upon the sun's surface. The Zodiacal Light is supposed to be a cloud of meteorites, and from it, it has been

---

some facts, lying on the surface as it were, that go to make it to some degree probable. How does the first paragraph, ll. **1-23**, contribute to such probability? Does it deal with an actual cause, or with a possible one? Does it deal with a cause which, if actual, would be adequate to produce the known effect? Exactly what, then, may we infer as looking toward the hypothesis here laid down?

24-38. What phenomenon is so accounted for here as to give color to the theory here propounded? Is this in itself a conclusive indication? How would you define its nature, from Rhet. p. 419? How does the author manifest toward this argument the caution inculcated Rhet. p. 419? From ll. **36-38**, in what line of questioning must the strength of the investigation be spent?

imagined, the rain of meteoric matter was derived. Now, the whatever be the value of this speculation, it is to be borne in mind that the pouring down of meteors in the way indicated would be competent to produce the light and heat of the sun. I shall develop the theory on a future occasion. With regard to its probable truth or fallacy, it is not necessary that I should offer an opinion; the theory deals with a cause which, if in sufficient operation, would certainly be competent to produce the effects ascribed to it.

* * * * * *

The total amount of solar heat received by the earth in a year, if distributed uniformly over the earth's surface, would be sufficient to liquefy a layer of ice one hundred feet thick, and covering the whole earth. It would also heat an ocean of fresh water sixty-six miles deep, from the temperature of melting ice to the temperature of ebullition.

Knowing thus the annual receipt of the earth, we can calculate the entire quantity of heat emitted by the sun in a year. Conceive a hollow sphere to surround the sun, its centre being the sun's centre, and its surface at the distance of the earth from the sun. The section of the earth

---

This first part of the treatment, which lays down the hypothesis and shows what makes it antecedently probable, is taken from the early part of the treatise; what follows, taken from near the end of the volume, is the fulfilment of the promise made in line 34.

In order to reason rightly from a known effect to its unknown cause, two things must be presented with care and clearness: 1. Exactly the extent of the effect to be accounted for; 2. The adequacy of the postulated cause to account for it.

With which of these do ll. **39–64** deal? How does the author's aim, expressed at the beginning, explain the manner in which he gives these estimates, in terms of combustion, liquefaction, and ebullition, instead of by some scientific unit? Why expressed in several ways? Trace

cut by this surface is, to the whole area of the hollow sphere, as 1 : 2,300,000,000; hence, the quantity of solar heat intercepted by the earth is only $\frac{1}{2300000000}$ of the total radiation.

55 The heat emitted by the sun, if used to melt a stratum of ice applied to the sun's surface, would liquefy the ice at the rate of 2,400 feet an hour. It would boil, per hour, 700,000 millions of cubic miles of ice-cold water. Expressed in another form, the heat given out by the sun, 60 per hour, is equal to that which would be generated by the combustion of a layer of solid coal, ten feet thick, entirely surrounding the sun; hence, the heat emitted in a year is equal to that which would be produced by the combustion of a layer of coal seventeen miles in thickness.

65 This, then, is the sun's expenditure which has been going on for ages, without our being able, in historic times, to detect the loss. When the tolling of a bell is heard at a distance, the sonorous vibrations are quickly wasted, and renewed strokes are necessary to maintain the sound. Like 70 the bell —

"Die Sonne tönt nach alter Weise."

But how is its tone sustained? How is the perennial loss made good? We are apt to overlook the wonderful in the common. Possibly to many of us — and even to some 75 of the most enlightened among us — the sun appears as

---

what part each of the three paragraphs in these lines fulfils in working out the general object.

Lines **65-70** draw the conclusion of the foregoing stage of the argument, and suggest by an analogy the condition of things to be explained. Is the analogy of use, either as exposition or argument, or otherwise than as a means of increasing the literary interest? — The German quotation, which is the first line of the Prologue to Goethe's Faust, means "The sun sounds after the ancient manner."

a fire, differing from our terrestrial fires only in the
magnitude and intensity of its combustion. But what is
the burning matter which can thus maintain itself? All
that we know of cosmical phenomena declares our brotherhood with the sun — affirms that the same constituents 80
enter into the composition of his mass as those already
known to chemistry. But no earthly substance with which
we are acquainted — no substance which the fall of meteors
has landed on the earth — would be at all competent to
maintain the sun's combustion. The chemical energy of 85
such substances would be too weak, and their dissipation
too speedy. Were the sun a block of burning coal, and
were it supplied with oxygen sufficient for the observed
emission, it would be utterly consumed in five thousand
years. On the other hand, to imagine it a body originally 90
endowed with a store of heat — a hot globe now cooling —
necessitates the ascription to it of qualities wholly different
from those possessed by terrestrial matter. If we knew
the specific heat of the sun, we could calculate its rate of
cooling. Assuming the specific heat to be the same as 95
that of water — the terrestrial substance which possesses
the highest specific heat — at its present rate of emission,
the entire mass of the sun would cool down 15,000° Fahr.
in five thousand years. In short, if the sun be formed of
matter like our own, some means must exist of restoring 100
to it its wasted power.

The question being propounded, ll. **72, 73**, a natural stage in the inquiry would be to ask whether there may be some other answer than the one under consideration.

Accordingly, what is the office, in the argument, of ll. **74–116**, and how explained by Rhet. p. 431?

Beginning with the supposition apparently most near and natural (cf. Rhet. p. 442, bottom), on what grounds must we rule out the possi-

The facts are so extraordinary, that the soberest hypothesis regarding them must appear wild. The sun we know rotates upon his axis once in about twenty-five days; and the notion has been entertained that the friction of the periphery of this wheel against something in surrounding space produces the light and heat. But what forms the brake, and by what agency is it held, while it rubs against the sun? Granting, moreover, the existence of the brake, we calculate the total amount of heat which the sun could generate by such friction. We know his mass; we know his time of rotation; we know the mechanical equivalent of heat; and, from these data, we can deduce, with certainty, that the force of rotation, if entirely converted into heat, would cover less than two centuries of emission. There is nothing hypothetical in this calculation.

I have already alluded to another theory, which, however bold it may at first sight appear, deserves our serious attention — the Meteoric Theory of the Sun. Kepler's celebrated statement, that "there are more comets in the heavens than fish in the ocean," implies that a small portion only of the total number of comets belonging to our system are seen from the earth. But, besides comets, and planets, and moons, a numerous class of bodies belong to our sys-

---

ble answer suggested in ll. **74-90**? How does it come into collision with observed facts? — What is the second supposition, ll. **90-101**, and what consideration rules it out? — What is the force in assuming the sun's specific heat to be the same as that of water? — Observe, in ll. **90, 91**, how scientific modes of expression are simplified for ordinary readers. Another example is seen below, in ll. **107-109**. — **99. If the sun be formed of matter like our own,** — this condition is the only basis on which the author can reason; what color has he for it, as expressed above, ll. 78, 79? It will be observed, accordingly, that all solar phenomena throughout the argument are estimated by standards afforded

tem, which, from their smallness, might be regarded as 125
cosmical atoms. Like the planets and the comets, these
smaller asteroids obey the law of gravity, and revolve in
elliptic orbits round the sun. It is they which, when they
come within the earth's atmosphere, and are fired by friction, appear to us as meteors and falling stars. 130

On a bright night, twenty minutes rarely pass at any
part of the earth's surface without the appearance of at
least one meteor. Twice a year (on the 12th of August
and 14th of November) they appear in enormous numbers.
During nine hours in Boston, when they were described 135
as falling as thick as snow-flakes, 240,000 meteors were
observed. The number falling in a year might, perhaps,
be estimated at hundreds or thousands of millions, and
even these would constitute but a small portion of the total

---

by phenomena of the earth; aside from these there is no intelligible basis of comparison.

What is the third supposition, ll. **102-116**, and how invalidated? What does the last sentence, l. **116**, imply as to the conclusiveness of the consideration against it?

The way being thus cleared by the removal of more plausible but untenable theories, we may advance without obstacle to the statement, more in full, of the hypothesis already propounded. What attitude toward the argument does the author profess (see ll. 117, 118; 201-206), and how does it agree with Rhet. p. 417? — **117. I have already alluded, etc.**, — see above, l. 34, and note on that part of the treatment. — **119.** It is quite in accord with the literary habit of our author's mind, as well as with his object, that he should begin his statement with this striking assertion from Kepler; see similar instances of popular treatment, ll. 16, 71. — Also it is natural and necessary that he should begin with an observed fact, and work as far as possible in the realm of observed facts. What parallel does the earth furnish, ll. **128-130**, to make our hypothesis more natural? — **125. Might be regarded as cosmical atoms,** — derivation and meaning of *cosmical?* How different from ordinary atoms? To the readers of the whole volume

crowd of asteroids that circulate round the sun. From the phenomena of light and heat, and by direct observations on Encke's comet, we learn that the universe is filled by a resisting medium, through the friction of which all the masses of our system are drawn gradually toward the sun. And though the larger planets show, in historic times, no diminution of their periods of revolution, it may be otherwise with the smaller bodies. In the time required for the mean distance of the earth to alter a single yard, a small asteroid may have approached thousands of miles nearer to the sun.

Following up these reflections, we should be led to the conclusion that, while an immeasurable stream of ponderable meteoric matter moves unceasingly toward the sun, it must augment in density as it approaches its centre of converg-

---

from which this argument is taken, an illustration and corroboration of our theory is supplied in an earlier section, to which these words are an allusion. "Our theory," he says, "is applicable not only to suns and planets, but equally so to atoms. Most of you know the scientific history of the diamond — that Newton, antedating intellectually the discoveries of modern chemistry, pronounced it to be an unctuous or combustible substance. Everybody now knows that this brilliant gem is composed of the same substance as common charcoal, graphite, or plumbago. A diamond is pure carbon, and carbon burns in oxygen. Here is a diamond, held fast in a loop of platinum-wire; heating the gem to redness in this flame, I plunge it into this jar, which contains oxygen gas. See how it brightens on entering the jar of oxygen, and now it glows, like a little star, with a pure white light. How are we to figure the action here going on? Exactly as you would present to your minds the idea of meteorites showering down upon the sun. The conceptions are, in quality, the same, and to the intellect the one is not more difficult than the other. You are to figure the atoms of oxygen showering against this diamond on all sides. They are urged toward it by what is called chemical affinity; but this force, made clear, presents itself to the mind as pure attraction, of the same mechanical quality,

ence. And here the conjecture naturally rises, whether 155
that vast nebulous mass, the Zodiacal Light, which embraces the sun, may not be a crowd of meteors. It is at least proved that this luminous phenomenon arises from matter which circulates in obedience to planetary laws; hence the **entire mass of** the zodiacal light must be con- 160
stantly approaching and incessantly raining its **substance** down upon the sun.

It is easy to calculate both the maximum and the minimum velocity, imparted by the sun's attraction to an asteroid circulating round him. The maximum is generated 165
when the body approaches the sun from an infinite distance; the *entire pull* **of** the sun being then exerted upon it. The minimum is that velocity which would barely en-

---

if I may use the term, as gravity. Every oxygen atom as it strikes the surface, and has its motion of translation destroyed by its collision with the carbon, assumes the motion which we call heat; and this heat is so intense, the attractions exerted at these molecular distances are so mighty, that the crystal is kept white-hot, and the compound, formed by the union of its atoms with those of the oxygen, flies away as carbonic-acid gas." "In short," he concludes his chapter on the Theory of Combustion, "all cases of combustion are to be ascribed to the collision of atoms which have been urged together by their mutual attractions." It seems no more than fair that what the readers of the volume had in their possession for the understanding of this argument, should also be put in ours. What then, in our present theory, corresponds to the *atoms* of the above note?

In constructing an argument *a priori* (and indeed any argument dealing with cause and effect), Rhet. represents, p. 419, that three things must be shown or made evident. How do ll. **131–150** meet the *first* of these? Show how the statements are made probable from observed phenomena, and how possible objections or difficulties are answered.

151–162. It is in this paragraph that conjecture begins, — what conjecture? What proved fact gives color and plausibility to the conjecture?

able the body to revolve round the sun close to his surface. The final velocity of the former, just before striking the sun, would be 390 miles a second, that of the latter 276 miles a second. The asteroid, on striking the sun, with the former velocity, would develop more than nine thousand times the heat generated by the combustion of an equal asteroid of solid coal; while the shock, in the latter case, would generate heat equal to that of the combustion of upward of four thousand such asteroids. It matters not, therefore, whether the substances falling into the sun be combustible or not; their being combustible would not add sensibly to the tremendous heat produced by their mechanical collision.

Here, then, we have an agency competent to restore his lost energy to the sun, and to maintain a temperature at his surface which transcends all terrestrial combustion. In the fall of asteroids we find the means of producing the solar light and heat. It may be contended that this showering down of matter necessitates the growth of the sun; it does so; but the quantity necessary to maintain the observed calorific emission for four thousand years would defeat the scrutiny of our best instruments. If the earth struck the sun, it would utterly vanish from perception; but the heat developed by its shock would cover the expenditure of a century. . . .

How do ll. **163–181** meet the *second* condition required Rhet. p. 419, and what conclusion is accordingly drawn, ll. **182–186**? How is the expression popularized, as to measurements and quantities of heat described? — What objection is met, ll. **186–193**? How does this answer meet the *third* condition, Rhet. p. 419? How, in accordance with former procedures, is it made striking and palpable to an ordinary reader?

193. The periods here mark the omission of a page of matter relat-

Such is an outline of the Meteoric Theory of the Sun, as extracted from Mayer's "Essay on Celestial Dynamics." 195 I have held closely to his statements, and in most cases simply translated his words. But the sketch conveys no adequate idea of the firmness and consistency with which he has applied his principles. He deals with true causes; and the only question that can affect his theory refers to 200 the quantity of action ascribed by him to these causes. I do not pledge myself to this theory, nor do I ask you to accept it as demonstrated; still, it would be a great mistake to regard it as chimerical. It is a noble speculation; and, depend upon it, the true theory, if this, or some form 205 of it, be not the true one, will not appear less wild or less astounding.

From HEAT CONSIDERED AS A MODE OF MOTION.

---

ing to broader considerations regarding the structure of the sun and "the permanence of our present terrestrial conditions"; which matter is not at all essential, and indeed seems disturbing, to our present argument.

In conclusion, what gives weight to this theory, ll. **199-201**, as an inductive argument? How is the thought of its boldness met, in ll. 204-207? How was this thought forestalled and prepared for, ll. 102, 103?

XXV.

THOMAS BABINGTON, LORD MACAULAY.

QUEEN ELIZABETH A PERSECUTOR.

It is vehemently maintained by some writers of the present day that Elizabeth persecuted neither Papists nor Puritans as such, and that the severe measures which she occasionally adopted were dictated, not by religious intol-
5 erance, but by political necessity. Even the excellent account of those times which Mr. Hallam has given has not altogether imposed silence on the authors of this fallacy. The title of the Queen, they say, was annulled by

---

The present Selection lends itself to study in two ways. As to principle, it exemplifies the main procedures of Deductive reasoning (Rhet. pp. 424-429), being concerned with establishing a truth expressed virtually in a syllogism. As to form it is a Refutation (Rhet. pp. 432-439), being concerned with exposing and tearing down, point by point, a fallacy. This mode of putting a course of reasoning in the form of refutation is quite characteristic of Macaulay. "His great powers of debate," says Professor Minto, "appear chiefly in refutation. He is critical rather than constructive. He takes delight in exposing false analogies and false generalities, and in showing that anticipations are not warranted by previous experience."

Let us first examine the refutation, with its main and minor points; and then, by way of recapitulation, note the force of the whole as a positive syllogistic argument.

Lines 1-13. What is the position that Macaulay sets out to refute, and on what does it principally turn? Explain how his opponents arrive at their position, by Rhet. p. 428. — **7. This fallacy,** — the word

the Pope; her throne was given to another; her subjects
were incited to rebellion; her life was menaced; every
Catholic was bound in conscience to be a traitor; it was
therefore against traitors, not against Catholics, that the
penal laws were enacted.

In order that our readers may be fully competent to
appreciate the merits of this defence, we will state, as
concisely as possible, the substance of some of these
laws.

As soon as Elizabeth ascended the throne, and before
the least hostility to her government had been shown by
the Catholic population, an act passed prohibiting the
celebration of the rites of the Romish Church, on pain of
forfeiture for the first offence, of a year's imprisonment
for the second, and of perpetual imprisonment for the
third.

A law was next made in 1562, enacting, that all who
had ever graduated at the Universities or received holy

---

fallacy is a general term to denote any error by which reasoning is
made inconclusive. Such error may lie either (1) in the fact alleged;
or (2) in the use of terms; or (3) in the course of reasoning. It is the
business of refutation to expose whatever is fallacious in an opponent's
argument, according to the need of the occasion.

With which aspect of the fallacy do the four paragraphs, ll. **14–58**,
deal? Does the author understate or overstate his object, ll. **14, 15**?
It will be observed that not only are facts stated, but in each case such
accompaniments and aspects of the facts are also given as will lend an
argumentative force to them. This of course is fair, but it is also wise.

18–24. In giving the substance of this first enactment, does the force
lie in the enactment itself, or in some accompaniment which invalidates
it as argument? How is this brought out in the structure of the first
sentence? Cf. Rhet. p. 181, 4.

25–52. The argumentative force of this statement lies in the bald
and direct way in which the obnoxious character of the law is made to

orders, all lawyers, and all magistrates, should take the oath of supremacy when tendered to them, on pain of forfeiture and imprisonment during the royal pleasure. After the lapse of three months, the oath might again be tendered to them; and, if it were again refused, the recusant was guilty of high treason. A prospective law, however severe, framed to exclude Catholics from the liberal professions, would have been mercy itself compared with this odious act. It is a retrospective statute; it is a retrospective penal statute; it is a retrospective penal statute against a large class. We will not positively affirm that a law of this description must always, and under all circumstances, be unjustifiable. But the presumption against it is most violent; nor do we remember any crisis, either in our own history, or in the history of any other country, which would have rendered such a provision necessary. In the present case, what circumstances called for extraordinary rigor? There might be disaffection among the Catholics. The prohibition of their worship would naturally produce it. But it is from their situation, not from their conduct, from the wrongs which they had suffered, not from those which they had committed, that the existence of discontent among them must be inferred. There were libels, no doubt, and prophecies, and rumors,

---

stand out, free from any disguise of verbiage. This, also, is the reasoner's fair privilege. — Point out how rhetorical strength is given to the characterization of the law, in ll. **32–37**; especially what figures of emphasis. — In answering it, what consideration would naturally come first in order, according to Rhet. p. 442 (middle), and how does this agree, in ll. **37–43**? — Having established an antecedent presumption against it, what further answer does he make, ll. **43–52**, and in what consideration does it centre? Does it break down the defence, as regards this enactment?

and suspicions, strange grounds for a law inflicting capital penalties, *ex post facto*, on a large body of men.

Eight years later, the bull of Pius deposing Elizabeth produced a third law. This law, to which alone, as we conceive, the defence now under our consideration can apply, provides that, if any Catholic shall convert a Protestant to the Romish Church, they shall both suffer death as for high treason.

We believe that we might safely content ourselves with stating the fact, and leaving it to the judgment of every plain Englishman. Recent controversies have, however, given so much importance to this subject, that we will offer a few remarks on it.

In the first place, the arguments which are urged in favor of Elizabeth apply with much greater force to the case of her sister Mary. The Catholics did not, at the time of Elizabeth's accession, rise in arms to seat a Pretender on her throne. But before Mary had given, or could give, provocation, the most distinguished Protestants attempted to set aside her rights in favor of the Lady Jane. That attempt, and the subsequent insurrection of Wyatt, furnished at least as good a plea for the burning of

---

53-58. What gives force to the statement of this enactment, — the law itself, or its occasion? How is this indicated in the manner of stating it? — **54. To which alone the defence can apply,** — show on what grounds, by comparison with ll. **8-13** above.

The fallacy in the fact alleged is clear enough, in Macaulay's view (ll. **59-61**), to invalidate the opponent's position; but he proceeds to make his answer doubly strong, in what he calls "a few remarks."

How does the paragraph, ll. **64-74**, exemplify Rhet. p. 438, 1, top? As to kind of argument, how explained by Rhet. p. 421, bottom? Trace its character on this line. — And yet, after all is done, what estimate does Macaulay set upon it, l. **75**? What is the use then, rhetorical or other, in introducing this argument at all?

Protestants, as the conspiracies against Elizabeth furnish for the hanging and embowelling of Papists.

75 The fact is that both pleas are worthless alike. If such arguments are to pass current, it will be easy to prove that there never was such a thing as religious persecution since the creation. For there never was a religious persecution in which some odious crime was not, justly or unjustly, 80 said to be obviously deducible from the doctrines of the persecuted party. We might say that the Cæsars did not persecute the Christians; that they only punished men who were charged, rightly or wrongly, with burning Rome, and with committing the foulest abominations in secret 85 assemblies; and that the refusal to throw frankincense on the altar of Jupiter was not the crime but only evidence of the crime. We might say, that the massacre of St. Bartholomew was intended to extirpate, not a religous sect, but a political party. For, beyond all doubt, the proceed- 90 ings of the Huguenots, from the conspiracy of Amboise to the battle of Moncontour, had given much more trouble to the French monarchy than the Catholics have ever given to the English monarchy since the Reformation; and that too with much less excuse.

95 The true distinction is perfectly obvious. To punish a man because he has committed a crime, or because he is

---

The division of the argument, ll. **75-111**, as indicated by ll. **75-78**, deals with the use of what term, and accordingly takes up what aspect of the fallacy, as indicated above? — Explain the two arguments, ll. **81-87** and **87-94**, by which he first meets the fallacy, by Rhet. p. 421, 1; also by Rhet. p. 438, 1. What is there of an *a fortiori* force in the second of these? What exposition of terms is necessary to break the force of these counter-arguments?

95-102. Explain the instruments of exposition here used by Rhet. pp. 387 and 392. — Explain the instrument of exposition used in ll. **103-**

believed, though unjustly, to have committed a crime, is
not persecution. To punish a man, because we infer from
the nature of some doctrine which he holds, or from the
conduct of other persons who hold the same doctrines with
him, that he will commit a crime, is persecution, and is, in
every case, foolish and wicked.

When Elizabeth put Ballard and Babington to death,
she was not persecuting. Nor should we have accused
her government of persecution for passing any law, however severe, against overt acts of sedition. But to argue
that, because a man is a Catholic, he must think it right
to murder a heretical sovereign, and that because he thinks
it right he will attempt to do it, and then, to found on this
conclusion a law for punishing him as if he had done it, is
plain persecution.

If, indeed, all men reasoned in the same manner on the
same data, and always did what they thought it their duty
to do, this mode of dispensing punishment might be extremely judicious. But as people who agree about premises often disagree about conclusions, and as no man in
the world acts up to his own standard of right, there are
two enormous gaps in the logic by which alone penalties

---

111 by Rhet. p. 394. Observe that the second of these examples, ll. 106-111, is not in the form of a specific case; it rather defines exactly what Elizabeth is admitted to have done, and puts it under the category established in general terms above, the category of persecution. This in the interests of exact usage.

With l. **112** a new section of the refutation begins, dealing, as gathered from ll. **117-119**, with what new aspect of the fallacy, as indicated above? — Let us trace the **two enormous gaps in the logic**, here alleged. What they are appears from Macaulay's negation of them:
1. From ll. **115, 116**, the argument of the opponents presupposes what? How is this presupposition proved fallacious, in ll. **119-138**? How does this manner of refutation exemplify Rhet. p. 438? What does Macau-

for opinions can be defended. The doctrine of reprobation, in the judgment of many very able men, follows by
syllogistic necessity from the doctrine of election. Others
conceive that the Antinomian heresy directly follows from
the doctrine of reprobation; and it is very generally thought
that licentiousness and cruelty of the worst description are
likely to be the fruits, as they often have been the fruits,
of Antinomian opinions. This chain of reasoning, we
think, is as perfect in all its parts as that which makes out
a Papist to be necessarily a traitor. Yet it would be rather
a strong measure to hang all the Calvinists, on the ground
that, if they were spared, they would infallibly commit all
the atrocities of Matthias and Knipperdoling. For, reason
the matter as we may, experience shows us that a man may
believe in election without believing in reprobation, that
he may believe in reprobation without being an Antinomian, and that he may be an Antinomian without being a
bad citizen. Man, in short, is so inconsistent a creature
that it is impossible to reason from his belief to his conduct, or from one part of his belief to another.

We do not believe that every Englishman who was
reconciled to the Catholic Church would, as a necessary
consequence, have thought himself justified in deposing or
assassinating Elizabeth. It is not sufficient to say that the
convert must have acknowledged the authority of the Pope,
and that the Pope had issued a bull against the Queen. We

---

lay call this argument, as to form (l. 126), and how does it correspond in this respect with the position refuted? What conclusion is drawn from the whole?

2. From ll. **116, 117** (cf. l. 113), the argument of the opponents, as a second "gap in the logic," presupposes what? By what parallel argument is this met, ll. **139-150**? By what concession (cf. Rhet. p. 445, 3) is the argument followed, and how is the concession answered? Does

know through what strange loopholes the human mind contrives to escape, when it wishes to avoid a disagreeable inference from an admitted proposition. We know how long the Jansenists contrived to believe the Pope infallible in matters of doctrine, and at the same time to believe doctrines which he pronounced to be heretical. Let it pass, however, that every Catholic in the kingdom thought that Elizabeth might be lawfully murdered. Still the old maxim, that what is the business of everybody is the business of nobody, is particularly likely to hold good in a case in which a cruel death is the almost inevitable consequence of making any attempt.

Of the ten thousand clergymen of the Church of England, there is scarcely one who would not say that a man who should leave his country and friends to preach the Gospel among savages, and who should, after laboring indefatigably without any hope of reward, terminate his life by martyrdom, would deserve the warmest admiration. Yet we doubt whether ten of the ten thousand ever thought of going on such an expedition. Why should we suppose that conscientious motives, feeble as they are constantly found to be in a good cause, should be omnipotent for evil? Doubtless there was many a jolly Popish priest in the old manor-houses of the northern counties, who would have admitted, in theory, the deposing power of the Pope, but who would not have been ambitious to be stretched on the rack, even though it were to be used, according to the

---

the *a fortiori* significance given to the answer serve adequately to make the "old maxim" conclusive? — The old maxim at least introduces a suggestion which gives point to the succeeding argument; compare ll. 155, 156 with ll. 170–178.

Explain how the counter argument, ll. 157–178 is *a fortiori*, from the suggestiveness of ll. 164–167.

benevolent proviso of Lord Burleigh, "as charitably as such a thing can be," or to be hanged, drawn, and quartered, even though, by that rare indulgence which the Queen, of her special grace, certain knowledge, and mere motion, sometimes extended to very mitigated cases, he were allowed a fair time to choke before the hangman began to grabble in his entrails.

But the laws passed against the Puritans had not even the wretched excuse which we have been considering. In this case, the cruelty was equal, the danger infinitely less. In fact, the danger was created solely by the cruelty. But it is superfluous to press the argument. By no artifice of ingenuity can the stigma of persecution, the worst blemish of the English Church, be effaced or patched over.

From Essay on HALLAM'S CONSTITUTIONAL HISTORY.

Thus the refutation has met in turn the three successive aspects of the fallacy, and has exposed them all. Note also, as indicated in ll. **179-182**, the wisdom displayed in refutation (Rhet. p. 438), in meeting the stronger case first (for there were two cases, that of the Catholics and that of the Puritans; cf. ll. 1-3), and having demolished that, leaving the other to fall of itself.

As intimated at the beginning, this argument, though in form a refutation, is in principle a syllogism (Rhet. p. 424), with major premise, minor premise, and conclusion fully involved, though not expressed in plain words. The syllogism may be expressed thus:

MINOR PREMISE: Elizabeth put Catholics to death for holding doctrines presumably tending to crime.

MAJOR PREMISE: So to do is persecution.

CONCLUSION: Hence Elizabeth was guilty of persecution.

By what various means is the first premise (the minor coming here first in order) established? How explained by Rhet. p. 427? — From the nature of the major premise, what means of establishing it do you expect, and what means are used here? How does the exposure of the "two enormous gaps in the logic" affect the strength of the major premise? — Point out where and how the conclusion is expressed.

XXVI.

GEORGE WILLIAM CURTIS.

THE PUBLIC DUTY OF EDUCATED MEN.

An oration delivered at the commencement of Union College, June 27th, 1877, the orator being at the time honorary Chancellor of Union University.

It is with diffidence that I rise to add any words of mine to the music of these younger voices. This day, Gentlemen of the Graduating Class, is especially yours. It is a day of high hope and expectation, and the counsels that fall from older lips should be carefully weighed, lest they chill the ardor of a generous enthusiasm or stay the all-conquering faith of youth that moves the world. To those who, constantly and actively engaged in a thousand

---

This final Selection will be studied for the manner in which it exemplifies the principles of Persuasion, as embodied in Oratory; and presupposes a knowledge of the Rhetoric as far as page 474. The present Oration, being somewhat recent, is selected for study, not only as exhibiting the essential and perennial requisites of oratorical discourse, but also as fairly and favorably illustrating the kind of oratory especially adapted to move the vigorous and practical mind of this day.

I. **The Introduction, or Exordium**: — A brief inquiry will suffice, in the case before us, to reveal the speaker's alliance with his audience (Rhet. p. 449). The speaker — a man thoroughly familiar with public affairs, and eminent in activities devoted to the country's good. The audience — a class of young men, just at the end of their college course, and looking forward into the untried life of sterner duties that lies before

pursuits, are still persuaded that educated intelligence moulds states and leads mankind, no day in the year is more significant, more inspiring, than this of the College Commencement. It matters not at what college it may be celebrated. It is the same at all. We stand here indeed beneath these College walls, beautiful for situation, girt at this moment with the perfumed splendor of midsummer, and full of tender memories and joyous associations to those who hear me. But on this day, and on other days, at a hundred other colleges, this summer sun beholds the same spectacle of eager and earnest throngs. The faith that we hold, they also cherish. It is the same God that is worshipped at the different altars. It is the same benediction that descends upon every reverent head and believing heart. In this annual celebration of faith in the power and the responsibility of educated men, all the colleges in the country, in whatever state, of whatever age, of whatever religious sympathy or direction, form but one great Union University.

But the interest of the day is not that of mere study, of

---

them. How does the speaker, in ll, **45–51**, define his relation to his hearers, and how does he make common cause with them? See Rhet. p. 449, 1. To what character, assumed as existing in his audience, does the speaker address himself, ll. **1–7**? What kind of adaptation to his audience does the speaker recognize as incumbent on him? See Rhet. p. 453, 2. How is the occasion, combined with the character attributed to the audience, utilized toward the suggestion of the theme, ll. **23–25**? Finally, report how the subject is broadened in its application, and in what graceful play upon words this occasion is connected with similar occasions.

14. These College walls, beautiful for situation, — the buildings of Union College are on a broad plateau at the summit of a gentle slope northeast of the city of Schenectady, and command a beautiful view of the Mohawk valley westward. Compare ll. 58, 49, below.

sound scholarship as an end, of good books for their own sake, but of education as a power in human affairs, of educated men as an influence in the commonwealth. "Tell me," said an American scholar of Goethe, the many-sided, "what did he ever do for the cause of man?" The scholar, the poet, the philosopher, are men among other men. From these unavoidable social relations spring opportunities and duties. How do they use them? How do they discharge them? Does the scholar show in his daily walk that he has studied the wisdom of ages in vain? Does the poet sing of angelic purity and lead an unclean life? Does the philosopher peer into other worlds, and fail to help this world upon its way? Four years before our civil war, the same scholar — it was Theodore Parker — said sadly: "If our educated men had done their duty, we should not now be in the ghastly condition we bewail." The theme of to-day seems to me to be prescribed by the occasion. It is the festival of the departure of a body of educated young men into the world. This company of picked recruits marches out with beating drums and flying colors

---

How is the theme of the oration expressed, ll. **51-54**? Show how this is a true oratorical theme, as defined Rhet. p. 447. How does the order and manner in which it is introduced exemplify Rhet. p. 267, note? As contributing thoughts toward the suggestion of it, what does the first paragraph, ll. **1-27** supply? What does the second paragraph, ll. **28-54**, add to this? In the style of this second paragraph much is left to implication. Fill up the implication conveyed by the quotation, ll. **31-33**. Also the implication of ll. **41-44**. How do these illustrate Rhet. p. 300?

II. **The Body of the Oration.** — Let us first study, and write out in tabular form, the plan of the discourse; compare Rhet. p. 264.

Express in brief terms the approach made to the discussion, in ll. **55-96**, and indicate by subdivisions how it is developed. Perhaps Rhet. p. 291, 2, may be suggestive here. — What is the office of the

to join the army. We who feel that our fate is gracious which allowed a liberal training, are here to welcome and to advise. On your behalf, Mr. President and Gentlemen, with your authority, and with all my heart, I shall say a word to them and to you of the public duty of educated men in America.

I shall not assume, Gentlemen Graduates, for I know that it is not so, that what Dr. Johnson says of the teachers of Rasselas and the princes of Abyssinia can be truly said of you in your happy valley: "The sages who instructed them told them of nothing but the miseries of public life, and described all beyond the mountains as regions of calamity where discord was always raging, and where man preyed upon man." The sages who have instructed you are American citizens. They know that patriotism has its glorious opportunities and its sacred duties. They have not shunned the one, and they have well performed the other. In the sharpest stress of our awful conflict, a clear voice of patriotic warning was heard from these peaceful Academic shades, the voice of the

---

paragraph, ll. **97–114**, and why necessary at the outset? See Rhet. p. 387, and cf. p. 440, 1.— Having answered the question *what*, explain in what way the orator, ll. **115–178**, answers the question *how*. Subdivide this section.— Lines **179–266** represent the scholar in what broad relation?— In what narrower relation do ll. **267–507**, the longest main division of the oration, represent the scholar?— In what deeper relation is he represented, ll. **508–552**, and how does this aspect of the theme follow naturally upon the foregoing?— The answer to the above questions will give a scheme for the main plan of the oration.

The sub-divisions will be better left, perhaps, to the more detailed study of the oration, on which let us now enter.

62–73. It is not only graceful and courteous, but also the most practical means of promoting his object, for the orator to begin his treatment of his theme by illustrations drawn from the students' daily

venerated teacher whom this University still freshly deplores, drawing from the wisdom of experience stored in 70 his ample learning, a lesson of startling cogency and power from the history of Greece for the welfare of America.

This was the discharge of a public duty by an educated man. It illustrated an indispensable condition of a pro- 75 gressive republic, the active, practical interest in politics of the most intelligent citizens. Civil and religious liberty in this country can be preserved only through the agency of our political institutions. But those institutions alone will not suffice. It is not the ship so much as the skilful 80 sailing that assures the prosperous voyage. American institutions presuppose not only general honesty and intelligence in the people, but their constant and direct application to public affairs. Our system rests upon all the people, not upon a part of them, and the citizen who 85 evades his share of the burden betrays his fellows. Our safety lies not in our institutions but in ourselves. It was under the forms of the republic that Julius Cæsar made

---

surroundings and companionships. What use in employing the quotation from Johnson's Rasselas? — **69. The venerated teacher, etc.**, — the reference is to Dr. Tayler Lewis, professor of the Greek and Oriental languages and literature in Union College, who died May 11, 1877, only a month and a half before this oration was delivered. The **clear voice of patriotic warning** here mentioned refers to a work of his entitled "State Rights a Photograph of the Ruins of Ancient Greece," published in 1864.

How is this illustration directly applied to the theme? How is its application defined and broadened? Point out the striking figure by which the thought of ll. **74-96** is enforced. — What is the exact point of the two illustrations, ll. **87-91**? — What is the practical use of the personification, ll. **93-96**?

As exposition, how do ll. **97-114** exemplify Rhet. p. 391, 3, and

himself emperor of Rome. It was professing reverence
for the national traditions that James the Second was destroying religious liberty in England. To labor, said the old monks, is to pray. What we earnestly desire we earnestly toil for. That she may be prized more truly, heaven-eyed Justice flies from us, like the Tartar maid from her lovers, and she yields her embrace at last only to the swiftest and most daring of her pursuers.

By the words public duty I do not necessarily mean official duty, although it may include that. I mean simply that constant and active practical participation in the details of politics without which, upon the part of the most intelligent citizens, the conduct of public affairs falls under the control of selfish and ignorant, or crafty and venal men. I mean that personal attention which, as it must be incessant, is often wearisome and even repulsive, to the details of politics, attendance at meetings, service upon committees, care and trouble and expense of many kinds, patient endurance of rebuffs, chagrins, ridicules, disappointments, defeats — in a word, all those duties and services which, when selfishly and meanly performed, stigmatize a man as a mere politician, but whose constant, honorable, intelligent and vigilant performance is the gradual building, stone by

---

as amplification how do they exemplify Rhet. p. 292, 2? Observe that the exposition is introduced not merely for its own sake, though it does make a needed explanation; but it also, in the true oratorical spirit, holds up the expounded idea in the light of duty and motive, that is, gives it a practical *issue* in conduct. See Rhet. p. 447. Observe further that the exposition is not applied to all aspects of the idea, but confines itself to the single discrimination needed for the enforcement of the object. What is that?

115-178. The section included in these lines has been represented above as a general answer to the question *how* to discharge public duty;

stone, and layer by layer, of that great temple of self-restrained liberty which all generous souls mean that our government shall be.

Public duty in this country is not discharged, as is so often supposed, by voting. A man may vote regularly, and still fail essentially of his political duty, as the Pharisee who gave tithes of all that he possessed, and fasted three times in the week, yet lacked the very heart of religion. When an American citizen is content with voting merely, he consents to accept what is often a doubtful alternative. His first duty is to help shape the alternative. This, which was formerly less necessary, is now indispensable. In a rural community such as this country was a hundred years ago, whoever was nominated for office was known to his neighbors, and the consciousness of that knowledge was a conservative influence in determining nominations. But in the local elections of the great cities of to-day, elections that control taxation and expenditure, the mass of the voters vote in absolute ignorance of the candidates. The citizen who supposes that he does all his duty when he votes, places a premium upon political knavery. Thieves welcome him to the polls and offer him a choice, which he has done nothing to prevent, between Jeremy Diddler and Dick Turpin. The party cries for

---

but in answering this question it really does much more. Show how it also *applies* the answer to the hearer's will, and how it makes evident that the duty is (1) important, (2) practicable, (3) one for whose neglect he only is responsible. — How is the duty defined negatively? How is it defined positively? — How does the allusion, ll. **117-120**, exemplify Rhet. p. 299, bottom? — **123. Is now indispensable,** — what considerations go to the proving of this? — **135. Jeremy Diddler and Dick Turpin,** — these are names of characters so notorious as to have become symbolical. Jeremy Diddler, in Kenney's play *Raising the Wind*, is "an

which he is responsible are: "Turpin and Honesty," "Diddler and Reform." And within a few years, as a result of this indifference to the details of public duty, the most powerful politician in the Empire State of the Union was Jonathan Wild, the Great, the captain of a band of plunderers. I know it is said that the knaves have taken the honest men in a net, and have contrived machinery which will inevitably grind only the grist of rascals. The answer is, that when honest men did once what they ought to do always, the thieves were netted and their machine was broken. To say that in this country the rogues must rule, is to defy history and to despair of the republic. It is to repeat the imbecile executive cry of sixteen years ago, "Oh dear! the states have no right to go; and, Oh dear! the nation has no right to help itself." Let the Union, stronger than ever and unstained with national wrong, teach us the power of patriotic virtue — and Ludlow street jail console those who suppose that American politics must necessarily be a game of thieves and bullies. If ignorance and corruption and intrigue control the primary meeting, and manage the convention, and dictate the nomination, the fault is in the honest and intelligent workshop and office, in the library and the parlor, in the church and the school. When they are as constant and faithful to their political rights as the slums and the grog-

---

artful swindler, a clever, seedy vagabond, who borrows money or obtains credit by his songs, witticisms, or other expedients." Dick Turpin was a noted English highwayman, executed at York in 1739. Note the ironical correspondence between the party cries here given and the characters of the men. — **140. Jonathan Wild, the Great,** — a noted English villain, cool, clever, heartless, utterly wicked, who lived from 1682 to 1725, and was executed at Tyburn for housebreaking. Both Defoe and Fielding have made him the hero of romances. The name

shops, the pool-rooms and the kennels ; when the educated, industrious, temperate, thrifty citizens are as zealous and prompt and unfailing in political activity as the ignorant and venal and mischievous, or when it is plain that they cannot be roused to their duty, then, but not until then — if ignorance and corruption always carry the day — there can be no honest question that the republic has failed. But let us not be deceived. While good men sit at home, not knowing that there is anything to be done, nor caring to know ; cultivating a feeling that politics are tiresome and dirty, and politicians vulgar bullies and bravoes ; half persuaded that a republic is the contemptible rule of a mob, and secretly longing for a splendid and vigorous despotism — then remember it is not a government mastered by ignorance, it is a government betrayed by intelligence ; it is not the victory of the slums, it is the surrender of the schools ; it is not that bad men are brave, but that good men are infidels and cowards.

But, gentlemen, when you come to address yourselves to these primary public duties, your first surprise and dismay will be the discovery that, in a country where education is declared to be the hope of its institutions, the higher education is often practically held to be almost a disadvantage. You will go from these halls to hear a very common sneer at college-bred men — to encounter a jeal-

---

is used here to designate William M. Tweed, the leader of a New York political ring. These symbolical names give to the passage, ll. 133–141, the color of what figure? — **141-154.** These lines are the answer to what implicit question here arising? In what trenchant sentence is the answer condensed? Compare a similarly trenchant way of putting the thought in ll. 131–133 above. These sentences illustrate the value of aphoristic expression in the defining part of orations ; see Rhet. p. 286.

How does the paragraph, ll. **155-178,** bring the thought of this

ousy of education as making men visionary and pedantic and impracticable — to confront a belief that there is something enfeebling in the higher education, and that self-made men, as they are called, are the sure stay of the state. But what is really meant by a self-made man? It is a man of native sagacity and strong character, who was taught, it is proudly said, only at the plough or the anvil or the bench. He was schooled by adversity, and was polished by hard attrition with men. He is Benjamin Franklin, the printer's boy, or Abraham Lincoln, the rail-splitter. They never went to college, but nevertheless, like Agamemnon, they were kings of men, and the world blesses their memory.

So it does; but the sophistry here is plain enough, although it is not always detected. Great genius and force of character undoubtedly make their own career. But because Walter Scott was dull at school, is a parent to see with joy that his son is a dunce? Because Lord Chatham was of a towering conceit, must we infer that pompous vanity portends a comprehensive statesmanship that will fill the world with the splendor of its triumphs? Because Sir Robert Walpole gambled and swore and boozed at Houghton, are we to suppose that gross sensuality and coarse contempt of human nature are the essential secrets of a power that defended liberty against tory intrigue and

---

section home to the hearers? To what motive (see Rhet. p. 464, 3) is appeal here made? Is the appeal direct or implicit? By what figurative means is the thought made pointed and cogent at the end?

The section, ll. **179–266**, which treats of the Scholar in Politics, is in form a refutation. What call to put it in this negative form is apparent in the opening lines? To what fallacious definition of terms (ll. **190–193**) does the refutation address itself? What argument from example (Rhet. p. 421, 1) is referred to as supporting the fallacious definition?

priestly politics? Was it because Benjamin Franklin was not college-bred that he drew the lightning from heaven and tore the sceptre from the tyrant? Was it because Abraham Lincoln had little schooling that his great heart beat true to God and man, lifting him to free a race and die for his country? Because men naturally great have done great service in the world without advantages, does it follow that lack of advantage is the secret of success? Was Pericles a less sagacious leader of the state, during forty years of Athenian glory, because he was thoroughly accomplished in every grace of learning? Or, swiftly passing from the Athenian agora to the Boston town-meeting, behold Samuel Adams, tribune of New England against Old England — of America against Europe — of liberty against despotism. Was his power enfeebled, his fervor chilled, his patriotism relaxed, by his college education? No, no; they were strengthened, kindled, confirmed. Taking his Master's Degree one hundred and thirty-four years ago, thirty-three years before the Declaration of Independence, Samuel Adams, then twenty-one years old, declared in a Latin discourse — the first flashes of the fire that blazed afterward in Faneuil Hall and kindled America — that it is lawful to resist the supreme magistrate if the commonwealth cannot otherwise be preserved. In the

---

A series of examples is adduced to expose the sophistry of this view, and they answer it in various ways. The two examples quoted from his opponents are how answered, in ll. 211–218? What suggestion does each of the three examples, ll. 201–211, furnish toward this answer? How do these three examples illustrate Rhet. p. 438, 1, top? In what different aspect do the two examples, ll. 219–239, present the argument? What call for presenting all these examples in interrogation, and what is gained by it? What circumstance is used to give the last adduced example a special interest for the present audience?

235 very year that Jefferson was born, the college boy, Samuel Adams, on a Commencement day like this, on an academical platform like this on which we stand, struck the keynote of American independence, which still stirs the heart of man with its music.

240 Or, within our own century, look at the great modern statesmen who have shaped the politics of the world. They were educated men; were they therefore visionary, pedantic, impracticable? Cavour, whose monument is United Italy — one from the Alps to Tarentum, from the 245 lagunes of Venice to the gulf of Salerno: Bismarck, who has raised the German empire from a name to a fact: Gladstone, to-day the incarnate heart and conscience of England: they are the perpetual refutation of the sneer that high education weakens men for practical affairs. 250 Trained themselves, such men know the value of training. All countries, all ages, all men, are their teachers. The broader their education, the wider the horizon of their thought and observation, the more affluent their resources, the more humane their policy. Would Samuel Adams 255 have been a truer popular leader had he been less an educated man? Would Walpole the less truly have served his country had he been, with all his capacities, a man whom England could have revered and loved? Could Gladstone so sway England with his serene eloquence, as

---

The next paragraph, ll. **240-266**, continues the refutation and summarizes it; compare ll. 261-266 with 199, 200. What advantages, for the present audience, in choosing modern examples, ll. **243-249**? What force in mentioning the work that each has done? How are the repeated examples, ll. **254-261**, varied, in each case, from their first introduction?

Why does the next section, ll. **267-507**, which treats of the Scholar in his Party, need to be the longest and most elaborate of the oration?

the moon the tides, were he a gambling, swearing, boozing 260
squire like Walpole? There is no sophistry more poisonous to the state, no folly more stupendous and demoralizing, than the notion that the purest character and the highest education are incompatible with the most commanding mastery of men and the most efficient adminis- 265
tration of affairs.

Undoubtedly a practical and active interest in politics will lead you to party association and co-operation. Great public results — the repeal of the corn-laws in England, the abolition of slavery in America — are due to that 270 organization of effort and concentration of aim which arouse, instruct and inspire the popular heart and will. This is the spring of party, and those who earnestly seek practical results instinctively turn to this agency of united action. But in this tendency, useful in the state as the 275 fire upon the household hearth, lurks, as in that fire, the deadliest peril. Here is our republic — it is a ship with towering canvas spread, sweeping before the prosperous gale over a foaming and sparkling sea : it is a lightning train darting with awful speed along the edge of dizzy 280 abysses and across bridges that quiver over unsounded gulfs. Because we are Americans, we have no peculiar charm, no magic spell, to stay the eternal laws. Our safety lies alone in cool self-possession, directing the forces of

---

How does the paragraph, ll. **267-297**, first set forth the question and its answer in general terms? What casual preliminary definition do you find in ll. **270-272**? **Point out the strong** and striking figures by which the importance of the subject is made palpable. Point out some of the tropes and epithets by which the figures themselves are expressed in more vivid terms. What relation does the paragraph bear to the emotions of the audience, and how does its style illustrate Rhet. p. 460, 2? In the orator's speech on Civil Service Reform in New York,

he is reviled as a popinjay and a visionary fool. Seeking
with honest purpose only the welfare of his country, the
hot air around him hums with the cry of "the grand old
party," "the traditions of the party," "loyalty to the
party," "future of the party," "servant of the party;" and
he sees and hears the gorged and portly money-changers
in the temple usurping the very divinity of the God.
Young hearts! be not dismayed. If ever any one of you
shall be the man so denounced, do not forget that your own
individual convictions are the whip of small cords which
God has put into your hands to expel the blasphemers.

The same party spirit naturally denies the patriotism of
its opponents. Identifying itself with the country, it
regards all others as public enemies. This is substantially
revolutionary politics. It is the condition of France, where,
in its own words, the revolution is permanent. Instead of
regarding the other party as legitimate opponents — in the
English phrase, His Majesty's Opposition — lawfully seeking a different policy under the government, it decries that
party as a conspiracy plotting the overthrow of the government itself. History is lurid with the wasting fires of this
madness. We need not look to that of other lands. Our
own is full of it. It is painful to turn to the opening years

---

these expressions exemplify what has been pointed out (see Bain, Composition Grammar, p. 206), that the language of abuse resorts most
naturally to the Saxon derivatives, as stronger and nearer to the emotions.
The words *renegade* and *popinjay*, if not Saxon in origin, are at least
thoroughly naturalized and old words, while the words *rat* and *fool* derive their very energy from being homely and brief. — **329-334** sq.
Explain the allusion by John ii. 13-17, and point out how ingeniously the
incident referred to is turned to the duty that should be potent here.

335-378. Point out the short sentence in which the thought of this
paragraph is defined. How does it exemplify Rhet. p. 433, 1? — **341.**
His Majesty's Opposition, — what argument for more wholesome

of the Union, and see how the great men whom we are taught to revere, and to whose fostering care the beginning of the republic was entrusted, fanned their hatred and suspicion of each other. Do not trust the flattering voices 350 that whisper of a Golden Age behind us, and bemoan our own as a degenerate day. The castles of hope always shine along the horizon. Our fathers saw theirs where we are standing. We behold ours where our fathers stood. But pensive regret for the heroic past, like eager anticipa- 355 tion of the future, shows only that the vision of a loftier life forever allures the human soul. We think our fathers to have been wiser than we, and their day more enviable. But eighty years ago the Federalists abhorred their opponents as Jacobins, and thought Robespierre and Marat no 360 worse than Washington's secretary of state. Their opponents retorted that the Federalists were plotting to establish a monarchy by force of arms. The New England pulpit anathematized Tom Jefferson as an atheist and a satyr. Jefferson denounced John Jay as a rogue, and the 365 chief newspaper of the opposition, on the morning that Washington retired from the presidency, thanked God that the country was now rid of the man who was the source of all its misfortunes. There is no mire in which party spirit wallows to-day, with which our fathers were not befouled, 370 and how little sincere the vituperation was, how shallow a fury, appears when Jefferson and Adams had retired from public life. Then they corresponded placidly and familiarly,

---

politics lies implied in this phrase? What is the advantage of choosing the examples here adduced from our own past history? To what useful appeal to the spirit of the present audience does this lead? Observe how this implicit appeal, ll. **350–357**, serves to relieve what might otherwise seem too prevailingly dark a picture, and thus infuses hope instead of discouragement. — How is the picture of past party bitterness turned

each at last conscious of the other's fervent patriotism; and when they died, they were lamented in common by those who in their names had flown at each other's throats, as the patriarchal Castor and Pollux of the pure age of our politics now fixed as a **constellation** of hope in our heaven. The same brutal spirit showed itself at the time of Andrew Johnson's impeachment. Impeachment is a proceeding to be instituted only for great public reasons, which should, presumptively, command universal support. To prostitute the power of impeachment to a mere party purpose, would readily lead to the reversal of the result of an election. But it was made a party measure. The party was to be whipped into its support: and when certain senators broke the party yoke upon their necks, and voted according to their convictions, as honorable men always will, whether the party whips like it or not, one of the whippers-in exclaimed of a patriotism, the struggle of obedience to which cost one senator at least, his life — " If there is anything worse than the treachery, it is the cant which pretends that it is the result of conscientious conviction; the pretence of a conscience is quite unbearable." This was the very acridity of bigotry, which in other times and countries raised the cruel tribunal of the Inquisition, and burned opponents for the glory of God. The party madness that dictated these words, and the sympathy that approved them, was treason not alone to the country but

---

against itself? — **377. The patriarchal Castor and Pollux,** — explain the allusion.

379–415. What is the general lesson embodied in this paragraph? How is it defined in ll. **395–397**, and how is the party cry turned against itself in ll. **411–415?** — **386. To be whipped,** — another example of energy gained by a plain Saxon word. — Observe how unsparingly the orator reduces the conduct he is combatting to its plainest

to well-ordered human society. Murder may destroy great 400
statesmen, but corruption makes great states impossible;
and this was an attempt at the most insidious corruption.
The man who attempts to terrify a senator of the United
States to cast a dishonest vote, by stigmatizing him as a
hypocrite and devoting him to party hatred, is only a more 405
plausible rascal than his opponent who gives Pat O'Flana-
gan a fraudulent naturalization paper or buys his vote with
a dollar or a glass of whiskey. Whatever the offences of
the president may have been, they were as nothing when
compared with the party spirit which declared that it was 410
tired of the intolerable cant of honesty. So the sneering
cavalier was tired of the cant of the Puritan conscience,
but the conscience of which plumed Injustice and coroneted Privilege were tired, has been for three centuries
the invincible body-guard of civil and religious liberty. 415

Gentlemen, how dire a calamity the same party spirit
was preparing for the country within a few months, we can
now perceive with amazement and with hearty thanksgiv-
ing for a great deliverance. The ordeal of last winter was
the severest strain ever yet applied to republican institu- 420
tions. It was a mortal strain along the very fibre of our
system. It was not a collision of sections, nor a conflict
of principles of civilization. It was a supreme and tri-

---

moral portraiture (see especially ll. 397–411); this is one of the strong
resources of oratory, to "call a spade a spade," and to unmask the real
significance of what is opposed. How does this exemplify Rhet. p.
466, 3dly, also p. 433, 1? — **413. Plumed Injustice and coroneted
Privilege,** — what figure is involved? How do the epithets exemplify
Rhet. p. 57, 3dly?

416–454. What is the fitness of introducing this more encouraging
example as the last of the illustrations of party spirit? Exactly what
does the paragraph illustrate? — **419. The ordeal of last winter,** —

umphant test of American patriotism. Greater than the
declaration of independence by colonies hopelessly alienated
from the crown and already in arms; greater than emanci-
pation, as a military expedient, amid the throes of civil
war, was the peaceful and reasonable consent of two vast
parties — in a crisis plainly foreseen and criminally neg-
lected — a crisis in which each party asserted its solution
to be indisputable — to devise a lawful settlement of the
tremendous contest, a settlement which, through furious
storms of disappointment and rage, has been religiously
respected. We are told that our politics are mean — that
already, in its hundredth year, the decadence of the American republic appears and the hope of the world is clouded.
But tell me, scholars, in what high hour of Greece, when,
as De Witt Clinton declared, "the herb-woman of Athens
could criticise the phraseology of Demosthenes, and the

---

the orator refers to the contested election of 1876. A quotation from
the Civil Service Reform Speech already mentioned will illustrate the
somewhat less impassioned, but still equally earnest, language employed
with an older and more matter-of-fact audience : "The exigencies and
tests of liberty in this country have been many and great, but a more
crucial hour the country never saw than that of the contested election
of 1876. Constitution, law, and precedent, were all obscured. Party
was arrayed angrily against party, and the peaceful continuance of the
Government itself was involved. It was a strain along the very fibre
of the American people and by the grace of God it did not give.
Party spirit yielded to patriotic instinct, and the great victory of popular government was won. In that supreme hour who was the traitor to
liberty, to Republican Government, to America? It was any man who
vociferated that party discipline must be maintained, and that every
man must stand by his party, because only by party could the Government be carried on. Happily the cry was vain. The crisis was beyond
party, and only because the people for that high hour rose superior to
party was the Government maintained and the country saved." —
437. But tell me, scholars, — how do the examples adduced make

meanest artisan could pronounce judgment on the works of Apelles and Phidias," or at what proud epoch of imperial Rome or millennial moment of the fierce Italian republics, was ever so momentous a party difference so wisely, so peacefully, so humanely, composed? Had the sophistry of party prevailed, had each side resolved that not to insist upon its own claim at every hazard was what the mad party spirit of each side declared it to be, a pusillanimous surrender: had the spirit of Marius mastered one party and that of Sylla the other, this waving valley of the Mohawk would not to-day murmur with the music of industry, and these tranquil voices of scholars blending with its happy harvest-song; it would have smoked and roared with fraternal war, and this shuddering river would have run red through desolated meadows and by burning homes.

It is because these consequences are familiar to the knowledge of educated and thoughtful men that such men are constantly to assuage this party fire and to take care that party is always subordinated to patriotism. Perfect party discipline is the most dangerous weapon of party spirit, for it is the abdication of the individual judgment: it is the application to political parties of the Jesuit principle of implicit obedience.

It is for you to help break this withering spell. It is for you to assert the independence and the dignity of the individual citizen, and to prove that party was made for the voter, not the voter for party. When you are angrily

---

this appeal to scholarship appropriate? — What offset does this illustration furnish to the implication of ll. 261-266 above, and how does it correspond to the speaker's feeling of responsibility at the outset? See ll. 4-7.

455-462. From the knowledge of history just appealed to, what sentiment is drawn, and how does this correspond to the prevailing

told that if you erect your personal whim against the regular party behest, you make representative government impossible by refusing to accept its conditions, hold fast by your own conscience and let the party go. There is not an American merchant who would send a ship to sea under the command of Captain Kidd, however skilful a sailor he might be. Why should he vote to send Captain Kidd to the legislature or to put him in command of the ship of state because his party directs? The party which to-day nominates Captain Kidd, will to-morrow nominate Judas Iscariot, and to-morrow, as to-day, party spirit will spurn you as a traitor for refusing to sell your master. "I tell you," said an ardent and well-meaning partisan, speaking of a closely contested election in another state, "I tell you it is a nasty state, and I hope we have done nasty work enough to carry it." But if your state has been carried by nasty means this year, success will require nastier next year, and the nastiest means will always carry it. The party may win, but the state will have been lost, for there are successes which are failures. When a man is sitting upon the bough of a tree and diligently sawing it off between himself and the trunk, he may succeed, but his success will break his neck.

The remedy for the constant excess of party spirit lies, and lies alone, in the courageous independence of the individual citizen. The only way, for instance, to procure the party nomination of good men, is for every self-respecting voter to refuse to vote for bad men. In the medieval theology the devils feared nothing so much as the drop of

---

motive to which appeal is made throughout the oration? How does this paragraph summarize the previous paragraphs, and what implied duty is deduced, **by contrast, from** the summary?

holy water and the sign of the cross, by which they were exorcised. The evil spirits of party fear nothing so much as bolting and scratching. *In hoc signo vinces.* **If a farmer** would **reap a good crop, he** scratches the weeds out of his field. **If we** would have good men upon **the** ticket, we must scratch bad men off. **If the** scratching breaks down the party, let it break: for the success of the party by such means would break down the country. The evil spirits must be taught by means that they can understand. "**Them** fellers," **said the** captain of a canal-boat of his men — "them fellers never think you mean a thing until you kick 'em. They feel that, and understand."

It is especially necessary for us to perceive the vital relation of individual courage and character to the common welfare because **ours is a government of** public opinion, and public opinion **is but** the aggregate **of** individual thought. **We have** the awful responsibility as a community of doing what we choose; and it is of the last importance that we choose to do what is wise and right. In the early days **of** the anti-slavery agitation, a meeting was called **at** Faneuil Hall, in Boston, which a good-natured

---

Having thus brought to a practical conclusion **the** thought of this section, for what purpose does the orator append the next two paragraphs, ll **463–507**? See Rhet. p. 457, 2, and p. 463, 1. In ll. **466–470**, what motive is appealed to? What is the practical force of the illustrations given in ll. **470–489**? What is effected, by way of suggestion, **in** the copious repetition of the word **nasty**, ll. **481–485**? How is epigram employed to give point to the thought?

490–507. How is "the remedy" here defined related to what has already been implied, ll. 458–462? Once defined, how is it translated into practical deeds? — **498. In hoc signo vinces,** — what *signum* is referred to here, and how is it emphasized by utilizing the suggestiveness of a word, as in ll. 481–485 above? How do ll. **503–507** illustrate Rhet. p. 468, top? — **505.** "**Them fellers**" is repeated after

mob of soldiers was hired to suppress. They took possession of the floor and danced breakdowns and shouted choruses and refused to hear any of the orators upon the
520 platform. The most eloquent pleaded with them in vain. They were urged by the memories of the Cradle of Liberty, for the honor of Massachusetts, for their own honor as Boston boys, to respect liberty of speech. But they still laughed and sang and danced, and were proof against
525 every appeal. At last a man suddenly arose from among themselves, and began to speak. Struck by his tone and quaint appearance, and with the thought that he might be one of themselves, the mob became suddenly still. "Well, fellow-citizens," he said, "I wouldn't be quiet if
530 I didn't want to." The words were greeted with a roar of delight from the mob, which supposed it had found its champion, and the applause was unceasing for five minutes, during which the strange orator tranquilly awaited his chance to continue. The wish to hear more hushed
535 the tumult, and when the hall was still he resumed: "No, I certainly wouldn't stop if I hadn't a mind to; but then, if I were you, I *would* have a mind to!" The oddity of the remark and the earnestness of the tone, held the

---

the interpolation; see also a similar instance, l. 481 above. This repetition is how dictated by the kind of discourse and occasion?

The next section of the oration, ll. **508-552**, which treats of the scholar in his relation to Public Opinion, may be shorter and less elaborated than the previous ones, perhaps *because* of them. How do the previous sections involve the thought of this, and how is this accordingly related to them? How is the sentiment here enforced made to grow out of what has been said regarding the individual? — A single well-told incident is sufficient to suggest the thought of this section. Exactly what does it illustrate as to the power of public opinion? It also suggests something as to the way in which public opinion may be controlled and directed; how does the quaint orator's

crowd silent, and the speaker continued: "Not because this is Faneuil Hall, nor for the honor of Massachusetts, nor because you are Boston boys, but because you are men, and because honorable and generous men always love fair play." The mob was conquered. Free speech and fair play were secured. Public opinion can do what it has a mind to in this country. If it be debased and demoralized, it is the most odious of tyrants. It is Nero and Caligula multiplied by millions. Can there then be a more stringent public duty for every man — and the greater the intelligence the greater the duty — than to take care, by all the influence he can command, that the country, the majority, public opinion, shall have a mind to do only what is just and pure, and humane?

Gentlemen, leaving this college to take your part in the discharge of the duties of American citizenship, every sign encourages and inspires. The year that is now ending, the year that opens the second century of our history, has furnished the supreme proof that in a country of rigorous party division the purest patriotism exists. That and that only is the pledge of a prosperous future. No mere party fervor, or party fidelity, or party discipline, could fully

---

success with the mob illustrate Rhet. p. 467, bottom? Distinguish the motives appealed to in that incident, and the motives that were actually operative. — Show how the summary of this section may stand as the summary of all that has been inculcated; and how does it illustrate Rhet. p. 281, 2?

III. The Conclusion, or Peroration. — What is there in the audience and the occasion to make a forward-looking conclusion appropriate, and how does this correspond with the speaker's attitude assumed at the beginning? What concrete instance does he choose (ll. 555-559) as the suggester and guarantee of a hopeful outlook? — 556. Has **furnished the supreme proof**, — see ll. 416-454, above, and **note** thereon. — The reversion to this instance furnishes also occasion to

restore a country torn and distracted by the fierce debate of a century and the convulsions of civil war; nothing less than a patriotism all-embracing as the summer air could heal a wound so wide. I know, — no man better, — how hard it is for earnest men to separate their country from their party, or their religion from their sect. But nevertheless the welfare of the country is dearer than the mere victory of party, as truth is more precious than the interest of any sect. You will hear this patriotism scorned as an impracticable theory, as the dream of a cloister, as the whim of a fool. But such was the folly of the Spartan Leonidas, staying with his three hundred the Persian horde and teaching Greece the self-reliance that saved her. Such was the folly of the Swiss Arnold von Winkelried, gathering into his own breast the host of Austrian spears, making his dead body the bridge of victory for his countrymen. Such was the folly of the American Nathan Hale, gladly risking the seeming disgrace of his name, and grieving that he had but one life to give for his country. Such are the beacon-lights of a pure patriotism that burn forever in men's memories and answer each other through the illuminated ages. And of the same grandeur, in less heroic and poetic form, was the patriotism of Sir Robert Peel in recent history. He was the leader of a great party and the prime minister of England. The character and

---

lead the thought to a culmination, in the sentiment that has been all along the supreme motive of the oration; what is that? Accordingly, how does the theme, in its highest outcome, correspond to the ideal of an oratorical theme, as shown Rhet. p. 258, top, and p. 456, top? Put in words the *imperative* of the oration.

563. A patriotism all-embracing as the summer air, — how is this applied to the recent task of government? How to the hardships and scorns of practical political activity? — **571. Such was the folly,**

necessity of party were as plain to him as to any man. But when he saw that the national welfare demanded the repeal of the corn-laws which he had always supported, he did not quail. Amply avowing the error of a life and the duty of avowing it — foreseeing the probable overthrow of his party and the bitter execration that must fall upon him, he tranquilly did his duty. With the eyes of England fixed upon him in mingled amazement, admiration and indignation, he rose in the House of Commons to perform as great a service as any English statesman ever performed for his country, and in closing his last speech in favor of the repeal, describing the consequences that its mere prospect had produced, he loftily exclaimed: "Where there was dissatisfaction I see contentment; where there was turbulence, I see there is peace; where there was disloyalty, I see there is loyalty. I see a disposition to confide in you, and not to agitate questions that are the foundations of your institutions." When all was over, when he had left office, when his party was out of power, and the fury of party execration against him was spent, his position was greater and nobler than it had ever been. Cobden said of him, "Sir Robert Peel has lost office, but he has gained a country;" and Lord Dalling said of him, what may truly be said of Washington: "Above all parties,

---

— this manner of introducing the examples here adduced makes them continually maintain what antithesis? — The three examples from history, ll. 571-579, are regarded by the speaker, according to the implication, l. 582, as having what character? How, therefore, suited to this audience? — If the grandeur of Sir Robert Peel's patriotism, as described, ll. 582-611, is "less heroic and poetic" in form, what is there in it to make it after all a true climax with the preceding illustrations? Is there anything in its occasion and manifestation to give it more interest and cogency for present affairs? — 608. What may truly

himself a party, he had trained his own mind into a disinterested sympathy with the intelligence of his country." A public spirit so lofty is not confined to other ages and lands. You are conscious of its stirrings in your souls. It calls you to courageous service, and I am here to bid you obey the call. Such patriotism may be ours. Let it be your parting vow that it shall be yours. Bolingbroke described a patriot king in England; I can imagine a patriot president in America. I can see him indeed the choice of a party, and called to administer the government when sectional jealousy is fiercest and party passion most inflamed. I can imagine him seeing clearly what justice and humanity, the national law and the national welfare require him to do, and resolve to do it. I can imagine him patiently enduring not only the mad cry of party hate, the taunt of "recreant" and "traitor," of "renegade" and "coward," but what is harder to bear, the amazement, the doubt, the grief, the denunciation, of those as sincerely devoted as he to the common welfare. I can imagine him pushing firmly on, trusting the heart, the intelligence, the conscience of his countrymen, healing angry wounds, cor-

---

be said of Washington, — thus the historical instance drawn from another nation is connected in a lofty sentiment with the heroic life of our own.

In the last paragraph, ll. 612-637, how is the theme brought home to the present audience and occasion? — The portrayal of a patriot president, ll. 616-633, furnishes occasion for an informal summary of the most practical things that have been inculcated; trace them. — What standard, highest and most comprehensive of all, is brought in the last sentence, ll. 634-637, to bear on the sentiment that has inspired the oration? — 636. The celestial secret, — what is the force of the epithet?

How does the style of the peroration correspond to what is said of the conclusion, Rhet. p. 282?

recting misunderstandings, planting justice on surer foundations, and, whether his party rise or fall, lifting his country heavenward to a more perfect union, prosperity and peace. This is the spirit of a patriotism that girds the commonwealth with the resistless splendor of the moral law — the invulnerable panoply of states, the celestial secret of a great nation and a happy people.

www.ingramcontent.com/pod-product-compliance
Lightning Source LLC
Chambersburg PA
CBHW031902220426
43663CB00006B/727